D0248501

On Equal Terms

The first disabled crew to sail
round the world – racing in the
BT Global Challenge

MARINA CANTACUZINO

Foreword by Sir Chay Blyth CBE BEM

SIMON & SCHUSTER
A VIACOM COMPANY

Picture on p1: © Mark Pepper/MPP

First published in Great Britain by Simon & Schuster Ltd, 1997
A Viacom company

Copyright © The Time & Tide Challenge Limited and Marina Cantacuzino, 1997

This book is copyright under the Berne Convention.
No reproduction without permission.
All rights reserved.

Data source for results tables: BT Information System.
Copyright © British Telecommunications plc 1996

The right of the Time & Tide Challenge Limited and Marina Cantacuzino to be
identified as authors of this work has been asserted by them in accordance with
sections 77 and 78 of the Copyright, Designs and Patents Act, 1988.

Simon & Schuster Ltd
West Garden Place
Kendal Street
London W2 2AQ

Simon & Schuster Australia
Sydney

A CIP catalogue record for this book is available from the British Library

ISBN 0-684-81935-X

Designed by Dan Newman
Printed and bound in Great Britain by Butler & Tanner Ltd, Frome and London

Dear Lionel,

    Your government hounded the disabled so much that they took up sailing + buggered off.

        Best wishes

        Domin

    (the last Majorite in town)

On Equal Terms

Contents

On behalf of the crew I would like to dedicate this account
of the struggle of *Time & Tide* to

Susan Preston Davis and Lucy Quinlan

A big Thank You –
Without your tireless efforts it would never have happened

James Hatfield MBE
Skipper

Foreword

When Susan Preston Davis first asked me to consider a disabled crew for one of the Challenge yachts I thought the idea impossible. We were preparing for the world's toughest yacht race yet devised which takes no prisoners and certainly no passengers and if they did compete and fail, whose fault would it be but mine. Worse still, if there was a serious accident or loss of life I'd be hanged, as I am directly responsible for the interviewing, selecting and training of every crew volunteer and skipper going on these races.

Yet, curiously, the more I thought about it, the more the idea actually appealed. Throughout my life I have always believed we are all responsible for ourselves and if these disabled yachtsmen and women believed they could compete who was I to stop them.

Time & Tide deserved their place at the starting line because they believed they should be there – and how right they were.

Achievement in any walk of life is about belief in yourself and as I write my thoughts turn to those I served with in The Parachute Regiment who faced and successfully endured great hardship and adversity in the performance of their duty.

I also think about the indomitable Douglas Bader who, despite losing both legs in a flying accident before the Second World War, went on to distinguish himself in the fight against the Nazis.

The climber Norman Croucher, twice voted Man of the Year, is another wonderful example of the strength of the human spirit. He too lost his legs and yet he is one of the few to have conquered Everest, the highest mountain in the world – a feat most able-bodied people can only wonder at.

What marks Douglas Bader, Norman Croucher, those men of The Parachute Regiment and now the crew of *Time & Tide* out from the rest is their unshakeable belief in themselves. It is for others to doubt, just as I did, and it is a lesson for us all.

The *Time & Tide* crew have had a wonderful adventure and a thrilling race. Their story will, I am sure, encourage other disabled people to pick up the gauntlet of life's challenges and, with equal determination, succeed.

I am delighted to write this foreword and am grateful for the opportunity to add my tribute to the skipper and crew of *Time & Tide* who proved so conclusively, for all the world to see, that if you want to do something enough you will do it. It has been an honour to know and work with them – I salute them.

Sir Chay Blyth CBE BEM

Acknowledgements

The Trustees and Crew of Time & Tide would like to thank:

Marina Cantacuzino
Mark Bosanquet-Bryant and Eric North for designing our yacht livery
Lynn Faulds Wood for being Godmother to the yacht
HMS *Belfast* & Livett's Launches for help at our naming ceremony

Ken Simons & Sandy Giddings
Eddie & Pam Edrich and Bulldog Sailing School, Southampton
Jeni Graham & Mike Russell for help during the race, but especially in Boston
Parceline and DPE International for providing all our freight facilities
Henri-Lloyd for the best foul-weather clothing in the world
Isabella Cornini, Carlo Gambuzzi & ItalBrokers Food Service for the best pasta in the world
Olivetti U.K. and Mitsubishi Electric for computer equipment
Richard Gough & Silent Alert Clofield Ltd
Rosie & Peter Mackie & MaST International
British Airways Cabin crews
Steve Wyre, Motorola sponsors and crew for fundraising
John & Harriet Anderson
Marius Harte & The Rover Group

Leyland Daf Trucks for providing the Supporters' Boat at the start
Northside Trucks for lending us the van in Southampton
Charles Sidney for the Boat Hi-fi System

Mercedes Benz UK and Mercedes Benz Brazil for loan of a minibus in Rio
Tom & Carlotta Richardson for all their help during the Rio stopover

Jane Hunter MBE and Hunters Wines New Zealand
Dale Adams our Boat Buddy in Wellington
Chicago - Life is Good Bar, Wellington

The Management & Staff of the Ritz-Carlton Hotels in Sydney
Lauda Air for flights to Sydney
Phil Vardy & Sailability Australia
Rover Australia for transport in Sydney

Suzanne Weil and Nicky Wimble of Sun International
Jan Mestriner and staff of the Table Bay Hotel, Cape Town
Mercedes Benz S.A. for loan of a minibus in Cape Town
Ferryman's Bar and Restaurant, Cape Town

Steve Spinetto, Commissioner for Persons with Disabilities, Boston
The Boston Harbour Police Force

Steve Denning, Dave Hodgson & General Atlantic Partners
Arron Toffler, Carolyn Bess & Outdoor Explorations
Ed Beard & Echoing Green
Devra Cohen & Concert Management Services Inc
Sondra Arkin, Wendy Ellman & ProMarket, Inc
Michael W. Cover & Aviance Marketing
Management and Staff at the Palm Restaurant, Westin Hotel, Boston
Massachussets Institute of Technology

Management & Staff of New Place Management Centre for the world's best ever homecoming party.

But very special thanks to:

Elena Preston Davis for lending us her Mummy

Martin Preston Davis, Tim Quinlan and Sarah Rowe for all their patience, understanding and support

Gary Champion & Bitcom International

Michael Nicholson & ITN

Maureen Ogg and all families, friends and supporters

Our sponsors: BT Community Programme, Church & Co., Deutsche Morgan Grenfell, Henri-Lloyd, IPC/IxNet, Lloyd Thompson, The Ritz-Carlton Hotel Company, the *Sunday Times*, Sun International, Symbol Technologies and Zurich Insurance – who believed we could accomplish our dream and were brave enough to back us

Bob Semaine, Peter Winmill, Tony Gledhill, Jennie Nicholson, Frances Pilcher and Wendy May – who stuck with us when the going was tough

The BT Global Challenge Team, especially Kim Fitzsimmons

Race Officers, Adrian Rayson, Liz Botting, Paul White & Anne Prees who kept watch over us day and night at sea

All at The Challenge Business

Sir Chay Blyth for giving us a unique opportunity and believing that we, too, could be pioneers and become part of sailing history.

Glossary

Aft	near or towards the stern of a boat
Backstay	a rigging wire connecting the top of the mast to the stern of the boat
Battens	flexible strips of wood or plastic slipped into pockets in the leech of a sail to help it maintain an efficient shape
Batten cars	attached to the end of the battens, connecting them to the mast
Bilge	the part of a boat's bottom beneath the floorboards
Boom	a spar running along the bottom edge of the main sail, fixed to the mast at one end
Bow	The front point of the boat
Broach	to cause the boat to veer so that she is broadside to the waves
Cleat	a fitting with projecting horns, for securing ropes
Cockpit	the aft working area of the vessel
Fore and aft	the boat's major or longitudinal axis: fore – towards the front (bow); aft – towards the back (stern)
Foulies	abbreviation for Henri-Lloyd foul-weather clothing
Gash bin	trash/garbage bin
Genoa	a type of sail
Growler	a small iceberg
Gybe	altering the boat's direction by steering to swing the boat's stern through the wind; causes the boom and mainsail to whip across the boat at speed. *Also see: tacking*
Guy	usually refers to a rope which adjusts the trim of the spinnaker pole
Halyard	rope for hoisting a sail or flag
Heads	toilet
Headsail	a sail set forward of the mast
Heel	the lean of a boat away from the wind; to level the boat (and improve racing efficiency) crews sometimes sit along the windward, 'uphill' side
Helm	tiller or wheel/the driver
Jury	makeshift
Leeward	opposite side to windward (on *Time & Tide* often described as downhill side because of the way the yacht was heeling)
Kite	spinnaker
Leech	trailing (aft) edge of a sail
Luff	front edge of a sail (to 'luff up' is to turn towards the wind)
Main	an abbreviation of mainsail
Mainsail	the large sail hoisted on the mast and along the boom
Port	the left-hand side of a boat (when looking forwards to the bow)
Reach	a sailing direction at an angle of (at least) 90° to the wind
Reef	to reduce a sail's area, for instance by tying folds into it; done in very high winds to slow the boat down (and stop sails being damaged)
Rigging	wires which secure the mast and are trimmed to adjust mast shape

Scuppers	the edge of the deck (where debris is washed overboard and lost – hence 'scuppered')
Sheet	a rope attached to the clew (bottom corner) of a sail by which it is trimmed (it is named after the sail to which it is attached eg staysail sheet, yankee sheet)
Smoke	to release a sheet quickly
Spinnaker	a large full-bellied sail set when reaching or running before the wind. Described by cloth weight: .75, 1.5, 2.2 (lighter sails are for gentler winds)
Starboard	the right-hand side of a boat (when looking forwards to the bow)
Stays	fore and aft rigging wires
Staysail	one of the smaller sails
Stern	the rear of the boat
Tacking	to direct a boat to windward by sailing alternately on port and starboard tacks, where the boat makes a small angle to the wind. Changing tack involves swinging the bow across the wind, when the sails flap wildly until they catch the wind on their other side
Trim	to alter the set of the sails or mast
Trysail	a small strong sail set instead of the mainsail in heavy weather
Watches	periods of duty for crew members
Winch	a drum around which the sheets/halyards are turned to pull in and ease out the sails. Contains gearing to give a mechanical advantage
Windward	the side of the boat nearest to the wind (ie 'uphill' side)

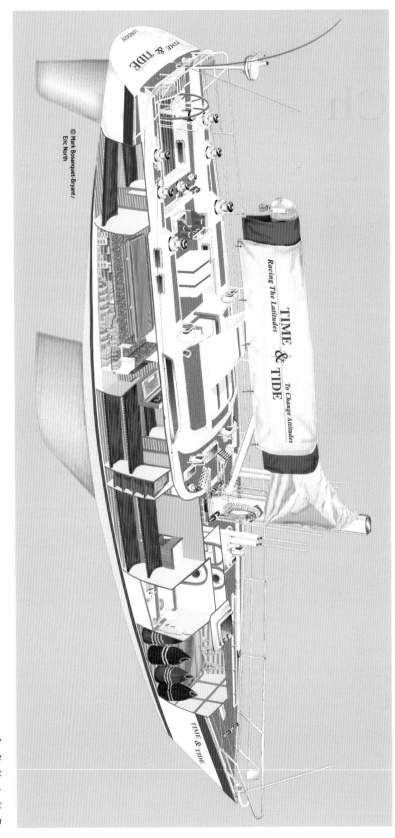

Cutaway diagram of Time & Tide *by Mark Bosanquet-Bryant/Eric North*

© Mark Bosanquet-Bryant / Eric North

Preface
Christmas Day 1996

Opening presents on Christmas Day (© Carolyn Davis)

For the crew of *Time & Tide*, Christmas Day 1996 was not a day they would ever forget. Somewhere in the latitudes of the Southern Ocean, as the boat pitched and rolled in mountainous seas, those on deck wrestled under three feet of water, barely able to work the waterlogged sails as they flapped and banged in shrieking winds gusting at forty-five knots.

With no sign of respite, the boat fell off the top of fifty-foot waves and slammed into deep troughs, flinging the crew across the foredeck. The most apprehensive among them crawled on all fours, desperately trying to cling to whatever they could grab hold of. It would have been easy to lose impetus in such wet, frightening and freezing conditions; but amidst the panic they tried to hold on to Chay Blyth's simple assessment of a Southern Ocean storm as being nothing more than 'wind and water'. The skipper, James Hatfield, was at the helm as always during sail changes, watching out to make sure the sail came down safely, ready to react quickly if anyone was knocked over the side. As the boat kept digging in her bow with waves sweeping down the deck, he tried to keep her steady as his crew were swept along the deck in front of him.

Everyone was bruised and battered, and several crew members came close to going over the rail that day. Carol Sear, thirty-five, recorded in her log:

> *I started crawling in the direction of the bow, waves in my face all the way. I wasn't too happy when I got there. Then a big wave came over and lifted me, smashing my legs into the cleats. For a while I was in terrible pain and couldn't move. By now I was shaking with fear. The boat was lurching about, with waves crashing over the bow ... Next thing I knew, I was washed over the side. My lifeline saved me from disappearing completely over the guard rail but I was petrified, cursing, swearing and crying, and the odd scream escaped from my mouth too ... We had just started pulling the sail away from the edge to drag it back to the cockpit when luckily the second cavalry arrived.*

The second cavalry amounted to other members of the crew appearing from below deck, having been hauled out of the relative warmth and safety of their bunks to help with what later became known as 'the sail change from hell'. In a sea whose surface would curl and break and then lash out again, with hissing white caps pouring water across the deck and cockpit, several crew members experienced an unfamiliar sensation that the boat was about to break apart. But the real danger was not so much that the boat would be swamped (after all, it had been built for heavy seas and was buoyant enough to take several tons of water on board) but that a person with only one leg or with insufficient muscle power might fall overboard and not have the strength to keep afloat. For the first time in this ten-month voyage the race felt more like a survival course than a first-to-the-finish contest, and on each crew member the full realization gradually dawned as to what it meant to have fourteen disabled sailors racing in the Southern Ocean.

That evening, while most of the crew were enjoying their evening meal at leisure (a valiant attempt at traditional Christmas fare cooked by James, infinitely preferable to the usual freeze-dried stodge) Paul Burns and David Tait, two of *Time & Tide*'s more resilient crew members, were up on deck – one helming, the other riding shotgun in the cockpit. In lumpy seas with spray everywhere and thirty knots of breeze, they could just about make out, through the steamed-up deck hatch below, Christmas decorations and flashing cameras, and hear muffled shouts of laughter and bursting balloons as the rest of the crew sat round the galley table playing cards and opening their presents. David recorded in his log, 'I knew then how Tiny Tim from *A Christmas Carol* must have felt being on the outside looking in.'

For some, despite the perilous location, it was a festive occasion; but for those in more sombre mood Christmas Day was not only much like any other day in the Southern Ocean but also, in sailing terms, considerably worse. With dampened spirits, a few were questioning their capabilities and wondering whether they had the stamina to carry on. 'Life is about setting challenges and seeing them through, good and bad,' were Mike Austin's thoughts in his log that evening. A British Airways pilot and one of the oldest crew members on board, he continued, 'I can't wait to get to Wellington, as much needs to be done to the yacht. She's taken a pounding and so have we. We need some healing.'

Chapter One

Ready... About

James Hatfield had always insisted that the British Telecom Global Challenge race, which lasted ten months and involved sailing round the world against prevailing winds and currents, was less of a challenge for his disabled crew than for the other crews in the fleet. 'Our people have already had to overcome greater hurdles than this,' he said. 'We see this as an opportunity to be judged on equal terms.'

James's interest in sailing began in 1977 at the age of twenty-one. He was in Middlesex hospital at the time, having undergone eight major open-heart operations over a period of two years. Although he'd been born with a hole in his heart, he'd become accustomed to the murmuring his heart made with every beat and the condition had never particularly debilitated him, until one day, in April 1975, he ruptured his aorta while out jogging.

There followed a traumatic period when he endured recurrent infections and major surgery resulting in an inch-wide scar that criss-crossed his body like lattice-work. By then he'd stopped wanting or expecting to live, as being made better simply hurt too much. But one day, as he lay in his hospital bed feeling more despondent than he had for a long while, his brother brought him a pile of magazines, *Playboy* and *Mayfair* hidden discreetly within copies of various Sunday supplements. Thinking it was a boring sort of gift, James decided to share them out with the other male patients on his ward, leaving just one for himself. But when, later that evening, he came to look at it, it wasn't quite what he'd expected. Instead of the rounded breasts of topless models, he discovered the rounded hulls of some of the world's finest yachts.

'I was glad it wasn't a mountaineering magazine, as I'm scared of heights but I wasn't wild about sailing either,' recalled James. 'However, as I flicked through the pages of *Yachting Monthly* my eyes fell on a report about a single-handed transatlantic race for boats under twenty-one feet. I don't know why, but for some reason I decided there and then to enter. Somehow it seemed like a good idea, even though I didn't have a boat, had no experience of sailing and was more dead than alive.' This impromptu decision provided James with a badly needed lifeline, and for the first time in several months he felt a small surge of energy – enough to release him from the confines of his hospital bed and eventually take him across the Atlantic. Already sailing had become a powerful metaphor for the liberty he so craved after two years of incarceration.

In January 1977, when eventually James was allowed out of hospital, despite being warned not to go anywhere crowded he headed straight for the London Boat Show at Earls Court. There he fell in love immediately with a twenty-foot Corribee. 'The owner of the company started

*James Hatfield
(© Mark
Pepper/MPP)*

taking down my details, assuming, I think, that I was a doctor, because I said I'd come straight from hospital. But when I asked him if he had a first-aid kit on his stand because my wound was seeping, he realized I'd never be able to afford the boat and lost interest.' Undaunted, James left the Boat Show determined he would somehow go it alone. And so, in the course of the next few months, he bought a hull and deck, and set about building a boat himself.

In October that year he set out on his first single-handed transatlantic race on the twenty-one-foot *British Heart I* with just sixteen hours of single-handed experience under his belt. It was a baptism of fire. Within forty-eight hours he had hit winds in excess of 60 miles an hour, capsized twice, hit a whale and broken his hand. Three days after the start of the race he returned to Penzance, beaten but not broken. In hindsight he was one of the luckier ones – two contestants died in ferocious storms during the first few days of that race.

It was a chance encounter with a journalist from a local newspaper that rekindled his competitive spirit. Indignant at the way this journalist had introduced him as someone who never completed what he'd set out to do, he vigorously denied the accusations. He couldn't remember exactly what was said. The following day his father woke him up by dropping a newspaper on his bed. The front page had James splashed across the headlines telling of his forthcoming adventures at sea.

And so it was that in May 1978 he set off single-handed again on *British Heart I*, this time sailing down to Madeira, the Canaries, across to Bermuda and then up to Newport Rhode Island in a trip that lasted fifty-six days. Arriving at his destination unscathed and within schedule, he felt exhilarated. 'I hadn't been particularly bright at school and it gave me such a buzz to realize that I'd made it. When you see land coming over the horizon and you're in the right place at the right time there's an enormous sense of achievement. Sailing had given me the world. It transformed me from the person I was to the person I am.'

There followed a world trip in a Cornish Crabber, *British Heart II*, during which, halfway between New Zealand and Cape Horn, with heavy seas giving his boat a particularly savage battering, he was reduced to buckets and bailing, until there came a gradual dawning that he was no longer sailing but sinking. Feeling like a traitor, he gathered up as many belongings as he could and prepared to abandon ship. Fortunately, after eight days a container ship bound for Panama came to his rescue. As James attempted to berth alongside the *Ellen Hudig*, *British Heart II* rolled over on to her side. Yelling for a line, James walked up the hull to the bow and was winched to safety. It was the last he saw of *British Heart II*.

Insurance money and the generosity of a number of New Zealand companies paid for the building of *British Heart III*, a Whiting 29 New Zealand design. To show appreciation to all the people who had helped rescue him from the Southern Ocean and get him afloat again, James then completed a single-handed circumnavigation of New Zealand to test the new craft, check his nerves and raise funds for the children's hospitals of New Zealand.

Eventually he returned to England, via the Straits of Magellan and the Falklands, having completed his first round-the-world voyage, so becoming the first person to sail single-handed round the world from the Pacific to the Atlantic via the Straits of Magellan, and raising in the process over £360,000 for research into heart disease. 'I felt terrific,' he said. 'For the first time ever I liked myself and I could see the genuine wonder that people had in what I'd achieved. It then occurred to me that there were hundreds of people out there who had had things happen to them that seemed to be the end of the world, and I thought that if they could only see an example of someone achieving something that no one thought they were capable of, they might have an idea to try something themselves, or at the very least feel better inside.'

By 1987, having made twenty-two Atlantic crossings, eight of which were single-handed, James was trying to put together a campaign for the Whitbread round-the-world yacht race, but he abandoned the idea when his father fell ill with cancer. Instead, he did the Carlsberg single-handed transatlantic race, in the middle of which he discovered he'd been awarded an MBE for services to sailing and charity. Then in January 1988 he was made Yachtsman of the Year. Slowly things were coming together, and sailing was giving him a confidence and a lust for life that he'd never experienced before.

He spent the next period of his life sailing big boats in the Caribbean, but after three years of working with other people's toys he'd had enough and returned to England eager for another adventure.

It was at this time that he first heard about the Dolphin circumnavigation project, put together by the Venture Abilities Trust, who were looking for an all-disabled crew and skipper to sail in the Whitbread Round the World Race. Within days of talking to the organizer, James was given the job, the Sports and Arts Foundation had been approached and the project was granted £1 million to build its boat.

When the boat was launched and James returned from his first sail he announced to the trustees that it was the fastest boat he'd ever sailed, adding as a joke that it was also the first time he'd ever considered making a will. But the lighthearted remark set off alarm bells among the trustees who, in view of the boat's speed, became wary of the safety factor and decided it was too fast for a disabled crew to handle without dire consequences. In the end, *Dolphin* merged with *Youth*, a crew in their early twenties also planning to sail the Whitbread, and the original all-disabled crew members were whittled down to just three. James, who was feeling increasingly disheartened by the turn of events, soon also found himself squeezed out of the project.

'I was told at first that I'd be joint skipper; then I was told I'd be the owner's representative on board. Either way, I knew that whatever went wrong on the boat would be my fault. It was a complete no-win situation, so I walked out of the project and began a legal battle to try to recoup some of the money I was owed. It was a very unpleasant time and like others I felt totally betrayed.'

Bruised but far from finished, James turned his mind to putting together another disabled crew, this time with the aim of sailing in Chay Blyth's 1996–7 Global (eventually to be called the BT Global) Challenge round-the-world yacht race.

Even though Chay Blyth is respected and admired for sailing alone and non-stop the wrong way round the world in 1971, and even though he has been fêted by fellow international mariners, he has always been a renegade figure in the yachting world, regarded with suspicion for publicly denigrating what he calls 'grotty yachties' and criticizing the élitist image of yacht racing. Even before he began transatlantic racing, this former-paratrooper-turned-professional-yachtsman viewed sailing as 'half art, half science and with an arcane language to match': in other words as an extremely complicated business that needed to be made available to all. But despite never being fully accepted as one of the yachting establishment, he is nonetheless admired for his daredevil attitude and brilliant seamanship.

The first 1992–3 British Steel Challenge race (the forerunner of the 1996–7 race) was originally devised by Chay not so much for those interested in racing round the world against prevailing winds and currents as for those who wanted to have the adventure of a lifetime. However, as the British Steel Challenge pushed along its upwind westerly course, it wasn't long before it developed into a serious and highly competitive race.

Chay's intention was to make serious amateur sailing available to anyone, regardless of their social background, knowledge and experience. The whole ethos of the Challenge was that anyone could take part and that sailing no longer had to be seen as an exclusively élitist club. The idea was that you could take a dozen people off the quayside and put them on a Challenge yacht with a skilled skipper, and in a relatively short period of time they would not only be able to sail long distances round the world but also be changed and enriched by the experience.

Not surprisingly the degree of scepticism from the yachting community was massive and many cast aspersions on the belief that ordinary people could lead by extraordinary example. To professional sailors the fact that the principal qualities Chay was looking for in his crews were determination and enthusiasm – not knowledge and experience – seemed both incongruous and ill-advised.

Apart from that, no one believed that amateur sailors, some with no experience at all, would be prepared to give nearly three years of their lives to fundraising, training and preparation and pay the necessary £15,000 berth fee to suffer the most arduous and uncomfortable eight

Time & Tide *needed a livery design which could include the names and logos of all their sponsors, with room for additions. (© Peter Viccari)*

months of their lives. While the Global Challenge race might indeed be the adventure of a lifetime (or, as Chay put it, 'the responsible embracing of risk') it was also bound to be a test of physical and mental endurance capable of breaking anybody. The sceptics were soon put to shame, however, when the Challenge recruitment campaign – which began on 3 January 1989 with an announcement on the ITN and BBC television news – attracted a massive response and resulted in over 1000 application forms being sent out by British Steel for 200 crew places. It was proof enough that this had genuinely become a race with universal appeal. In the final selection, done on a first-come-first-served basis, crew volunteers included a butcher, a baker and an undertaker.

The 1992–3 British Steel Challenge was a phenomenal success. Not only did it establish The Challenge Business as the event organisers, with Chay Blyth as managing director and the

Royal Ocean Racing Club overseeing race rules, it also became a high-profile media event that seemed to capture the interest of the public as well as change the age-old perception of ocean racing as a hobby only for the well-heeled.

As a result, Chay set his sights even higher for the second Global Challenge race, due to start in Southampton in September 1996 and to return in July 1997. The route of the previous race had been via Rio de Janeiro, Hobart, Cape Town and back to Southhampton. This time it would take two months longer, stopping in Wellington, New Zealand instead of Hobart, Tasmania and the race was to include two extra ports of call, Sydney and Boston, with the intention of attracting new media and business interests along the way. Chay was already also looking ahead to the year 2000, in which he wanted to add for the first time an international dimension to the race. For the Challenge 2000 the plans were for a yacht design that would carry a crew of eighteen, rather than fourteen, thus keeping costs down even further.

In organizing the second Global Challenge race, Chay had to find not only a title sponsor but also fourteen individual yacht sponsors who would have a boat chartered to them for the duration of the race and whose company name would become the name of the racing yacht. The companies who were acting as sponsors had to pay £450,000 for the privilege of leasing a boat for a year and having their logos boldly stamped across the hull – although inevitably the final cost amounted to much more. Most sponsors doubled their initial outlay due to project management costs such as accommodation, clothes and PR communications with the boats.

While the skippers were paid employees of The Challenge Business, crew volunteers had to pay £18,750 to take part. Most people signed up to do the whole race, but some, known as leggers, only wanted to do one or two legs. It was also likely that some crew volunteers would drop out during the course of the race and replacement crew were also needed.

Crew volunteers had to be interviewed by Chay, whose criteria for selection relied on his own instincts and intuition rather than a candidate's sailing knowledge. Training consisted of an induction weekend, sailing weekends on the boat, placement sails with the skipper observing how a crew performed and specialist courses. It also included the 800-mile Fastnet course in July 1996, a test race from the Ushant in the English Channel round the Fastnet lighthouse off the south-west coast of Ireland and back again. It was an ideal opportunity to test crews, test equipment and whet the appetite of the press.

In order for James Hatfield's disabled crew to take part in a major round-the-world race it seemed sensible to apply for charitable status; and so in November 1993 the *Time & Tide* Trust was formed, its aim being to support and promote the abilities of those who had overcome a disability to take part in a sporting challenge. There were three trustees: James Hatfield, Guy Chandler and public relations consultant Susan Preston Davis.

Trustee Guy Chandler, who suffers from cerebral palsy, initially hoped to be one of *Time & Tide*'s first crew volunteers. In terms of prejudice Guy has been battling with disability all his life. When his cerebral palsy was diagnosed at birth his parents were told that he wouldn't live beyond six months. When he defied this first fateful prediction he was told he would never walk or ride a bicycle. However, by the time he was twenty-six he was playing for the London Scottish Rugby Club and in 1994 he completed the London Marathon. He had been through mainstream education and worked for Lloyd's Insurance Brokers for twelve years, where his greatest challenge had been 'making it in an able-bodied world as an able-bodied person.'

Although Guy passed his interview with Chay to become one of *Time & Tide*'s crew members, he failed his crew selection sail because he was just too weak. It was a huge

The three trustees on the morning of the race start: Guy Chandler, James Hatfield and Susan Preston Davis (©Time & Tide)

disappointment, which he tried to get round by asking the Challenge Business to allow him to compete in a single leg instead. Several months later he was given a second chance at a crew selection sail, but this time Challenge left it to James to make the crucial decision. Reluctantly James had to conclude that Guy was not fit to sail in even one leg, because if someone on deck was in trouble he wouldn't be strong enough to keep himself and the other person safe, and therefore he was likely to be a liability to the boat. By now the two men had become firm friends and James knew just how gutted Guy would feel being passed over like this. But Guy was determined that, as a trustee, he would help the *Time & Tide* project get on the water; and after being made redundant, just a year before *Time & Tide* was due to sail, he was able to put all his energies into working for the Trust and exploiting his contacts in the marine insurance business.

For Susan the call for help came shortly after the premature birth of her daughter, Elena, weighing just 1 lb 10 oz. Susan had been told that her daughter wouldn't survive more than forty-eight hours and although this proved not to be the case, tests then revealed that she had bleeding of the brain and chronic lung disease. No one could yet say whether or not the baby had suffered severe brain damage. 'Although I was in a highly charged emotional state and Elena was still on oxygen, there was no way I could turn down this project because I knew that if my daughter was handicapped I would want her to have an opportunity like this,' recalled Susan. 'But my husband and I had been badly hit by the recession and we had our own separate businesses to run. I thought being a trustee just meant giving advice on media matters, attending a few meetings and making sure that the ethos of the Trust was upheld. I had no idea how much *Time & Tide* was going to take over my life.'

Susan, who was the public relations adviser for the yachting wear manufacturers Henri-Lloyd and a number of other important sponsors in the sailing world and marine trade, had also looked after the PR campaign for *United Friendly*, the yacht Chay Blyth had skippered in the 1981–2 Whitbread round-the-world race. This ultimately proved a great advantage when it came to convincing him that a charity and disabled team were capable of taking part in his race. Initially he was extremely reluctant and when Susan first approached him the answer was a straightforward 'No'.

'The problems were threefold,' explained Chay. 'First, *Time & Tide* was a charity that had no money; second, the whole point of the race is that the yachts are all the same, so there was no way we could accommodate special needs; and third, if we were supposed to be running a level-playing-field race how would that square with people who were disabled? To put it mildly, I was not excited.'

Over and above all this was the factor that Chay did not believe that disabled people would be safe on his boats: a general rule of thumb with ocean racing, which he thought they might not all be able to heed, is one hand for yourself and one for the boat. He was concerned that people would think he was sending a disabled crew off to their deaths. If someone was lost overboard in one of the other boats, it would be seen as a legitimate risk, but if it happened to a crew volunteer on *Time & Tide* his decision to let them enter would be considered highly irresponsible. It would also do untold damage to the image of the Challenge Business and could even signal the end of the four-yearly Challenge round-the-world race.

James remembered Chay's initial response as candid and unconvinced. 'I market and bill this race as the toughest yacht race in the world,' the master yachtsman had told him, 'so how do you think it'll be viewed if a disabled crew wins the race?' James insisted that this was exactly the kind of attitude they were trying to change and that if *Time & Tide* did well in the race it would simply confirm the excellence of the Challenge training.

'At first we didn't see eye-to-eye,' admitted James. 'He thought I was a grotty yachty and I thought he was a pompous prat. I tried to point out to him that one of the things we were trying to change was the way people perceived disability, to the extent that even if a disability was unseen and didn't evoke instantaneous public sympathy, it still affected people's lives and prevented them from achieving things.'

At this time Chay had still not found a race sponsor and he was concerned that having a disabled crew in his race might put off potential clients. He was also anxious about what the individual sponsors of other yachts would think when they realized that with a disabled crew taking part in the race most of the publicity would be likely to focus on that crew. For sponsors, how often they got their company name or logo into the press was important and anything that took away from their moment of glory could make them have second thoughts.

All in all, as far as the Challenge Business was concerned, there was clearly nothing to be gained from involving *Time & Tide*. For several months Chay stuck resolutely to his position. What eventually persuaded him was an ingenious piece of emotive marketing on the part of Susan. She showed Chay a short video of two runners competing in a race, shot at an angle that showed only their heads and shoulders. You could see the two figures raise their bodies to the sound of the starting gun and begin to pound down the track. Running neck and neck, with sweat pouring off their faces, both were putting huge effort into the race, demonstrating equal amounts of will and tenacity. At the end of the film, the camera panned down from the backs of their heads to their feet, at which point it became clear that one of the runners was an amputee.

Visibly moved by what he had seen, Chay began to question his own resolute stance and his mind turned to Sir Douglas Bader, famous for overcoming the loss of both legs, whom he'd known and had great admiration for. The overriding question in Chay's mind now was how fair was he being to exclude the disabled from his race? 'The thought occurred to me, what right did I have to stop these guys having an adventure of a lifetime? We live in an "umbrella" society but I've always believed people should take responsibility for themselves. So I said to Susan and James that, providing each member of the crew could take responsibility for themselves and didn't put anyone else or the boat at risk, I thought we should run with it.'

Chay had always maintained that the ethos of the world's toughest amateur yacht race was about ordinary people achieving extraordinary things. In his book about the previous race, *The Challenge*, he wrote, 'The achievements of a perfectly representative selection of ordinary people, whose only common denominator was the ambition and determination to do something difficult and extraordinary, to my mind stands for everything that is unconquerable about team spirit and co-operation.'

The difference with the *Time & Tide* crew was that they were not ordinary people, in so far as they had either been born with, or acquired in adulthood, a disability that marked them out as different and for the most part less physically able than their counterparts on the other boats. For the *Time & Tide* crew, therefore, the meaning of the word 'challenge' was different. The challenge for them was not only to do something 'difficult and extraordinary' but also to convince others that they were capable of doing it well, safely and above all on equal terms.

Chay's change of heart was *Time & Tide*'s first moment of real triumph. But although it meant that one huge hurdle was overcome many more still lay ahead – not least raising the £445,000 now due to the Challenge Business in order to allow it to compete in the race.

With Susan's considerable PR skills and sailing experience, it seemed obvious that she should manage the PR for the *Time & Tide* Trust and its sponsors; but first she had to check that as a trustee she could legally undertake these dual roles. Under the Charity Commission rules a trustee cannot derive any benefit from a charity unless working in his or her professional capacity – and only then if he or she receives a 'reasonable' remuneration, below the going market rate.

Although it was now clear that her daughter's premature birth had had no long term effects, Susan had become not only indispensable to the project but was totally wrapped up in it. She and James were never under any illusion that *Time & Tide* would make them rich – it was the kind of all-absorbing, ground-breaking project you got involved in almost against your better judgement, and only because you believed passionately in what it stood for. The *Time & Tide* Trust hoped that by participating in the BT Global Challenge race it would demonstrate to the world how people with disabilities could achieve their goals in life and, by example, inspire other people with disabilities to set and achieve their own goals.

Unfortunately just as *Time & Tide* was working hard at putting its message across, some alleged irregularities were uncovered and a complex legal battle ensued, which is still ongoing, with a former *Time & Tide* fundraiser. Thus efforts and funds that should have been put into finding sponsors and new crew members were going towards fighting a court case instead, and for a long time it looked as if *Time & Tide* would never make it to the quayside.

The name '*Time & Tide*' had originally been chosen from the sixteenth-century proverb, 'Time and tide wait for no man,' but in view of the legal problems now associated with this name the three trustees were keen to find another one. Certainly if a sponsor had come forward with a big-enough pot of money, they would gladly have renamed their boat after it, just as most of the other boats had done. But that wasn't going to happen with a small charity like *Time & Tide* and a more suitable name could not be found. So *Time & Tide* it was: the name stuck and soon the image and ethos of the project overrode all the former bad publicity that had been thrown in its way. Indeed the name eventually became such a source of pride to crew members that the idea of ever having wanted to change it seemed incongruous. Then, in a moment of inspiration, James came up with the strap line 'racing the latitudes to change attitudes,' which splendidly summed up the ethos of the Trust – not just as a versatile marketing gimmick but also as a heartfelt statement of intent.

Time & Tide's spinnaker, commonly referred to as the 'kite'. (© Mark Pepper/MPP)

At the same time disabled designer Mark Bosanquet-Bryant came up with an ingenious logo and design for the hull that managed to feature all the sponsors without making the boat look like a floating billboard, by using a rope to link all the sponsors together. Mark had been in the Royal Air Force when an accident left him a quadriplegic; as a result he had learnt how to design with the aid of a special headset which controlled computer keys.

In the meantime, fundraising and the search for more crew had to continue. Many potential crew members were enthralled by the whole notion of sailing round the world, but failed spectacularly on their first interview with Chay. 'One factor they all had in common was vanity,' said Chay. 'They all insisted they wanted to be treated like everyone else, but really what they wanted was special treatment. They simply had no idea what they were looking for.'

In the early days the bulk of the fundraising work was in selling £2 competition tickets at boat shows and other exhibitions. But the nightmare and heartache came from touting industry for sponsorship deals in order to raise enough to meet the deadlines for stage payments set by The Challenge Business. Despite the very welcome support from the chief sponsors they already had – Church's (the shoe manufacturers), Zurich Insurance and BT Community Programme – it was a slow and demoralizing process. As James recalled, 'We would sweat blood making a presentation which would cost us money and take up a whole day's work. While we were making the presentation everyone would be charming to us but then afterwards they'd stop taking our calls. I've lost count of the number of presentations I've made and God knows how many miles I've driven.'

At times Susan and James felt like packing it all in but their decision would have let down too many people – the sponsors who had stuck with them through thick and thin, and the signed-up crew volunteers for whom this had become a huge personal goal – not to mention *Time & Tide*'s first volunteer fundraisers, Stuart Boreham and Guy Chandler. Stuart, like Guy, had cerebral palsy and initially hoped to sail with *Time & Tide*, and had dedicated much time and effort to the project. Some of them had been living *Time & Tide* too long and too intensely, often having put their lives on hold to the detriment of their work and their families. All, however, knew that they were now in the project too deep to throw in the towel. For James particularly, the project was beginning to weigh heavily, and his natural enthusiasm and robust sense of humour, which normally enabled him to gain the confidence of just about anyone, were beginning to wear thin and be submerged by the enormity of the task ahead.

As 1995 drew to a close, the prospect of raising sufficient sums to take part in the BT Global Challenge seemed remote. Consequently the Trust decided it was time to put all its cards on the table and notify the sponsors of their continuing legal battle. So on 22 December the trustees called a meeting at BT's office with BT Community Programme, Church's and Zurich Insurance. 'We sat them all round the table,' recalled Susan, 'told them what had been going on and gave them the opportunity to pull out. They heard what we had to say and then asked us to leave the room. At the time, James and I both felt quite fatalistic – I'd had enough of the endless hassle and James had been offered a job running a marina in the Bahamas. We thought, if they pull out – well, perhaps that's the way things should be.'

But clearly it wasn't. Following a brief consultation, the sponsors called James and Susan back into the room to give the project their wholehearted vote of confidence. They told them that they still believed in everything *Time & Tide* stood for and would continue to finance them, and agreed jointly to write as sponsors to The Challenge Business, pledging support for the project and asking them to give the Trust a few more months' grace to come up with its final payment. It was the green light *Time & Tide* had been looking for, a boost to its flagging morale and the beginning of a turn in its fortunes that would take it to the start line.

It was James's vision, drive and charisma that gained *Time & Tide* support and sustained its high profile during this initial period of the project. In order to help with finance and dedicate more time to fundraising, he sold his successful Ipswich wine bar and invested a great deal of his own personal savings. He had hoped to find another skipper for *Time & Tide* but none came forward, so his role became that of both chairman and skipper. At the same time Guy kept searching for sponsorship leads in the City; and Stuart Boreham, a former employee of Barclay's whose knowledge of analysing accounts had proved invaluable to the Trust, was taken on in the office for a while but when money became scarce he volunteered his services for nothing.

The Trust would never have survived without Susan's total dedication in terms of time and commitment; and the sacrifices that she made with regard to her own PR business were colossal. Although quite apart from a PR person the project needed a project manager, there was no money to take anyone of that calibre on, so Susan agreed that the Trust headquarters could be moved into her own office, from where she would take on the role of project manager as well as PR manager. She was ably assisted by Lucy Quinlan, who also took the Trust book-keeping under her wing. As the *Time & Tide* project took shape Susan found herself becoming more and more embroiled in Trust work, dealing not only with the media and sponsors, but also with every other aspect of the race. Quite apart from this, the excessive workload meant

Richard Horton-
Fawkes
(© Time &
Tide/BT)

that she was unable to take on any new clients, as so much of her office resources were being channelled into this one project.

By Christmas 1995 there were nine crew members who had been accepted by Chay and who were already busy raising £18,750 each for their berth fees. These were cerebral palsy sufferer Stuart Boreham and profoundly deaf Paul Hebblethwaite, who had been the first selected crew members; polio sufferer Brian Beveridge; Chris Ogg, who suffered from a rare muscle-wasting disease; Richard Horton-Fawkes, who was almost totally blind; a young diabetic woman, Julie Ventris; David Tait, a bond trader suffering from asthma; Greg Williams, who had lost a leg in a road accident and had been appointed first mate; and the crew's medic Naomi Smith. The following January Paul Burns and Nigel Smith, both amputees, were accepted. Four more were still needed.

By now *Time & Tide* had secured additional sponsors in the form of Henri-Lloyd, who supplied over £250,000 worth of sailing and onshore clothing to the crew, including survival suits which crew had to take under race rules; and Symbol Technologies, manufacturers of barcoding equipment who had overseas offices in some of the ports of call. A few months later *Time & Tide* secured its biggest sponsor to date – Deutsche Morgan Grenfell. David Tait, who had recently been headhunted by the bank, had instigated a meeting, and as a result Susan and James put forward a proposal and successfully raised the final sum, just four days before the naming ceremony on 24 May 1996. Although *Time & Tide* asked for £250,000, DMG agreed to only £150,000, but introduced them to their suppliers IPC/iXnet, who put in the extra £100,000. The deal was another huge boost to morale and for the first time *Time & Tide* could legitimately claim to have a place in the race.

At long last the project was beginning not only to move people's hearts but to bring in the badly needed cash as well. Barriers that Chay had thought insurmountable at the beginning

Time & Tide
crew with
television
presenter Lynn
Faulds Wood at
the naming
ceremony.
(© Peter
Viccari)

were at last beginning to break down – although money was still urgently needed for hotels, clothing and administration. The crew volunteers who had been involved in training throughout, and who had all been assured places on other boats if *Time & Tide* didn't manage to raise the necessary funds, now knew that they would be the first fully disabled crew to attempt to sail around the world.

Without any royal patronage, the *Time & Tide* Trust desperately needed someone who was sympathetic to disability to christen its yacht at the naming ceremony. So Susan approached television presenter Lynn Faulds Wood who herself had battled with and overcome colon cancer. Sympathetic to a cause that would help disabled people to take part in the challenge of a lifetime, Lynn Faulds Wood gladly accepted the invitation and at the naming ceremony, along with a priest to bless the yacht and the Royal Parachute Regiment Band, added an extra dimension of style and celebration to the day's proceedings. In a short speech James thanked his sponsors for backing *Time & Tide* in its quest, ending up with a final tribute to The Challenge Business for its enduring 'tolerance, faith and vision'.

As early as 1994 Church's had been enthralled by the idea of *Time & Tide*, even though there was no guarantee that the boat would sail. From a promotional point of view this was the only boat worth sponsoring, since Church's was never going to be a major player in the race and there was no point in it joining another boat just to have its name round the toe rail of the hull. Also, in media terms it knew that *Time & Tide* would be more attractive than any other boat. But, like most of *Time & Tide*'s sponsors, Church's was in this for more than just raising its own company profile: it felt a strong moral obligation to a boat that sought to overcome prejudice and promote the sporting abilities of the disabled.

Through Tony Gledhill, its marketing director, the company had taken customers and staff on day sailing activities in order to raise awareness of the aims and ethos of the project. Recognizing that with any sponsorship deal it helps to have someone who's passionate about the subject, Tony Gledhill found himself getting more and more involved. 'I found it was beginning to enchant me,' he said. 'It was more than putting a bit of money into the boat – it had now become both a commercial and personal interest of mine and I had to see it through.' Indeed his commitment to the project was such that he was to sail with the crew in the so-called 'chairman's leg' from Wellington to Sydney.

James was impressed by Church's high level of commitment to the project and was under no illusion about the returns that commercial and personal involvement could bring. He wanted *Time & Tide*'s sponsors to have a hands-on experience during the corporate days on the boat, so that by the end of the day 'the guest would feel part of the *Time & Tide* family'.

BT Community Programme and Zurich Insurance were also sponsors who supported *Time & Tide* in more ways than just by handing over a sum of money. Like Church's, BT Community Partnership Programme (as it became known) stuck its neck out and had agreed to give £75,000 in three annual instalments well before the yacht was guaranteed a place in the race. Project manager Peter Winmill believed that *Time & Tide* typified his programme's objective, to promote people's abilities through spending £15 million of BT's profits each year on community activities; and like most of the other sponsors he felt *Time & Tide* was significantly different to his other projects, in that he and his staff had come to feel passionate about it.

This was also true of corporate communications manager Frances Pilcher and public relations executive Wendy May at Zurich Insurance. If James wanted his sponsors to be part of the *Time & Tide* family, then they and their staff were surely at the heart of it. 'It captured our imaginations because they were such a unique crew,' explained Wendy May. 'We couldn't afford to spend a million pounds on leasing our own boat but we reckoned that just as *Maiden* in the 1989 Whitbread had received an enormous amount of media attention because they were an all-woman crew, the same would happen to *Time & Tide* because they were disabled. From that point of view we more than justified our investment of £20,000. But within the corporate affairs teams it soon became far more than just that for us. It was almost like a crusade that we became intimately involved in.'

There had been ten yachts competing in the original British Steel Challenge, nine of which had now been refitted for the BT race; and another five had been added to the fleet. Sponsoring yachts must have been considered a worthwhile investment, as a number of companies had come forward as sponsors for a second time, including Nuclear Electric who had won the first race and returned to defend its title. Its spokesman, Martin Kay, summed up what was to be gained from a major company taking part in a global race: 'In media terms we featured extensively on regional and national television and the radio and press coverage was exceptional. To have achieved the same profile through advertising would have cost many millions of pounds.'

Of course *Time & Tide* hoped to achieve the same. With the loss of revenue it had suffered from fighting the court case, it now needed all the good publicity it could get to attract more sponsorship; and despite the colossal cost of taking part in the race (which would continue to be a constant drain on resources and manpower throughout the succeeding ten months) the trustees were convinced that competing on equal terms in a race that was billed as the toughest yacht race in the world would in the end pay dividends for the Trust's credibility.

The Challenge Business had been enormously helpful to *Time & Tide*, frequently turning a blind eye when it lagged behind with payments. The huge efforts the Trust had made by now to get the boat to the start line had won Chay's full commendation. He was hugely impressed by the fact that a charity had raised and secured so many sound sponsorship deals, even if the total amount of money still fell short of that raised by other yachts. The bottom line was that he admired anyone who came from the position of underdog and fought their way to the top. After all, wasn't that the whole ethos of the Challenge – and hadn't it proved the greatest motivator of all for the *Time & Tide* crew?

James was adamant that *Time & Tide* was taking on the fleet and the race on equal terms, and he was extremely vocal on this point. But from the start his relationship with the crew hadn't always been an easy one, perhaps because he never attempted to massage their egos or because they couldn't quite understand where he was coming from. He often spoke of his struggles on shore as being far tougher than his struggles at sea.

'One of the major problems we had early on,' confessed James, 'was that the crew thought I wasn't motivated to win, but I was. I just knew that I could race the boat only as fast as they could race it. They were the ones who would have to do it and if we came in between fifth and tenth in the first leg that to me was winning. If, on the other hand, the boat didn't do well I could see them laying the blame on me.'

What the crew perceived as a lack of motivation in James was more a sign of seasoned resignation. He had come to know the other skippers either personally or by repute and was in awe of the skills they possessed. Here was a wealth of talent – indeed some of the most experienced skippers in the business – all competing to come in first, most of whom had considerably more corporate money behind them than he did. While at the end of the day in rough seas no amount of money would prevent the mast from breaking or a spinnaker from blowing, and while all sponsors had an undertaking not to offer their crew incentives, nevertheless having a strong sponsor who was involved and committed to the race could help considerably in building team morale and therefore ensuring a smooth running yacht and an effective crew.

On the other hand the very fact that *Time & Tide* didn't have one major sponsor and the sponsors it did have had no expectations that their yacht should be leading the fleet was a relief to James, as it meant he was under no corporate pressure to win. The attitude from some of the other sponsors was 'I've paid so you'd better deliver', with the effect that for some of the skippers the pressure was immense.

Tensions were also created by the fact that James, like all the skippers, was a paid employee of The Challenge Business, there to ensure first and foremost that he got his crew safely round the world, while the crew were all clients who had paid for their berth fee and therefore had particular expectations of the way things should be. As Chay had often said, '£18,750 buys you a seat at the table.'

James's manner could sometimes seem cool and abrupt, but it was a distance he cultivated by design, for the sake of his own sanity as well as the safety and good management of the boat. If a skipper was too matey with his crew, he believed, it would create the wrong team dynamics and foster a basic lack of respect. He felt it was necessary, therefore, to build a bubble of detachment around himself even if it did create what every captain experienced, the loneliness of command. On a deep level, however, he cared sincerely for his crew and spoke of them with pride and admiration, once claiming that if he'd had to go through what many of them had had to go through his whole world would have collapsed.

Another criticism of James was that he spent too much time involved in business concerning the *Time & Tide* Trust and not enough on the boat itself or on training the crew. To a certain degree this was true, but given the nature of the relationship between the Trust and the Challenge it was unavoidable. Because James was both the skipper and integral to the project's fundraising, his time was often taken up helping Susan to seek sponsorship deals or pursuing the publicity necessary to attract those deals. So while the *Time & Tide* crew had the advantage of knowing who they were sailing with and who their skipper was well before any of the other crew volunteers, James didn't have the time to take full advantage of this. As far as the other boats were concerned, thirteen different crews were put together based on the suggestions of The Challenge Business training skippers, and the names put into thirteen envelopes. In November 1995 the yacht sponsors were invited to a reception at the BT Tower, where each representative was asked to choose one of the envelopes and thus select their crew.

Whereas other skippers on the BT Challenge had the luxury of having one sponsor with a nice pot of money to provide everything they needed, this was certainly not so in James's

An exhausted James Hatfield after the Fastnet Qualifying Race (© Mark Hampshire)

case. As the start date approached most other boats had their stopover accommodation sorted out and paid for, but *Time & Tide* had yet to find and finance accommodation for Cape Town and Boston. Luckily a last-minute deal with the *Sunday Times* provided hotel rooms in Rio and the Ritz-Carlton Hotel in Sydney promised to sponsor the yacht by giving the crew a week's free accommodation. A couple of weeks before the race Lloyd Thompson Insurance came in as sponsors. Susan and Guy were left to raise the additional funds needed for the rest of the race.

Learning the ropes: crew training. Left to right: Paul Hebblethwaite, Nigel Smith and Dave Hodder. (© Peter Viccari)

Time & Tide had hoped that its Business Club Members would also get more involved with their project. Each one had paid The Challenge Business to have their names displayed along the toe rail of one of the Challenge yachts. These companies became involved with the race, got invited to Challenge functions, were given a certain number of corporate days on the boat and were encouraged to network with each other.

This worked well for yachts that had just one corporate sponsor, but *Time & Tide*, supported by a consortium of small sponsors, was disappointed that so many of the Business Club members didn't try to give more back in return. *Time & Tide* Trustees and crew were desperately trying to raise the funds needed for the costs that would be incurred during the race and it seemed that some Business Club members wanted their names on *Time & Tide* for the high publicity value a disabled crew would bring without ever attempting to find out how they could help. It was as if they presumed the money they'd paid to The Challenge Business bought them a slice of the *Time & Tide* project and that the crew should therefore oblige them by generally jumping through hoops.

Some, on the other hand, had been extremely supportive – in particular, Italbrokers, run by an Italian husband and wife team, who had supplied large quantities of their best pasta and meat products for the duration of the voyage. Similarly Olivetti and Mitsubishi Electric had given *Time & Tide* computer equipment, and Diodex had given it maps for promotion. Parceline, of which Chris Ogg was a director, were also extremely supportive of the project.

The Trustees decided that the vessel's port of registration should be London. (© Peter Viccari)

The crew meeting August 1996, with Susan Preston Davis on the far left. (© Peter Viccari)

Time & Tide could not afford to join the other yachts in sending crew luggage from port to port but Parceline had agreed to send one kit bag per crew member to each of the ports of call, thus ensuring that the crew had clean kit on arrival.

Rumours abounded about some of the other boats, whose crews, it was said, had been given spending money for every stopover and had been promised the reimbursement of some of their berth fee if they won the race. Chay dismissed these rumours, insisting that it was stipulated in the race rules and in the sponsor's contract that sponsors should not offer incentives during the race. But inevitably, having a wealthy sponsor gave a yacht certain advantages. After the 1992–3 British Steel Challenge, Group 4 had bought the boat outright to give their skipper, Mike Golding, a chance to sail her single-handed round the world. 'The vast amount of cash being pumped into their training has created a tough racing machine and a crew who have been psyched up to the eyeballs with winning jargon,' noted one *Time & Tide* crew member.

Time & Tide sometimes seemed like the poor relation. In the week preceding the race, some crews stayed together in luxury hotels and were seen wining and dining together in up-market restaurants paid for by their sponsors; but the *Time & Tide* crew had no major sponsor to pay for these luxuries and besides they were all independent individuals who seemed to prefer doing things separately. While no one was suggesting that this disparity in standards of accommodation or the number of team-building away-days organised by individual sponsors and skippers could establish who would win and who would lose the race, it was obvious to everyone what such activities could do to boost morale.

Realizing that morale and team-building still needed working on, James requested help from Peter and Rosie Mackie of MaST International, a leading management training company, who had been paid by The Challenge Business to hone up the skippers' management skills. Offering their services free to *Time & Tide* for a team-building day in Southampton just six weeks before the start of the race, MaST not only identified personality problems but also established that having a common goal was essential to the make-up of a unified team.

During the day's session it soon became apparent that doing well and being seen to compete on equal terms were the crew's main priority. They knew that the eyes of the media were on them and that if they failed to be taken seriously as competitors in the race they would be doing the disabled community no favours at all. MaST was also extremely useful in providing a forum for complaint and modification so that issues and anxieties were aired and to a large degree resolved.

As far as Dave Hodder, a crew member suffering from curvature of the spine, was concerned the MaST Self-Perception Test was pretty much spot on, identifying two contradictory traits in his character: namely that he had strong leadership qualities while at the same time was shy and reticent. 'MaST kicked people into shape,' said this forty-year-old company director from Gloucestershire, 'because from that day we devised the rule of no complaining as well as the objective to sort out problems straight away before they had time to linger and fester.'

On that initial team-building day in July 1996, Peter Mackie noticed that compared with other crews he had worked with, *Time & Tide* seemed to be finding it more difficult to settle down. This, he soon realized, 'was all to do with their situation, because in coping with their individual disabilities theirs had been a particularly singular struggle – a battle which they had waged all alone up until that point. I challenged them on this and said they wouldn't get very far until they realized it would take all fourteen of them working together to sail round the world.'

One thing was certain, however – they had the stamina. The hard lessons in life that each crew member had already learnt had prepared them – perhaps more than any other crew – for the rigours that lay ahead. Preparation was now all a matter of mental training. James particularly had the resilience and willpower to pull it off but only so long as he could keep the crew behind him. Peter Mackie had no doubts on this front: 'When MaST did the leadership training for all the Challenge skippers, James came across to us as one of the more sophisticated. I had no misgivings about him because of his social graces, his background and his obvious maturity.'

Differences between the crew arose from the fact that such a disparate group of people was gathered together under the 'disabled' banner, particularly as many of the *Time & Tide* crew had never had cause to classify themselves as disabled before. In the months leading up to the race the disability issue was never far from anyone's mind, forever brought home to them by a growing media presence that insisted on portraying them as heroic examples of human endurance and triumph. Annoying too could be the attitude of the other crews, which at times was unintentionally patronizing in its overt and steadfast admiration of the so-called 'disabled boat'.

The fact that from the beginning the *Time & Tide* crew fought to be taken seriously and viewed as equal contenders meant that when they were made to berth in Southampton between two other boats, obliging the crew to clamber across *Courtaulds* in order to disembark (especially awkward for the amputees and cerebral palsy sufferers among them), there was no question of changing positions to make life easier. When a crew member suggested complaining to the race organizers about the positioning of their boat, the only honest reply James could give was, 'How can we complain when we're doing this race to show that we're the same as everyone else?'

Racing Motorola in the Solent. (© Mark Pepper/MPP)

Chris Ogg was convinced that one of the greatest strengths their boat had was that each individual had fought hard to overcome the stigma of disability. 'If everyone could just harness that strength and leave the crap behind them we could become a very powerful team. We're kidding ourselves if we think we can go as fast as a well-trained, able-bodied boat in heavy weather, but in a normal situation we should be more competent than any other crew because we'll be that much more focused.'

The veteran sailing instructor Eddie Edrich – known by the crew as 'fast Eddie' – and his wife Pam had also volunteered their skills for nothing to help *Time & Tide* get into shape quickly. The Trust was immensely grateful to both MaST and the Edrichs as they provided a support team for the crew, which allowed the trustees to go out and pursue extra funds necessary for managing the project during the months ahead. By now all James's time was tied up with corporate days and getting the boat ready to sail.

When Eddie Edrich first started helping *Time & Tide* he was struck by just how green the crew were. 'Although they'd done the 800-mile Fastnet course most of them didn't have much sailing experience. So I set about helping them on the foredeck and showing them how to make best use of the sails.' He also observed that although the majority had come to terms with their disability, one or two were still quite angry and consequently found it difficult to blend in. 'The rest had become very tough mentally, all having coped with life through their own personal effort,' he noted, 'but because of this they had reached a stage where if someone wanted to help them, they'd say, "It's OK, I can manage."' Although he could see that *Time & Tide* had not yet quite gelled as a crew and still had a lot to learn in terms of handling the boat, he was absolutely confident that once they were at sea they would soon settle down into a team and make the boat go.

Prior to MaST's in-put and Eddie Edrich's training, James had been close to quitting. 'It reached a point when I was really fed up. I didn't want to be anywhere near the boat or the crew. It was enormously difficult because in the past I'd always chosen who I sailed with and now here I was stuck with a group of people I hadn't chosen and hardly knew.'

In the week before the start of the race (departure date was 29 September) it became apparent that Greg had still not raised the full berth fee. Consequently MaST was called in again to help. Peter Mackie explained, 'It was all a question of how we could present to the crew the decision not to have Greg as mate and instead appoint Chris Ogg – who would be able to see the whole project through and who we now felt was the person best suited for the job. Greg had the money for only one leg and we thought it was ludicrous, with just a few days to go, to let the situation continue when there was a real possibility we'd have to reshuffle the whole thing in Rio.'

Appointing Chris as mate relieved James. Here was someone with invaluable skills upon whom he could rely to keep everyone motivated during the crucial repair-and-preparation time in the days and hours leading up to the start. But he was also quick to acknowledge Greg's skills: 'In the early days of the pre-race the role of the mate was to help give my guys some knowledge of sailing on a big boat and Greg was great for that. But now that they had that knowledge, I was looking for someone with organizational skills, business aptitude, an ability to take an overview and a willingness to delegate. Chris's computer profile devised by MaST showed him to be the perfect man for the job.'

The pressure was on James during that last week in September 1996. Undoubtedly he had a greater responsibility than any of the other Challenge skippers. Safety was paramount in all the yachts but particularly on board *Time & Tide*, where muscle power was so crucially lacking. He was constantly anxious about what could go wrong and had sleepless nights imagining appalling scenarios. A few days before the start of race he said, 'Looking back over all the time I've been sailing, I can see how lucky I've been and can't help wondering what will happen if that luck runs out.' The crew were not privy to these pre-race anxieties; instead, they saw a skipper who seemed remarkably laid back and casual in his approach. The truth was, of course, that he was feeling far from laid back but was doing everything in his power to appear that way. The last thing the increasingly nervous crew needed was an anxious skipper.

Like most of the crew James was aching to get away. The intensity of the days leading up to the start cannot be overstated. There was the pressure of not only a seemingly never-ending list of last-minute tasks but also important goodbyes to be said. Precious moments that the crew thought they would have with friends and family were suddenly swallowed up by commitments to the boat and to the race. But everyone knew that the more thorough their preparation, the better their chances of avoiding unforeseen emergencies and time-consuming maintenance at sea.

As the hours ticked away Dave Hodder was beginning to feel increasingly fractious and unsettled, alarmed at the way the excitement he'd anticipated on departure seemed to be fading fast. And the reality of what lay ahead was also beginning to dawn on his wife, Jane. She had previously found it hard to understand how a busy and resourceful woman like Maureen Ogg could be concerned about loneliness while her workaholic husband, Chris, was away at sea. 'I understood what missing someone meant but I didn't understand about loneliness,' Jane said. 'However, by the week before the race I was beginning to get a picture of how it would be without someone there in the evening, without someone to share things with.' She was worried too that this big sea adventure might change her husband and that Dave would return to her subtly but somehow irrevocably changed.

At the same time Paul Hebblethwaite's mother, who had been so supportive and proud of her deaf son's achievements, suddenly felt a deep sense of sorrow and loss at the idea of being parted from him for the next ten months. 'There's nothing to compare it with,' she said, 'other than perhaps saying goodbye to a son who's leaving for war.'

As the time for the fleet's departure drew closer, the pressure from the media also intensified, particularly on amputee Paul Burns – an ex-serviceman blown up in Northern Ireland – and his family, whom the press considered more media-friendly than many of the others. In this context 'media-friendly' meant having the irresistible combination of looking disabled as well as being reasonably articulate. Because the IRA bomb, which killed eighteen British soldiers, had been headline news in 1979, and because Paul looked every bit a war hero, the press made a beeline for him. His wife and children were also put under enormous pressure and consequently the Burns family and the *Time & Tide* Trust tussled with their two vying agendas: on the one hand the Trust badly needed all the publicity it could get to ensure as high a media profile as possible, while on the other hand the family felt they were taking on the greatest burden of the media pressure by being placed centre-stage.

The atmosphere in Southampton immediately before the start of race was heavy with tension as moods changed from eager anticipation through to soul searching and naked anxiety. Little problems took on huge proportions, tempers flared and crew volunteers on all the yachts lay awake at night wondering what on earth they had taken on. Like most people involved in the race, the *Time & Tide* crew were left with conflicting emotions, both dreading and longing for the moment of departure. For James, waiting for the countdown to the race

The BT Global
Challenge Fleet
in the Solent.
(©Mark
Pepper/MPP)

was like treading water, a no-man's-land of unresolved problems and possibilities. As the departure date drew closer he became increasingly impatient to leave: 'That's my world out there,' he said, pointing towards the vast expanse of ocean that lay ahead of him.

Stuart Boreham recalled Chay Blyth standing on a rostrum in front of the assembled crowd on the Saturday before the race. 'He was telling all the crews about the bad weather that had been forecast. We thought he was then going to go on to say, "But don't worry, it's going to get better," but instead he said, "Don't worry – come what may you're going!"'

Chay Blyth was delighted that *Time & Tide* had made it to the start line and respected the crew immensely, as indeed he did the crew of all the yachts. In the *Daily Telegraph* that week he wrote, 'I identify strongly with each of the 290 amateur sailors recruited for a race that continues to capture the imagination. I see myself as their custodian. They are drawn from all ages, all backgrounds. They come from ten different countries, and have different attitudes, different characters. But there's a common spark, a thread of humanity that binds them together … It's nonsense to suggest such adventures are not the domain of so-called ordinary people. These crews have a tenacity, and quiet courage, that render such generalities meaningless.'

For everyone the harsh realization of leaving family and friends was at times unbearable; and though the crew got on well enough, who could tell how thirty days at sea would affect them? Between them they had a variety of disparate skills – a small minority had racing experience but most had done very little deep-sea off-shore sailing. As 29 September approached, many of the *Time & Tide* crew felt intensely ill-prepared for what lay ahead. While knowing that life 'waits for no man', some couldn't help wondering whether their harshest critics had in fact been right all along when they'd questioned the sanity of a disabled crew taking part in the world's toughest yacht race. Perhaps, after all, they were not, as the media had claimed, 'Hatfield's heroes' or 'the yacht of courage', but rather, as David Tait suggested, 'just a ship of fools'.

Next page:
We're off –
heavy weather,
a sign of things
to come.
(© Mark
Pepper/MPP)

Chapter Two

The Crew

People's motivation for joining the crew of *Time & Tide* varied, but loosely speaking the crew fell into three main categories: those whose physical strength was deteriorating and for whom the BT Global Challenge presented a final chance to wrestle with the elements and test their capabilities to the limit; those who desperately sought a diversion from a the humdrum of daily living, often made all the more pedestrian by the restrictions their disability placed on them; and those who had never particularly sought adventure but somehow came across the project by chance and got hooked. This was the core crew who, with the exception of Stuart Boreham, were expected to complete the whole race.

CHRIS OGG

Chris Ogg, from Worcester, fell into the first of these categories. Forty-one years old, he is an intensely private person, happy mostly in the company of his wife and daughters, unwilling to become intimate with anyone but those few friends who have broken through the barriers of acquaintanceship. He has two passions in life – his job as director of technical services for the delivery business, Parceline, and sailing. In his time he has owned a thirty-one-foot sailing yacht, two Miracle dinghies and a Heron, which at first he sailed with his wife Maureen and more latterly with his two daughters, Kathy and Susan – Maureen being all too happy to let the girls take her place. 'It is Chris's love, not mine,' she said. 'The competitive part of my nature doesn't include sailing.' Nevertheless she carried on supporting the rest of the family in their love for the water, eventually getting used to never seeing them on a Sunday morning or Tuesday evening. Kathy, who was seventeen when Chris became involved with *Time & Tide*, noted that sailing was the thing that brought the family together.

Whereas other fathers might have bought their teenage daughters a horse or a car, Chris bought Kathy and Susan their own small boat. His younger daughter, Susan, was eleven at the time and she contributed £250 of her own savings to the cost – a demonstration to Chris of her level of commitment. She was always the keener of the two daughters. While Kathy declined to sail in the winter because of the cold and wet, nothing would deter Susan, who soon began to show a special talent for the sport and consequently became known by the rest of the family as the 'secret weapon'.

Chris was one of *Time & Tide*'s greatest assets. Not only was he one of the most experienced yachtsmen on board, but also his managerial position for Parceline had given him a great deal of expertise in team-building and motivating people to work to their full capacity. He is a perfectionist in many ways, cautious and thorough, and a man who does not tolerate fools gladly. He is also the master of understatement, with a sharp wit that occasionally borders on sarcasm. While some appreciated his blunt, no-nonsense approach, for others it remained confusing and unhelpful.

A tired Time & Tide *crew after the five-day Fastnet course (© Mark Hampshire)*

Chris's phlegmatic temperament is perfectly matched by that of his supportive, open-hearted wife, Maureen, who, like his daughters, stood by him from the beginning. Susan had gone with Chris to a talk about the last race and they were on the point of signing up for a magazine when they spotted at the bottom left-hand corner of the page an advert for *Time & Tide*. 'I went home and showed it to Maureen, who took it marvellously. "Well, what are you waiting for?" she said. By eight o'clock that evening my application was in the post. In our family that's how big decisions are made. If we want a new carpet we'll debate the pros and cons for hours but big decisions are made instantaneously and spontaneously.'

While Chris wondered whether his application would be accepted, Maureen had every confidence in her husband's abilities. 'How could he be turned down when he was strong, hard-working, determined, a good manager of people and time, and with an extremely useful background in engineering?'

According to Chris, his interview with Chay was full of bizarre and unrelated questions – 'to be kind, one assumes they're meant to throw you,' he remarked. 'It was the text-book interview technique, so that within five minutes you know whether you're going or not. Chay bases his decisions entirely on a gut reaction and communicates whether you're in or out

Chris Ogg
(© Mark
Hampshire)

through his body language.' The one piece of advice he gave Chris was not to tell his boss until absolutely necessary.

The Ogg family have always been close, though it is the kind of closeness that goes unstated, which you sense through an ease and respect rather than through any great displays of emotion. The concern and apprehension the rest of the family felt about Chris taking part in the BT Global Challenge was not something that was ever really aired, but it helped that they all sailed and could appreciate his insatiable desire to circumnavigate the globe. 'A friend of mine,' said Kathy, 'told me that her mum would never have let her father do what Dad was doing, but in our family it's not a matter of "letting" someone do anything – Dad's free to come and go as he pleases.' Perhaps it would have been different, however, if Maureen had not been able to afford the air fares and the time off work to meet Chris at every port of call along the way, with the one exception of New Zealand, from where he was due to fly back and return to work for three weeks.

Unlike the families of some of the other crew members, Chris's decision to take part in the BT Global Challenge did not come like a bolt from the blue but was the obvious next step for someone who had always had a passion for sailing and whose progressive illness was beginning to bite in.

Chris was diagnosed with Charcot Marie Tooth disease in 1990 while on holiday in Greece. It is a little-known hereditary disease that results in the progressive loss of nerve and the wasting of muscle, normally in the hands or feet. There is no fixed rate of deterioration, but in Chris's case he had the rare complication of the loss of his right diaphragm, which gave him severe respiratory problems resulting in two-thirds' lung capacity. Bronchial pneumonia was a constant hazard and flu and colds were now life-threatening. Without ample quantities of antibiotics the Southern Ocean would have been a death trap for Chris. Consequently it took several months for him to navigate his way round the doctors and get them to agree to passing him fit to complete the entire six legs of the journey. Their concern was that he might set off relatively fit but end up not being well enough to do the final leg. At the time *Time & Tide* were keen for every member of the crew to complete the whole race, but the reality was that securing berths for disabled people was a great deal more difficult than for the able-bodied and therefore it soon became apparent that they would have to take on crew members who preferred to do just one or two legs.

Taking a year away from your family and colleagues can cause massive upheavals in your life. From the moment a person is accepted as a Challenge volunteer, daily life, in the ordinary sense of the word, is put on hold. Knowing how impotent a person can feel when it becomes plain to them that they are not as indispensable as they thought they were, Chay's advice to hold off telling his boss until the last moment proved prudent. However, being a director and having what he felt was a moral responsibility to the company, Chris didn't think it was fair to conceal his plans for too long, particularly at a time when the company was about to embark on a massive restructuring programme.

Thus twelve months before *Time & Tide* was due to sail he informed his boss of his plans, warning him that he would not be around during the crucial restructuring period. 'As it turned out my boss supported me 100 per cent,' he said, 'but initially it caused me a problem because work began to be taken away from me. I'd been very active in the business for fourteen years and for a while it was very tough. But then a number of things didn't go as they'd planned, which meant my position was reversed and instead of being backed out of the business I ended up right back in the middle of things.' He also chose this time to tell his employers about his progressive illness, explaining that what they'd assumed was no more than a slight rheumatic limp was actually the first symptoms of something far more sinister.

In the six months prior to the race, Chris's family – like the families of all the crew volunteers – had to make do with seeing much less of him. Most weekends were taken up with training and even during the few waking hours spent at home his thoughts were permanently with the race. What to put in the 19-x-16-x-10-ins. kit box allocated to every crew member was worthy of much speculation. Among other essentials, Chris packed plenty of thermal underwear, ten knickers, ten T-shirts, wet wipes, first aid medicine, Murray mints and two P. D. James books for a bit of light relief. To put your life in cold storage requires a massive amount of organization and the weeks leading up to the race in some ways were likely to be more fraught than days to come spent surmounting ninety-foot waves in prevailing seventy-five-knot winds.

Chris expects a high degree of professionalism from those around him, and admitted during the final training sessions to having suppressed his normal instincts and attitudes to life because here he was working with fellow volunteers not employees. 'I don't think some of the individuals involved would be ready for the true me – it would be destructive rather than constructive,' he once said. He is a workaholic, happiest when he is working fourteen hours a day, seven days a week, and responsible for several projects worth millions. This was the first time in his working life that he'd put a personal goal ahead of his career. His boss was understanding and supportive of the project from the beginning because he realized that the one thing Chris didn't have was the luxury or choice of time. By now, in addition to having lost his right diaphragm and having only partial lung capacity, his nerves were deteriorating, and the muscles in his lower legs and hands were wasting away.

Chris's experience with the other crew volunteers on *Time & Tide* convinced him that those born with a physical handicap had a far tougher time than those, like himself, for whom disability had struck later in life. 'Life really isn't fair for them,' he said, 'and as a result some of them carry chips – in some cases great sacks of chips – on their shoulders.'

Chris is a hard taskmaster – as much on himself as others, never allowing himself to pick up even a crumb of sympathy and despising the 'weak and exploitative' kind of self-pity that in his view disabled people were capable of indulging in. When asked how his diagnosis affected him, he thought for a minute before admitting, 'Well, it gets me down a bit from time to time but then I just throw myself even harder into work. What is upsetting is not so much the physical symptoms as what those symptoms mean – being uninsurable and no longer having the choice of movement as far as movement with my career is concerned.' For Maureen it was even harder to accept. 'At first I just couldn't believe he wasn't going to get better. It seemed so silly to think that he had this long-term health problem just because he'd been ill for a couple of weeks while on holiday.'

Maureen, who trains on accounting packages for a living (and who clearly needs to work as 'living with three people who value themselves quite highly can be a bit of a problem') was immensely supportive of Chris's needs and from the start took an active part in supporting the *Time & Tide* Trust. Frequently, however, as the race drew closer she found herself wishing her husband had never applied to take part in it. 'The bit of me that's his friend never has any doubts that he should be doing this,' she said, 'but the bit of me that's his wife is rather more selfish and thinks how could he possibly leave us for so long.'

One senses with Maureen that being married to such a single-minded and methodical man as Chris has meant suppressing something of her own wants and needs along the way, but all the same she remained the bedrock of that family. It wasn't always easy, however. Susan, who had a particularly close relationship with her father due to their shared love of sailing, had always had a tendency to withdraw into herself and when this became more exaggerated as the start date approached it became a source of some concern to her parents. The family rarely spoke of what the future held, and though at times they undoubtedly retreated into the relative safety of denial, there was a brave attempt to live each day to the full for as long as they could.

STUART BOREHAM

Stuart Boreham, a 31-year-old from Aylesbury, Buckinghamshire, with mild cerebral palsy, was the first crew member to be accepted by *Time & Tide* in August 1994. Like the other crew member with cerebral palsy, Liz Tring, Stuart's keen sense of independence had been fostered since childhood. Both had attended boarding school and both had parents who compensated for their child's disability by emphasizing autonomy. Stuart was the only disabled child in his school and no allowances were made for the extra effort he had to make to move around the building and its grounds. Though that was tough at times, he is grateful now that the teachers had never taken pity on him or passed him off into a side room for special treatment. It fostered a self-discipline and self-reliance that enabled him to fend for himself and forge his own way in the world. Like Liz, he is fiercely independent – with a kind of self-assurance that at times seems to border on arrogance – but what his independence shows is a determination to achieve and accept a challenge that even the most resolute crew members aboard the other Challenge yachts would have found hard to match.

From school Stuart went on to work at Barclay's Bank, where he hoped to be directly in line for promotion. He had his eye keenly set on a managerial post, for which he saw himself as eminently qualified.

At the same time, with the kind of craving for adventure and speed that so many people with limited physical capabilities have, he took up motor racing – a sport he could do sitting down. In 1992, however, he had a crash in which his right thigh was smashed in six places, and he was off work for nine months. Having already had a lot of orthopaedic surgery on this leg because of his cerebral palsy, he now had to have a metal plate and four screws inserted. The doctors warned him that if he broke his leg again he would lose it.

On holiday in Auckland, in the winter of 1989–90, along with three and a half million others, he got caught up in the euphoria surrounding the 1989–90 Whitbread round-the-world yacht race. Although ocean racing seemed to him to be the kind of thing that only the ablest of the able-bodied endeavoured to take part in, in the furthest reaches of Stuart's mind he could not let go of the image of himself out there on the ocean waves of the huge seas of the Southern Ocean. Before long it became a dream that he could not dislodge from his mind.

While off sick he indulged his new interest by keenly following the progress of Chay Blyth's British Steel Challenge, making full use of the publicity available through the BT faxing service. Some time later, in the spring of 1993, Stuart picked up a copy of the *Daily Telegraph* and read about a journalist with the paper who was sailing round the world in one of the Challenge yachts. With motor racing no longer an option, Stuart turned his thoughts instead to sailing and was drawn to the small print at the bottom of the page, which stated that in the 1996–7 Global Challenge race there would be a boat manned entirely by a disabled crew. Despite only having sailed dinghies at school, he thought there was nothing to lose by contacting the Challenge office.

In 1994, at Baden Powell House, London, Stuart met Chay Blyth. The interview was the customary brief, idiosyncratic assessment, resulting in Stuart securing a place on *Time & Tide*, subject to him raising the £18,750 berth fee. 'I knew it would be rough, cold, miserable and extremely frightening, but it caught my imagination and I was absolutely determined to succeed,' he said. Letters to companies asking for money proved fruitless so, realizing that they were constantly receiving a barrage of such requests, Stuart decided to raise all the berth fee

Stuart Boreham
(© Mark
Hampshire)

Paul Burns
(© Mark
Pepper/MPP)

himself. His fundraising campaign began with a sponsored cycle ride, included a round-the-world international evening sampling food from the different ports of call during the race, and ended with him standing in a shopping precinct shaking a box. In just nine months he had raised the entire £18,750.

Although Stuart was an immensely capable small business adviser, back at work his hopes of promotion remained unfulfilled and finally in July 1995, frustrated by a job that he felt held no future for him, he decided he'd had enough and handed in his notice, giving up nine and a half years of security and steady employment.

Despite having felt at work like some obsolete and hard-to-operate piece of machinery, with his resignation came a new determination to do everything he could to help James Hatfield and the *Time & Tide* team turn his dream of sailing in the second round-the-world Global

Challenge into a reality. At that time the project was still in jeopardy, badly in need of sponsorship money and extra hands to secure it.

His parents, though anxious about where Stuart's newfound passion might lead, supported him all the way. As for so many people who are captivated by the magic of the sea, the race became an addiction and before long he was living, breathing and sleeping it. He seemed to relish the spirit of obsession shared by all eager mariners.

From being someone who didn't want to make a crusade out of his disability, he now started to take up a more campaigning stance, fuelled by his determination to show that disabled people had abilities like everyone else. In some way sailing in the race became a way of getting his own back at his disability. While not wanting to be the sort who chains himself to government railings, Stuart saw *Time & Tide*'s role in the Challenge race as a chance to make disabled people more visible. Chay Blyth had boosted his confidence when he'd accepted him as a crew member by crediting him with the stamina and calibre of an ocean racer.

As the first crew member to be picked for *Time & Tide* Stuart saw crew members come, and some go, as well as some muddy water passing under the bridge. Like Brian Beveridge, an earlier recruit with polio, Stuart had been told by Chay Blyth and James after the Fastnet Race, and on the advice of doctors, that he would be unsafe in rough seas and therefore not fit or able to take part in the whole race. Whereas Stuart reluctantly, and not without a struggle, finally accepted the cup half full, Brian took the view that if he couldn't do the whole race there was no point in him doing any of it and consequently he eventually dropped out.

By the time of the start of the race, Stuart had got 5,000 training sea miles under his belt and had sailed six days at one stretch at a distance of 1,038 miles. He'd been sick every time he had been sailing but was confident he would find his sea legs within the first few days.

PAUL BURNS

Paul Burns joined the Army as a boy soldier at the age of sixteen. He had always been a sporty kind of kid and joining the Army seemed the obvious way to pursue what he did best, at the same time giving him an opportunity to see the world. Afterwards he intended to settle down in a regular job – at least regular by Paul's standards, namely the fire service. And it would all very probably have gone according to plan had Paul not joined the 2nd Battalion Parachute Regiment and been posted to Northern Ireland.

On 27 August 1979 Paul's world changed irrevocably. For it was on this day that Lord Mountbatten, who had been enjoying his annual family holiday at Classiebawn Castle in the Republic of Ireland, was blown up on his boat by the IRA, along with the Dowager Lady Brabourne, his fourteen-year-old grandson and a fifteen-year-old local boy who liked boats and had come along to help. On that same day eighteen British soldiers were killed at Warrenpoint in Ulster by 1200 lbs of explosive placed in a hay cart and detonated from across the border, and four British army bandsmen were injured in Brussels by a time bomb for which the IRA also claimed responsibility.

The Mountbatten killing overshadowed the tragedy at Warrenpoint. There had been twenty men in the lorry when it passed the hay cart that day, of whom only two survived – one of them being eighteen-year-old Paul Burns, who lost his left leg and part of the heel of his right, and suffered severe burns.

Now, seventeen years later, Paul had grown accustomed to speaking of that time and, though fed up with being hailed as a hero, he was still willing to tell people anything they wanted to know about the events of that fateful day. He was used to the morbid fascination people showed towards survivors of bomb atrocities, and, considering the trauma he had endured, he was a remarkably well-adjusted man, having come to terms with the loss of not only a limb but of a whole way of life as well. He seemed to have adapted, without bitterness or self-pity, to the new set of circumstances the tragedy had suddenly and violently thrust upon him. In fact his attitude was so reasonable and at times so matter-of-fact that it was easy to forget that Paul had very nearly lost his life at the hands of IRA terrorists. 'It wasn't a bad time for it to happen to me,' he would say, with a measured rationality hard to equate with such a horrendous massacre. 'You see, I was young enough to reconstruct my life then. I had no mortgage, no wife and no kids, so it was like starting from scratch.'

Feelings of guilt plagued him, however. 'It wasn't just that eighteen guys had died that day; there were eighteen families grieving, and I had got away with my injuries, I was alive. That spurred me on in a way, because the things I've done since I haven't just done for myself. I've done them to bridge the gap because the others were robbed of the chance to live their lives.'

He had spent a year at RAF Chessington – the joint services' rehabilitation centre – before regaining enough physical strength to step tentatively back into the outside world. From there he was offered a job as a mechanic for the parachute regiment, first in Cyprus and then in Germany. It was during this time that he met and married his wife Sheila. Finally, he moved to a job in Civvy Street, but the strain of full-time employment proved too much for him and eventually in 1994 Paul was medically retired. Although he fought against this decision up until the last minute, Sheila knew it was the only possible option for a man who was taking painkillers every morning and had turned into 'a walking zombie'.

So at thirty-three years of age Paul Burns was told he would never be fit enough to work again. Despite the fact that various invalidity pensions meant that he wasn't faced with any pressing financial concerns, in some ways becoming part of the army of unemployed was more difficult to come to terms with than the appalling injuries he had sustained. He had been blessed with a stoical attitude to what had befallen him, but he also had an immense pride and determination not to scrounge off society.

But Paul learnt to adapt to yet another change well. Once he had given up work he moved with his wife and three children from a four-bedroom semi in Farnborough to a smaller terraced house in Salisbury, near to where Sheila's parents lived. Having always put his job first, he now applied himself to his family.

Despite his injuries Paul was a tall, muscular man with a passion for adventure sports – or rather for anything that didn't require speed on two legs. Looking something like a life-size 'action man', he had tried everything from parachute jumping to deep-sea diving. Although he loved parachute jumping, the strain of landing on his so-called 'good' leg wasn't doing him any favours and it was at this point that sailing came into the picture as one of the few sports that didn't require excessive mobility. He became involved first in Sailability (an organization that gives disabled people an opportunity to sail) and then in BLESMA – the British Limbless Ex-Servicemen's Association – and it was during that time that, while visiting the Boat Show with his friend Nigel Smith in January 1996, he first met Stuart Boreham and heard about *Time & Tide*. That evening, after an interview with Chay Blyth, he went home and asked his wife if she would mind him going on a ten-month trip round the world.

From the beginning Sheila supported him, though in truth she longed for him to have a change of heart. She knew too that the chances of this were remote, since Paul was a man with a steel purpose who never lost sight of his goal. He was now determined to harness the elements and to become one of the first amputees to sail round the world. Sheila feared for his health and safety, knew she would miss him terribly and worried about how the children would fare without their father for so long. Yet she also knew that stopping a man like Paul from pursuing his dreams – no matter how fantastic they might be – would be like caging a wild bird.

Sheila voiced a concern felt by many of the wives, husbands and partners of the BT Global Challenge crews: that during their ten-month separation Paul would change, and to a certain degree she would too, and perhaps when they were reunited and it was all over things would never be quite the same again.

It was good news for Paul when a dressing manufacturer agreed to sponsor him to the tune of a year's supply of bandages, as the first aid equipment which Lesley Bowden had been supplied with, and which was identical throughout the fleet, was intended for everybody's use. This meant that Paul's kit box was crammed full of additional medical supplies for his own use; he also had a couple of spare legs.

Paul's sponsors were many and varied. He had managed to persuade former prime minister Margaret Thatcher to part with £1,000 by writing to her and saying since she hadn't visited him in hospital after Warrenpoint, how about donating to his round-the-world sailing adventure? He had parachuted into tycoon Richard Branson's back garden and elicited another £1,000 from him. The Honourable Company of Fishmongers also contributed, as did the 10th Battalion Regiment. But his most generous sponsor was Stannah Lifts: company owners Brian and Alan Stannah donated £3,000 each, while their staff raised an additional £3,000 – the result being that nearly half of Paul's berth fee was provided by just one sponsor. Paul had been concerned that he wouldn't be able to give his sponsors much back in return, but Stannah Lifts didn't seem bothered as it told Paul it was using his venture as a incentive for its workforce, who would be following the trip closely. *Time & Tide* gave Stannah use of the yacht for staff sailing, to help Paul repay Stannah for their generosity.

Out of all the *Time & Tide* crew members, Paul was probably the person who had to take greatest care of his health, and though he did his best to conceal it he was also probably the person in greatest discomfort and pain. He still had a lot of problems with the skin that had been grafted on to the foot of his left leg and his stump was constantly breaking out in sores and infections. Both he and his wife knew that it was a matter of time before his right foot was amputated as well. So taking part in the BT Global Challenge was in many ways his final chance to experience the sort of autonomy of adventure he'd always yearned for. 'My idea has always been to have ten or fifteen really good years even if I have to suffer a bit for the rest,' he explained. 'To me that's infinitely preferable to sitting at home wrapped in cotton wool for fifty years.'

NIGEL SMITH

Nigel Smith, thirty-one, had joined the Navy at the age of sixteen, but like Paul Burns his dream of a career in the armed forces was shattered when at the age of eighteen while on duty in Cyprus he was hit by a drunk driver. The severe injuries he suffered resulted in his right leg being amputated above the knee.

Always a master of understatement, Nigel is a shy man who has come to terms with his disability with remarkable equanimity. As his older brother remarked, 'Nigel just dealt with it like he dealt with everything. He got on and made the best of it without making a fuss. In many ways the family took it worse.' Nigel himself now thinks of the incident as something that had happened to him in the distant past and he insists he hardly gives it a second thought. So much so, in fact, that 'putting on my spare leg in the morning is just a part of getting dressed.' The £50,000 he'd received in compensation had been invested wisely, so that fifteen years later he still had a substantial sum and could put some of it towards his Challenge berth fee.

Although never one to cry loneliness, Nigel's life had grown empty in recent years before the race. He had never really got over the loss of first his father in 1991 and then his

Nigel Smith
(© Mark
Pepper/MPP)

grandmother and mother between Christmas '94 and the following February. The loss had been immense and especially hard to bear since Nigel's brother and sister now both lived overseas. As some sort of compensation he bought his parents' house, moved in and became involved in RYA Sailability. But his was an unfulfilled and unsatisfactory life. 'Suddenly there was no one there for me,' explained Nigel. 'One minute I seemed to have everything and then I had nothing.' The forbidding emptiness of his parents' house seemed to accentuate his solitude rather than alleviate it, and his work as tool-room grinder had long since ceased to be challenging, instead having taken on a monotonous predictability. 'Mum died at fifty-nine,' said Nigel, 'and it made me think about the inevitability of things. You're born, you bring up a family and then you go. I thought about myself and knew I had to do something different and drastic with my life.'

He first heard about the BT Global Challenge race while visiting the Boat Show with Paul Burns, whom he'd met through BLESMA. Susan Preston Davis and Stuart Boreham, who were there trying to raise awareness for *Time & Tide*, immediately realized they had in front of them two new potential crew members. By five o'clock that evening both Paul and Nigel had had an interview with Chay and been accepted. 'I was flabbergasted,' said Nigel. 'It was unbelievable, but I knew I shouldn't get too excited because *Time & Tide* hadn't raised all the money yet and there was no guarantee we would go.' But for the first time since he'd joined the Navy there seemed to be some point to what he was doing and for the first time since his accident it was as if his disability had actually done him a favour. From then on, with the interest of the world's media focused on *Time & Tide*, Nigel could no longer underplay his situation or dismiss his disability as a tedious irrelevance. 'None of us like the disability label,' he acknowledged, 'but all of us realize we can make it work to our advantage.'

Best of all he was now out of the rut that a series of unfortunate circumstances had wedged him into so firmly. At last he had every excuse to leave his job, rent out his house in Aylesford, Kent, put his car in the garage and set off with his cod liver oil capsules and a *Viz* annual for the adventure of a lifetime. With no family to help him fundraise and with a job that demanded all his daytime hours, the task of raising money for his berth fee didn't come easily and in the end Nigel cut his losses and decided to dig into his own pocket instead to fund the venture.

Sailing gave Nigel an enormous sense of achievement and boosted his self-esteem. What particularly caught his imagination was the thought that he would be doing something that no one else in his village or workplace would ever have contemplated doing.

GREG WILLIAMS

Greg's attitude to the head-on truck collision that resulted in the loss of his right leg at the age of twenty-six seemed less resolved than that of either Paul Burns or Nigel Smith. Whereas the others had adapted and come to terms with their disability with what seemed like remarkably little resistance, for Greg the pain, inconvenience and injustice of it all still seemed to linger on.

Single and living with his parents at the time of the accident, he was forced to give up his truck business and all the freedom that driving across the Continent had entailed. As he began to think about other ways of earning a living, sailing was the one activity that took his mind off his grim circumstances. As a result he started going to evening classes to gain qualifications, which not only provided him with something to get his teeth into but also helped train him in a new and highly challenging skill.

At the Boat Show one year he got talking to some people from Sailability, who invited him to demonstrate some of their boats at weekends. It was the break he needed and, despite racing against able-bodied people, he was surprised to find that he kept winning. As his

Greg Williams
(© Mark
Hampshire)

confidence grew, so did his passion for the sport and eventually he was offered a temporary job as a dinghy instructor at the sailing academy in Cowes on the Isle of Wight. In the meantime he got a number of lifeguard and first-aid qualifications and eventually he was offered a full-time job as a sailing instructor.

Well before *Time & Tide* set sail Greg admitted to disliking the politics of sailing: the big guys versus the little guys, long ocean sailing versus off-shore sailing, the professionals versus the amateurs. As someone who was used to being skipper, he sometimes found it difficult to have to stand back and take instructions, although the crew claimed that his role as first mate during the training sessions was invaluable in teaching them the basics of sailing.

Greg first heard about Chay Blyth's Global Challenge in l994 and he wrote to the Challenge Business asking for details about the race. At the time he wanted to prove that he was capable of more than taking people sailing on pleasant day trips. 'I wanted proper conditions, the rougher the better,' he said. When Challenge informed Greg that it would cost him upwards

Richard Horton-Fawkes (© Mark Pepper/MPP)

of £18,750, he dismissed the enterprise as being well beyond his means. However, several months later, when he was teaching some blind people how to sail, he was told about an all-disabled crew taking part in the Challenge race. Again Greg wrote off, hoping that the berth fee for this special boat would be cheaper. But again he was disappointed – even on the disabled boat the berth fee was to cost him the same amount. He had more or less put the whole idea out of his mind when in November 1995 *Time & Tide* got in touch, having heard of his sailing skills through Sailability, and asked him to come on board the project as they desperately needed someone with his experience. When he told them he was working full-time and could neither afford the fee nor the time to fundraise, they promised to help as much as they could.

It was unfortunate that for a number of reasons Greg was unlucky in his attempts to get sponsorship and as the start date approached he had still only raised enough money for the first leg of the race. As Chay had repeatedly said, 'no cash, no splash'. Everyone was disappointed, but none more so than Greg who joined the start in a mood of quiet resignation, knowing it was unlikely that he would be going beyond Rio.

RICHARD HORTON-FAWKES

At fifty-nine – a year under the cut-off age for Challenge crew volunteers – Richard Horton-Fawkes was the oldest member of the *Time & Tide* crew and also one of the most experienced. His family had been sea lovers for generations, as a boy he'd read Arthur Ransome avidly and had grown up messing about in dinghies on the lakes of Yorkshire. He was experienced in ocean sailing, had been to the Azores and back, and had raced in the Atlantic in his capacity as a partially sighted crew member.

His eyesight had been deteriorating since the age of twenty-five, when he was diagnosed with glaucoma – in those days a relatively new and little-understood disease. It succeeded in destroying fairly effectively the retina in both eyes and Richard was informed that within five years he'd go blind. Fortunately the doctors' predictions turned out to be inaccurate and deterioration, though steady, was slow. However, in 1991 his vision began to deteriorate alarmingly quickly and as a result he was forced to retire from his landscaping business.

At the time when the BT Global Challenge came into his life Richard had no vision in his left eye, other than a vague sense of light and dark, and just 25 per cent vision in his right eye. Like Stuart Boreham and Paul Hebblethwaite, he was one of the first crew members to become involved with *Time & Tide*, although his interview with Chay nearly put an end to it. 'It was a real argy-bargy meeting because that's the way we both are,' recalled Richard, 'but finally Chay reluctantly agreed that I might possibly be a suitable candidate.'

In the months before departure Richard wrote two secret lists – one with the names of the *Time & Tide* crew who he felt were likely to drop out along the way, and the other with the names of the people who he felt would end up actually running the boat. He put himself in the first list: perhaps if he'd been younger, he used to say, he might have considered staying on board no matter what, just to say he'd sailed round the world, but at the age of fifty-nine he was not prepared to waste months of his life on a thankless endeavour out of plain stubborn pride.

Well before the start of the race he had begun to have doubts about *Time & Tide* and the whole BT Global Challenge business. The endless changes to the rules and regulations regarding the yachts undermined his confidence in the project and sometimes he would wake up in the morning with images of himself at sea, cold, wet and miserable, while his friends and his partner, Marion, were enjoying all the creature comforts of home. At times like these he would think to himself, 'Well, that's it, there's no way I'm going!' However, he never did actually throw in the towel, partly because he loved the idea of ocean racing and partly because he'd told so many people he was going and didn't want to lose face.

His relationship with Marion was relatively new; before it he'd lived alone for twenty years in a tiny, cosy, cabin-like cottage in Lymington, Hampshire. He was well aware that over time he'd become a little set in his ways and wasn't the easiest person to live with. Sharing his home, as well as his passion for sailing, with Marion was one thing but living at such close quarters with near strangers was quite another and from time to time frightened the life out of him. While long-distance ocean sailing might be the experience of a lifetime, he knew too that it could be ruined by conflict among a crew crammed together in such a tiny space for weeks, even months, on end. Although he loved reading, his poor eyesight prevented him from escaping into the absorbing world of literature – but he had packed three books of the type you could dip into and which he hoped would provide some solace at times of loneliness – namely *Roget's Thesaurus*, a book of dirty rugby songs and a rag-bag anthology of poetry and prose.

Richard had never sailed with an all-disabled crew before; he had sailed only with crews who were partially sighted and even then 50 per cent had always been able-bodied. To begin with he had found the whole concept of *Time & Tide* extremely alarming but in time had come to appreciate people's strengths and weaknesses, seeing how as a team they could compensate for each other's disabilities. For a blind person, moving around the boat didn't create too many problems because it was a finite space but he told the rest of the crew to communicate with him verbally because he always needed to be made aware of what was happening on deck. He asked them always to put equipment back where it was stored and to replace the food and dishes in the same cupboards so that he knew where to find them.

Although he had some reservations about how well he would get on with James, he believed that 'at sea even the most insensitive of people become sensitized' and he was hopeful that the crew would come together when they were finally out in the ocean doing what they had been trained to do. But experience had taught him that it wasn't going to be easy. He felt that several of the crew had been carried along by all the publicity and media hype and had no idea of what real off-shore ocean racing was like. He knew there would be moments of intense loneliness, irritation and discomfort and that in boredom, hardship and prolonged enforced confinement everyone would undergo a huge mental struggle just to continue.

Although Richard's grown-up children all thought he was insane, none of them had actually tried to dissuade him from going. The only people who did that were two sailing companions who knew just how harsh the reality could be.

JOHN RICH

In 1993 Polish-born John Rich had been working at putting together an Australian entry for the 1992–3 Whitbread round-the-world yacht race from his home in Sydney when he was suddenly taken ill and diagnosed as having stomach cancer. Within days all his plans crashed around him as he underwent surgery and sunk from one apparent crisis to another. Just as he seemed to be making a good recovery from an operation to remove most of his stomach and spleen, the internal stitches collapsed, opening up a passageway from the stomach and allowing everything he was eating to end up in his lungs.

'They stuck tubes in my chest and drained my lungs, and I was hooked up to several machines,' recalled John. 'In a nutshell I was dying. I was thinking about things I'd done in my life – rather like a shopkeeper taking stock of his merchandise. I'd certainly been written off by the medical staff and I suppose I was getting ready to depart. But then I got talking to this nurse one evening and she made me realize that I could have a future. "John," she said,

*John Rich
(© Mark
Pepper/MPP)*

"you must start thinking about what you're going to do when you get out of here – because you will get out of here." The first thought that came into my mind was that I would go off-shore sailing. The next day the doctor came in and said I was looking better; the day after that he came in and said I was making good progress; and four weeks later, to everyone's amazement, I walked out of the hospital with the all-clear.'

Once out of hospital John turned his mind to work. The video and television production company he'd run previously as a one-man business had ground to a halt in his absence and besides, after months of lying in a hospital bed, he no longer had any wish to work on his own. So when a friend offered him a job evaluating the financial performance of companies he jumped at the opportunity.

While working on his Whitbread campaign John had met up with Susan Preston Davis, who had also been involved with the Whitbread race in her PR capacity for Henri-Lloyd, who were the official suppliers of foul-weather clothing. When she came to hear of John's illness and subsequent recovery she remembered that he had taken part in the 1992 Sydney Hobart race. Realizing that here was an ideal candidate for *Time & Tide*, she faxed him immediately with an urgent request to get in touch regarding the forthcoming 1996-7 BT Global Challenge.

It was the green light that John had been waiting for and when Susan asked him if he would like to join an all-disabled crew sailing from Southampton in September 1996 he leapt at the chance. Concerned at first that having cancer was not a genuine disability, he was reassured when he learnt that losing an internal organ was enough to qualify him for the race.

It then took another five months to be passed fit by the Challenge doctors and given the go-ahead by Chay. This time the interview took place over the phone and although John found himself nervously searching for words to describe his life-long ambition to sail round the world, at the end of just two minutes he was amazed to hear the voice on the other end of the line say, 'OK, John, you're in.' For John the notion of sailing round the world was the ultimate goal, a long-sought-after aspiration and a kick in the teeth for the cancer that had so nearly destroyed him.

He worked out that from the day he sent out his initial application to the day the race ended, including mandatory Challenge training in England, it would cost him roughly £50,000, and so with nearly two years still to go he began to put all his energy into raising the money. His first sponsor was the financial services company he was working for, followed by Blackmore – a large manufacturer of vitamins and minerals – who did not provide any hard cash but said they would give him a free supply of minerals and vitamins to monitor his health. 'It was the greatest thing that could happen,' said John, 'because finally a company said we believe in what you want to achieve – go on and do it.' By the time September 1996 arrived John had raised 25 per cent of the money he needed from sponsors, so for the rest, like so many crew volunteers, he sacrificed his own savings.

Of everyone, John seemed to have the most sanguine attitude towards the race – perhaps because he had harboured in his heart the dream of sailing round the world since his early twenties. He spoke of the race with childlike, rapturous enthusiasm, projecting life on board as a sanctuary of harmony and good will. 'Despite our differences we will put them aside and work together towards the common goal,' he announced optimistically. He was adamant that he would never drop out of the race – 'once I decide to do something, I have to do it,' he said – and, dividing the crew up into two categories of followers and leaders, he placed himself firmly and confidently into the latter.

Some of the other crew members regarded John as a very different animal from themselves. It was partly his Polish background, and partly the romanticized view he held of the race, but also the unintentionally officious tone he used to address them sometimes that made them feel this. One crew member remembered how after the Fastnet race, 'John jumped up and gave us a lecture on what we'd done wrong.' It was not something that endeared him to the other crew volunteers at the time, all of whom wondered what gave him the authority to tell them what to do. James, on the other hand, was clearly impressed by the strong signs of leadership John displayed and with Greg looking increasingly unlikely to take on the mantle of first mate, for a while John Rich seemed the most likely contender.

There was no doubt that John was a sincere, caring and committed member of the crew. If he could sound officious it was only out of a determination to succeed rather than any desire to lord it over others. The problem was that the crew did not feel he had the right skills for the job of mate and were concerned that James would hand over the post to him without consulting them first.

How much the decision not to make him first mate affected John was hard to tell. He wasn't present at the MaST meeting in July and never spoke about it afterwards, but it may have played a part in the subsequent turn of events as far as John's race was concerned.

Carolyn Davies
(© Mark
Pepper/MPP)

When, at the farewell crew party just three days before the fleet left Southampton, 39-year-old John stood up and declared that he had been brought up as an only child but now had found thirteen brothers and sisters, everyone applauded. Some, however, who knew the reality of living in a sixty-seven-foot cabin with people you hadn't chosen to sail with, saw John's dreams of a happy, mutually supportive family as sheer delusion. As Chay would often remark, 'I never promised anyone Utopia.'

CAROLYN DAVIES

Carolyn Davies is someone who has spent a lifetime disregarding her hearing limitations and she was eager to experience something other than the environment she'd grown up in. Chay Blyth's round-the-world yacht race provided her with an opportunity not only of leaving Cheshire behind but also of proving she had strengths and abilities the same – if not better – than the next person.

Carolyn was an enthusiastic, even-tempered 33-year-old who, despite initially knowing nothing about sailing, was determined to be as good as the old handers. Initially she found out about the race as a result of being a British Telecom employee. Visiting Cowes in 1995, she was invited for a day's sail on a yacht and, although she'd never sailed before, she was immediately struck by the intensity of this mental and physical challenge and it captured her imagination.

Originally she was intending to be a BT one-legger, which involved raising just £5,000 for the charity of her choice (the standard procedure when an employee of a sponsor was racing a leg), but a shortage of crew volunteers on *Time & Tide* meant that just three months before the start the crew asked her if she would consider taking part in the whole race. Although she was delighted to be given the opportunity to sail round the globe, the proposal presented a tricky problem as far as fundraising was concerned. Having raised her initial berth fee of £5,000 for the Save the Children Fund, she felt it would now be extremely awkward to go back to her sponsors and ask them to start coughing up towards the remaining £13,750. Colleagues had promised to carry on fundraising while she was away at sea but Carolyn knew that without her physical presence the momentum would all too easily be lost. Although she managed to raise a few thousand pounds more towards her berth fee, it was thanks to a generous loan from her grandparents that she was able to take part in the race at all. She wasn't the only member of the crew who had to borrow large sums of money towards the berth fee and although she was in no doubt that she would eventually pay the money back it couldn't help but put an additional strain on her during the weeks leading up to the race and beyond.

Although Carolyn was hugely optimistic about the voyage, she was also realistic about the dynamics of so many disparate people surviving together in such cramped conditions. 'We're all from very different backgrounds and have very different experiences, ideas and opinions, and there are bound to be a lot of personality clashes. But we can't walk away from each other and we're all going to have to learn patience and humility. In the end I think everyone will come out of it a better person.'

Unlike some of the crew, she wasn't worried about living at such close quarters with people she hardly knew. Like other members of the team – James Hatfield, Liz Tring, Stuart Boreham, David Tait and Richard Horton-Fawkes – she had been to boarding school – an experience that would surely help them to adjust to the communal way of life, the lack of privacy and the intermittent bouts of loneliness that life on board would inevitably bring.

Carolyn became deaf at the age of two following a bout of viral pneumonia. She has no hearing in her left ear and only very limited hearing in her right, but since she can hear her voice with the help of a hearing aid her speech is clear and intelligible – only a slight fuzziness in her pronunciation alerts you to the fact that she is deaf. She is also extremely adept at lip-reading, which meant that she played the useful role of acting as interpreter for the other deaf crew member, Paul Hebblethwaite, whose speech was far more difficult to understand.

PAUL HEBBLETHWAITE

While some crew members had made an attempt to learn sign language, most had not persevered and relied heavily on Paul's ability to lip read, and when that failed on Carolyn Davies's interpretation skills. Even before the race began Paul felt that not enough effort was being made to meet him on his own ground. It was fair criticism, yet sign language wasn't something that the crew could pick up easily by reading a book or going on a two-hour course; it required time, effort and above all the will to persist, and with time in such short supply the will to persist just wasn't there.

This meant that Paul's world was lonely and isolated from the start. Easily recognizable by his boyish good looks and thick mane of wavy, fair hair, which hung down over his eyes and earned him the nickname of Viking, this thirty-year-old joiner from Yorkshire was an extremely sociable, confident young man. On his own admission he was a 'party animal' who, feeling the pulsations of the music's rhythm through the floorboards, above all loved dancing. As he was well-known and popular throughout the fleet, it was no surprise that he had won the 'Man Oh Man' competition that BT had organized for a bit of inter-crew fun during start week.

Yet Paul felt that even before *Time & Tide* set sail there were tensions on board, stemming particularly from personality clashes and confusion over Greg Williams's role. In some ways he was right (though *Time & Tide* were certainly not the only yacht to have experienced this) and the MaST team-building day had correctly picked up on what was lacking and what needed to be addressed in order to create a crew who could work well and effectively together.

At the same time Paul knew that his world would shrink considerably as soon as he left port. Conversation wasn't easy and the relief he found from partying wouldn't be found from lying on his bunk 2,000 miles from nowhere and listening to music at a volume of ninety decibels. Even reading a book was not something he could easily indulge in, as Paul's vocabulary and comprehension were limited, due to his inability to hear and therefore understand the nuances and subtleties of language.

Paul was far from a novice in sailing, having cruised since 1988 and notched up 12,000 sea miles, including crossing the Atlantic to St Lucia. However, he had not done any deep-ocean sailing and this now became his greatest dream. Therefore when he saw a newspaper advertisement for the BT Global Challenge he immediately applied and became one of *Time & Tide*'s first crew members to be interviewed by Chay Blyth. 'It was the most difficult interview of my life because he seemed very wary of my deafness,' recalled Paul. Luckily, however, he had brought an interpreter with him, who helped convince Chay that in muscle power alone Paul would bring badly needed strength to the *Time & Tide* crew.

With the unstinting support of a loving family Paul managed to raise above and beyond the required berth fee in under two years, the small rural village in North Yorkshire where he lived being only too willing to back a local lad with a global dream. As the race got under way Paul's mother, Anne Hebblethwaite, was amazed by the amount of interest it generated. 'It was like throwing a stone in a pond,' she said. 'The ripples just went on and on, until people we didn't even know wanted to know about Paul.'

As one of the first crew members involved in *Time & Tide*, Paul was determined to be the first deaf person to sail round the world. When Carolyn Davies was then also given the

*Paul
Hebblethwaite
(© Mark
Hampshire)*

opportunity of completing the race, Paul's initial reaction was one of undisguised irritation, for it seemed that she had somehow appeared at the eleventh hour to steal his thunder. Eventually, however, Susan Preston Davis, who had an ingenious way of smoothing over the cracks and setting the most turbulent situations right, persuaded him that he would be the first profoundly deaf person to circumnavigate the world. After all, hadn't the BBC television deaf programme *See Hear* given him £5,000 towards his berth fee to make short documentary pieces for their Sunday morning programmes precisely because he was the first deaf person to sail round the world?

DAVID TAIT

Like Chris Ogg, David Tait is another unmistakable workaholic. As a bond trader now working for Deutsche Morgan Grenfell, he had risen quickly up the ladder of status and success, and at the age of thirty enjoyed a lucrative salary and a large flat in Paddington, which he shared with his South African girlfriend, Carol. The only trouble was that, given the immense demands placed on him by his job, he had little time to enjoy the advantages of his relative good fortune. Years of pressure and crazy working hours were beginning to tell and as a matter of survival he had started to look for a new and less stressful challenge.

Coming from an environment where news was being pumped through to him seven times a day he was concerned about how he would adjust to being suspended for weeks on end in a news-free zone where important events in the outside world would be viewed as minor irrelevancies. On the other hand the thought of leaving behind the financial community was something he relished. 'When my colleagues ask me about joining *Time & Tide* the first thing they want to know is how I'm going to keep in contact with the financial markets. But what they don't realize is that I don't give a damn about the financial markets – in fact one reason why I'm doing this is to find out whether I really want to carry on working in this same mad way for another ten years.'

David stumbled upon *Time & Tide* by accident. Browsing in a bookshop one day, he happened to pick up one of Chay Blyth's books and noticed at the bottom of the page an announcement about the next Challenge race and a number to call for further details. Having an irrepressible curiosity, he picked up the phone and asked them to send him an application form, though never for a moment believing that he would actually end up on one of the boats.

David has suffered from severe asthma since childhood but for a number of years now has largely got his symptoms under control. The strategy he developed while at school was to get to grips with the problem by finding ways round it rather than fighting it head on. 'Like most boys' public schools, mine was very sports orientated,' he explained, 'but because of my asthma I couldn't take part in them and that's hard if you're a competitive sort of person going to a competitive sort of school. The classroom didn't count and no matter how clever you were, if you weren't good at sport, you were out.' To compensate David took up skiing and found that suddenly, instead of being a kid who couldn't play games, he was now someone who everyone could relate to and wanted to be friends with. In the long term the experience taught him that every child needs to find a sport to excel in, in order to build up strength, stamina and self-esteem.

David saw his place on the boat as being part of a broader picture in which his own personal goal was included within the shared goal of giving disabled people a higher, more visible profile. Like Dave Hodder there was nothing very noticeably wrong with David and he too had borne the brunt of wisecracks about his 'bogus' status on board *Time & Tide*. A journalist from the *Daily Mail*, who had written a double-page spread on the crew a few weeks prior to the start date, had looked surprised when she met David and said, 'But I thought you were

David Tait
(© John Rich)

all supposed to be disabled?' Understandably irked, he replied, 'We don't have to look disabled to take part in this race, you know.'

Disability can indeed be invisible, and with 23 million people suffering from breathing disorders throughout Europe it was appropriate that an asthma sufferer should be one of *Time & Tide*'s crew members. Disability, after all, wasn't just about being physically disadvantaged; it was about being discriminated against on every level of life – whether financially, socially or in the workplace.

David understood this, despite the fact that he had never suffered from overt or blatant discrimination. An invisible disability like his at least allowed you to blend in with the crowd, didn't restrict your mobility or make eyes turn in the street – whether to stare or look the other away. Coming from an environment that advocated the survival of the fittest, he admitted what many thought – that 'however politically correct we may like to think we are, people prefer to hang around with cool people.'

David's bank was extremely supportive in his endeavours to sail round the world, not only by giving him the time off work but also by becoming one of *Time & Tide*'s primary sponsors. The idea of a group of individuals stretching themselves to new limits fitted well with Deutsche Morgan Grenfell's corporate identity and the strong emphasis it placed on pushing the barriers of achievement. As a result, David was asked to do some customer entertaining on corporate days during the stopovers. At one stage the bank had even requested that he fly his suits out to all the ports of call, but he wasn't having any of this and ignored the request, considering it unnecessarily conformist. As one of *Time & Tide*'s most vociferous and dynamic crew members, David had supreme confidence in his abilities and always said what he thought.

LIZ TRING

Liz Tring, a 28-year-old from Benfleet, Essex, suffering from cerebral palsy, has a restless energy. Never happy sitting still for long, she is a combative, compulsive person whose sheer determination and a refusal to take no for an answer means she usually gets what she wants, though not always without getting her fingers burnt in the process.

It was in May 1995 at the Birmingham Health and Safety Exhibition that Liz first came across people shaking a box for *Time & Tide*. She told them that they were welcome to her money but what she really wanted was to go ocean sailing with them, as pottering about in the Solent for a few days here and there no longer satisfied her needs. But *Time & Tide* already had one crew member with cerebral palsy and at that stage wanted to open up the challenge to as many different disabilities as possible. Instead Liz looked elsewhere and that October she got accepted on a boat in the Hong Kong Challenge, a race in which privately owned vessels and charter yachts offered berths for paying crew to travel in a racing flotilla around the world.

Unfortunately, however, having flown to Auckland to deliver the boat back to England, she got thrown off at Fort Lauderdale and never got to sail in the Hong Kong Challenge after all. Instead she began litigation, along with twenty other claimants, to recover the £120,000 that they had lost between them. While Liz knew she had little of hope of recouping the £1,500 owed to her, others had lost far more and she went to court as a matter of principle and out of solidarity for a crew whom she felt had been so badly cheated.

The episode left her bruised. She had been working as a safety adviser for a metal reprocessing firm at the time, but was bored with the job and determined to get out of the rat race as soon as possible – something her colleagues found hard to comprehend. With a company car, her own house and a salary that had doubled in three years, to everyone else she seemed to have made it, but for Liz it was small fry. She gave in her notice, rented out her house, moved back to her parents and thought about her next move.

In July 1996 a friend told her about an article in the *Daily Mail* in which James Hatfield had announced he was still looking for crew volunteers for *Time & Tide*, particularly those with upper body strength and balance.

Liz clearly did not fit the bill, so once again dismissed her dream of ocean racing as inappropriately timed. However, a month before the race start, on a whim she picked up the phone one day and rang the *Time & Tide* office just in case there was a place that hadn't been filled. To her amazement it seemed her hunch had been right and she was invited down to St Katharine's Dock on the river Thames later that week, where all the boats were then berthed. 'James couldn't make a decision about me,' she said, 'because he had just thrown a "wobbly" off the boat, but he told me to come back in a few days' time to help sail *Time & Tide* back to Southampton, after which he would decide.' In the meantime Chay had interviewed Liz and given her the go-ahead, so when James later told her that, despite her apparent weakness, he had decided she would make a valuable crew member and was indeed precisely the sort of person *Time & Tide* had been campaigning for all along, she was overjoyed.

One problem of joining the race so late was that there was precious little time to contact potential sponsors. She'd already raised some money for the Hong Kong Challenge, so there weren't many businesses or individuals left to ask. In the end she raised a small amount of the money herself, but the rest was lent by her family.

With less experience than most of the crew she felt every bit a novice; and she seemed to succeed immediately in rubbing the skipper up the wrong way. However, as the race momentum began to build up and she took part in various training sessions and sponsor days, she put her anxieties to one side, convinced that on the way to Rio the team would gel, undergo the toughest training yet and soon be better equipped to face the far more hazardous Southern Ocean.

From her experience of sailing to date, despite its uncomfortable and arduous nature, Liz found it an endlessly relaxing hobby, particularly as it required complete concentration and was the only thing that helped her switch off from the self-inflicted chaos of her life. Even when resting in her berth she was able to concentrate on a book in a way she found impossible on land, when little plans and concerns would constantly creep in and ambush her thoughts.

Her feisty independence came from a determination to outdo her disability, plus the fact that at the age of twenty while studying at Birmingham university she had become a practising Christian. 'I read the Bible and decided that I had only one life to live and that I was going to do what I wanted with it at every stage and take whatever opportunity came up.' Being at sea, she said, had deepened her faith because it had given her a greater sense of how insignificant and small she was.

Liz found the demands made on her at sea exacting and exhilarating precisely because they required a great deal of physical effort and self-discipline. Like Stuart Boreham, Chris Ogg and all the one-legged crew members she could not take walking for granted. Her balance and co-ordination have been badly affected by the cerebral palsy and every movement she makes takes immense consideration, concentration and effort. Whereas able-bodied crew did not have to think about how to get from A to B in order to perform a simple duty, many on board *Time & Tide* would have already used up much of their energy before even reaching the task in hand.

Liz wrestled with the disabled issue. Like most of the crew this was the first time she had voluntarily included herself as part of this particular minority group and unlike her fellow cerebral palsy crew member, Stuart Boreham, she felt decidedly uncomfortable with it. She had been to university, where she received a double honours in Engineering and Economics, and she had never found her lack of mobility to be a restriction there or at any other place of work. But now, all of a sudden, she was having to align herself with thirteen other people in a similar position to herself and was being asked to fly the disabled banner.

She is someone who has no time for disabled rights and believes in disabled people being accepted and assimilated into the mainstream, so any attempt to group them together under a label seemed to her to be counterproductive and ultimately disempowering. 'Sometimes I feel like an animal in a zoo,' she once admitted, 'and James's attitude seems to be, "You're a really good sailor even though you're disabled."' In Liz's mind there shouldn't have been an 'even though': the crew of *Time & Tide* were there to do a job and were as capable of doing it as the next man.

From the beginning she was wary of the whole concept of *Time & Tide*, wondering if Chay Blyth had agreed to let the Trust take part in the BT Global Challenge simply so that he could get maximum publicity for his race. As she trumpeted her case for individualism it

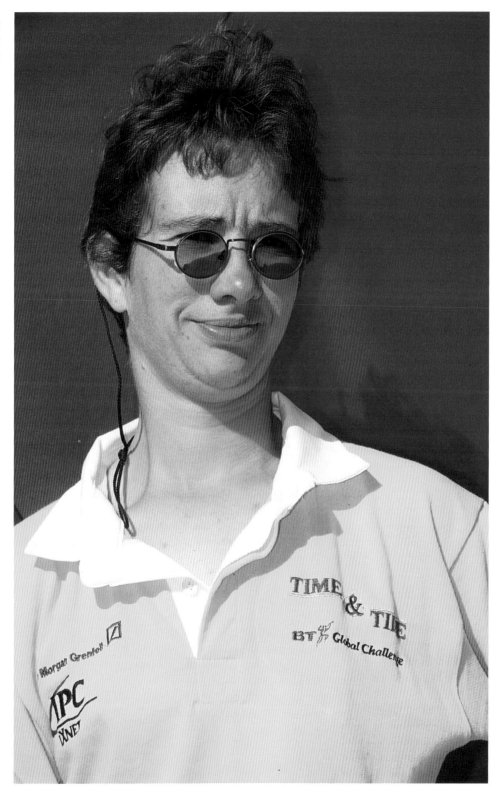

*Liz Tring
(© Mark
Pepper/MPP)*

became clear that her refusal to be seen as one of the crowd stemmed from having a disability that had turned her into a particularly determined fighter. Always having been praised for her ability to get on with life, despite her obvious physical limitations, suddenly she found herself with a group of disabled people all equally able and equally determined not to play on their disability. Perhaps not surprisingly, therefore, even before leaving Southampton, Liz was talking of her ambition to be the first disabled woman to sail single-handedly round the world. 'At least then I could say it was me who'd done it and no one else,' she said.

DAVE HODDER

A hankering for adventure and for breaking the monotony and predictability of his all-too-routine working life was what brought *Time & Tide* to the attention of company director, Dave Hodder. Up until then Dave's sailing experience had consisted of occasional day sails in the Solent and chartering yachts around the Greek islands on family holidays. Before that he had tried everything in the way of recreational sports from golf to shooting, but shooting had bored him and golf's slow progress and tedious social scene disheartened him. Even go-cart racing, which had started off promisingly as a boot-of-car kind of hobby, got too much for him when people started turning up with mechanics and behaving as if they were taking part in Formula One racing.

But then in the summer of 1996, just as the Challenge boats were undergoing their final preparations, Dave was invited by business associate, Chris Ogg, on a champagne and strawberries corporate day round the Solent. When Chris told him about *Time & Tide*, adding that they were still short of a couple of crew members, Dave's response was automatic – 'How disabled is disabled?'

As someone who had been born with his right leg shorter than his left, resulting in curvature of the spine and a crooked heel which had always given him severe back and leg pain, Dave narrowly qualified. In fact, the four-hour watch system, whereby crew worked on deck in four-hour shifts, would suit him down to the ground, since his back always gives him trouble if he stays in bed for longer than four or five hours at a stretch. That evening back at his home in Yate, Gloucestershire, he asked his wife whether she would mind him going. Jane Hodder was hardly ecstatic at the prospect but how could she deny her husband the opportunity of a lifetime when all their seventeen-year marriage had been based on trust and a mutual respect for each other's desires and ambitions?

'I put it down to the male menopause,' Jane said, seeming to understand his restlessness perfectly and taking it neither too personally nor too seriously. Dave had worked hard at building up his business for fifteen years and now at the age of thirty-nine he felt he'd reached a plateau from which there was no going up or coming down. He had a good standard of living and no particular wish to become a millionaire, and the obsessive drive he'd had in his twenties had long since disappeared. As his fortieth birthday approached from behind the horizon he realized that the single most important thing for him now was to have a happy family life, which meant each member of his family being fulfilled in whatever they wanted to do. For him personally this meant a need to achieve something new – a desire to take on another challenge.

But despite her support, Jane was not happy about her husband going and right up until the start week she felt churned up about the race, as it had left everything hanging in the air. 'It wasn't that I resented him going,' she explained. 'I just resented that he could go – that I'd given him the option and he'd taken it. You see, I knew I could never have gone and left him or the children.' She had hoped that at least in the two months before he left they would spend some quality time together, but it soon became apparent that what with training days and getting the boat ready to sail there would be precious little time left for the family. Most of the time she accepted what was happening to their family with good grace, but when Dave announced one evening that he wouldn't have allowed her to go because he couldn't have coped without her, the full weight of her sacrifice began to sink in and she told him so in no uncertain terms.

Raising the berth fee in such a short space of time wasn't a problem for Dave. In the two months he had available to him, he raised £8,000 from business associates and for the rest dug into his own pocket. To appease the family and to make the trip emotionally bearable for them all, he decided to fly them out to four of the five stopovers during the course of the race. But, as start week approached, he found himself becoming increasingly anxious and the idea of leaving his comfortable home, a wife whom he adored and their three children seemed far more of a wrench than he'd ever imagined. The Hodders had not only been happily married for seventeen years, and worked together as partners in the transport firm that Dave had built up from nothing and now ran; they hadn't been apart for a single night until a recent four-day sailing course had given them a taste of things to come. The children were included in everything their parents did and Dave, who greatly regretted not having spent more time with his two sons in the first few years of their life, had latterly had a complete role reversal and played a far greater part in the upbringing of his four-year-old daughter, Lois, whom he clearly worshipped. He knew he would miss his family immensely but the spirit of adventure took hold and he cast any misgivings aside, determined to make the most of this latest challenge.

In his kit box he packed his CD player with a number of CDs, including sing-along songs of the eighties to cheer him up at times of acute loneliness. Escaping into a good book was not an option, as he claims reading has always bored him.

With a disability that is minor compared to those of most of the *Time & Tide* crew, Dave initially felt uneasy about being grouped under the disabled flag. When a local newspaper headline screamed out 'Disabled Man in World First', he wondered who they were talking about. After that people would come up to him in the street saying, 'I didn't know you were disabled', and wanting to know all about it. The Hodders noted with interest that the children's grandparents were mildly horrified at the idea of Dave being labelled disabled. 'Oh dear, what will the children think?' was their initial reaction. The children, on the other hand, were far more accepting, having grown up at a time when it was thought important to assimilate disabled people into society.

Not since the age of eighteen, when his bones had started to harden and set, had Dave suffered the kind of excruciating and acute back pain that had made him punch the side of his head to change the nature of the pain. At the time he had the choice of surgery which carried the risk of making the condition much worse or a plaster jacket which would hold his spine still from the neck down to the waist for seven weeks. He chose the latter and at the end of seven weeks there was a dramatic improvement. The experience, however, made him pack in his job as an electrical engineer and start his own business. The most important thing for someone with chronic back problems, he realized, was to be able to get up and get out when he wanted.

Dave was impressed by the attitude of the crew towards their own disabilities and quickly caught on to their black humour, which at times was the only thing that kept *Time & Tide* buoyant. He admitted that being involved with the boat had changed his attitude towards the disabled. Whereas a year ago he would have walked the other way out of embarrassment if confronted by a disabled person, now he positively relished the chance of mucking in and being part of the team. He cut his moustache short so that the two deaf crew members would find it easier to lip read, and he was always watching out for those whose physical weaknesses

Dave Hodder
(© Mark
Hampshire)

made them unsteady on their feet. Dave's dry sense of humour, like that of his colleague, Chris Ogg, often went above people's heads. 'Take Paul Burns – the para blown up by the IRA,' said Dave. 'On top of everything else he's got a damaged eardrum and he said to me once, "You realize I'm a bit deaf, don't you?" "No," I said, "I just thought you were stupid." He looked at me a bit bemused because he didn't get my humour – he thought I meant it.'

Dave is a determined, self-confident but intensely private person – so much so in fact that on the eve of his wedding his own mother had ominously warned Jane: 'You'll be married to my son all your life but you'll never get to know him.' But Jane was in no doubt that she could make serious inroads into this man and prove her mother-in-law wrong. Now, seventeen years later, she knew instinctively what mood he was in even before he walked through the door.

By and large Dave gets on well with others – his loyal workforce of about thirty rated him highly as a boss – and he seldom has disagreements with people. His only concern about being shut up in a sixty-seven-foot boat with so many people for so long was that very occasionally he met someone with whom he couldn't stand to be in the same room for more than five minutes. 'I had a dog much the same once,' he revealed. 'He would watch other dogs walking past the house for days on end and take no notice of them, but then all of a sudden, for no apparent reason, a dog would come along and he'd want to rip its throat out. I guess I'm the same.' Dave vowed that if he came to feel such instinctive antipathy towards any crew member on board *Time & Tide* he'd be off at Rio.

LESLEY BOWDEN

Of all the *Time & Tide* crew members Lesley was probably the least sure of her motives for participating. Up until the summer of 1996 she had watched the build-up to the race from the comfort of the sidelines, as her son Simon, a BT employee, was doing the Rio to Wellington leg on *Save the Children*, skippered by Andy Hindley. Simon had known for two years that he was taking part in the race and Lesley had taken an active interest in his training, even visiting him in Plymouth to see the boat being built. And that was as far as her involvement would have gone – had it not been for the fact that Simon was seconded to work in the *Time & Tide* office for a few weeks in the spring of 1996 when Naomi Smith, the nurse who had been designated as the medic on board, failed to turn up for the naming ceremony and then wrote a letter of apology to the Trust saying that the pressure of raising the funds for her berth fee had proved too much and that regrettably she was bowing out of the project. With four months to go until the start of race it was now vitally important to find a replacement. Finding crew members for *Time & Tide* was difficult enough in the first place, but to find someone with medical qualifications was going to be an even more awesome task.

Simon's thoughts immediately turned to his mother. She was a Macmillan nurse in Devon who fitted the disability criteria in so far as she had suffered from ovarian cancer in 1985 when she was thirty-eight. He also knew she was at a crossroads in her life.

During the past ten years life had changed dramatically for Lesley. She had been divorced when she moved from Leicestershire to Devon to become a Macmillan nurse. There she met her second husband, while nursing his wife when she was dying from cancer. Sadly, however, they had only been married for eighteen months when he too died.

'I'd reached a stage in my life that wasn't a happy one,' explained Lesley, 'and so in some ways it was the ideal time to a make a dramatic change. I'd already considered doing one leg of the race, but sailing all the way round was not something that appealed. It was only after Simon came and talked to me one Sunday for several hours about it, and then got James to ring me and put forward all the positive things about the voyage, that I began to think that maybe it would be a good idea to go. After all, what did I have to leave behind? So the very next day I talked to my colleagues at work about my plans and they said I could take unpaid leave. Then it was all down to the interview with Chay.'

Chay warned Lesley that it would be hard work as the medic on board *Time & Tide* and asked if she had the money to go. It was too late to start raising money through sponsorship, so she told him that she had the money available now and had reconciled herself to working an extra five years to make up for the loss of income that would be incurred.

Joining the race so late, Lesley was only just in time to take part in the qualifying sail down to the Fastnet. She had virtually no sailing experience and it was a tough six days. With force seven gales and unrepentant seas, she spent most of her time below deck nursing Greg Williams, who had an infection on his stump, and Julie Ventris, whose diabetes became so out of control that she was later dropped from the crew as being clearly unfit and unsafe to sail. It was an exacting experience and a portent of things to come.

On several occasions Lesley thought seriously about dropping out. Common sense told her that her minimal sailing experience was a disadvantage; and she was saddled with the most awesome responsibility of all the Challenge crew medics, and was likely to be spending more time tending to injuries and infections than sailing the boat. On the other hand, she felt a keen sense of commitment to the *Time & Tide* project and had no desire to let James or the Trust down. Every time she voiced her doubts and concerns she was somehow persuaded by James and the rest of the crew to stick it out and stay with the project. It would, she knew, have been a major blow for them to lose their medic at this late stage, as under the Challenge rules no boat was permitted to sail without a doctor or nurse on board.

Lesley was hesitant, too, about living with so many people in such a close environment. She had lived on her own in a four-bedroom house with a large garden for the past four years and didn't quite know what it would be like sharing so much of herself with men and women she hardly knew. But she seemed to get on well with Carolyn Davies and was certain that at times, together with Liz Tring, they would need to form a force against the male members of the crew.

Lesley's doubts came to a head during the start of race week. On the Monday, as she herself said, 'I could quite cheerfully have turned round and gone home again,' but luckily by the end of the week the buzzing hub of activity around Southampton's Ocean Village, plus the excitement and anticipation felt by all the crew, had taken a grip and, though she was still far from convinced that she was doing the right thing, at least she knew that once the race had started she would be too occupied with the tasks at hand to carry on questioning the wisdom of her decision to go.

James recognized the immense pressure Lesley was under and determined to give her as much support as he could throughout the 30,000 miles voyage ahead.

*Lesley Bowden
(© Peter
Viccari)*

Chapter Three

Leg One

Southampton to Rio de Janeiro

Departure date 29 September l996; 5,300 miles,
mostly fair-weather sailing, down through the North East Trades,
across the Doldrums just north of the Equator and on through
the South East Trades.

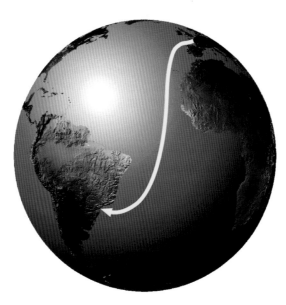

29 September 1996: First Mate's Log – Race Day

Left early for crew breakfast. The generator packed up. Normal Challenge bullshit, that we had broken something. Lost my temper – told them I knew more than the guy who fixes it. It was a good diversion for tension of the day. Saying goodbye was hard. Mo was good. Start was hard, very windy. Had to work so hard to sail the boat. Got to the Needles, had to nav – became seasick for next twenty-four hours. James broke his right hand. Paul B. cut his hand. Saw the spectator boat a few times but no time to wave. Being busy was good – the reality of what I was doing did not sink in!

Life jackets and safety harnesses were worn on deck in big seas and at night. (© Time & Tide)

At seven o'clock on Sunday morning, the day of the start of the race, the crew met at the tapas bar in Southampton's Ocean Village. Within sight of the boats, they had breakfast with their families and friends and tried to make the best of it. But for most it was a tense, miserable affair. Lesley Bowden was so overcome with a mixture of anxiety and emotion that she could hardly speak; Richard Horton-Fawkes was visibly distracted, wondering if he'd bitten off more than he could chew; and Dave Hodder, seated round the corner from the rest of the crew, had a horrible feeling in his gut that he had made a terrible mistake. From the strained faces of the families and friends that morning, it was plain to see that the race demanded a high level of involvement and commitment from everyone, even those on the fringes. Right from the beginning James had told his crew that the hardest part of the trip would be deciding to go; after that the hardest part would be actually going; and once they'd gone the hardest part would be to keep on going.

Possibly the only person not to be harbouring doubts that morning was Nigel Smith. After all, Nigel had no family to leave behind, just the all-too-familiar routine of a job that had begun to bore him. As he was waiting in the rain to embark, a journalist appeared from nowhere and stuck a camera in his face. 'Feeling emotional?' he asked. 'No, just wet,' replied Nigel.

There were problems with Greg Williams that morning, too. Turning up on the quayside he announced he didn't want to sign the contract *Time & Tide* had agreed with the *Sunday Times*, giving them exclusive UK rights to the story, because he already had his own deal with another newspaper. Although Greg was no longer first mate, he was still a key player in the crew, and his resistance did not bode well for the future.

'We had a blazing row,' said James. 'I told him what I thought of him and how unsupportive he was being, and he said he thought the same of me and that he would make a better skipper than me. He was sure I'd be off the boat by Rio and that then he would be the person with most experience to take over as skipper.'

At this point Chay got involved. It was against race rules to sign any contracts with the media without permission from The Challenge Business; therefore Greg's announcement that he was going to sign a newspaper deal of his own just an hour before the start of the race held no weight. 'Leave the guy at the quayside, if you want to,' Chay told James, knowing full well the trouble a reluctant and disgruntled crew member could cause.

Time & Tide operated a four-hour watch system. (© Time & Tide/BT)

The *Sunday Times* exclusivity deal was crucial because it was to pay the crew's hotel costs in Brazil. If Greg failed to sign, there would be no deal and no hotel rooms, and it would be up to Greg to explain to the rest of the crew why. Not surprisingly, and very late in the day, Greg gave in and signed the deal.

In the meantime Chris Ogg, with the help of an engineer from The Challenge Business, was busy trying to fix the broken generator. While a broken generator wasn't going to stop them setting off at the allocated time, it could mean being without a battery charger or fresh-water maker all the way to Rio.

By now James was feeling extremely uptight. 'There was a stink of diesel on the boat, my brother and sister had turned up to say goodbye and there was a decidedly tense atmosphere in the tapas bar. I was tired of people poking microphones in my face and asking me questions – all I wanted to do was be left alone. At the same time I knew full well that the start to every race is crisis management at its peak and I had to stay calm to get things done.'

The weather forecast for that day was for force ten gales, driving rain and turbulent seas. Not ideal fair-weather conditions for the start, but an equinoctial frenzy that would baptise everyone within minutes and give them a taste of the inclement weather to come. The only relief was that the bad weather had prevented much of the support fleet from turning out, which would mean that the Solent was likely to be less like the start of the Grand Prix on the M25, as Richard had feared, and rather more like an obstacle course on a roller coaster.

With just twenty minutes to go before the yachts were due to leave harbour, *Time & Tide*'s fuel system was still in pieces and the crew knew how embarrassing it would look if they were towed into the Solent for the start. Finally by 8.00 a.m. the generator was fixed, the emotional farewells over and the yachts began to leave the harbour one by one, to loud cheers and heartfelt applause. As *Time & Tide* cast off, a single voice could be heard shouting above the rest of the crowd: 'Take care of them, skipper!'

At that same moment Dave caught sight of the strained face of his wife and thought, 'What have I done?' As he turned away, Anne Hebblethwaite, who had come down from Yorkshire with her family and a number of Paul's deaf and hearing friends, caught sight of Jane Hodder and fell into her arms, both women weeping uncontrollably. As a mother who had wept buckets during the past few weeks at the thought of her son's departure, she had actually exercised remarkable self-restraint during the past forty-eight hours, but now all her pent-up emotions came tumbling out. 'But at the same time I was very relieved he'd finally gone and after a while I was all right again,' she said. 'But I'm not so sure about Jane Hodder.'

For the next few hours on board *Time & Tide* no one had time to reflect on the wisdom of their decision to go, as all fourteen crew members were forced to concentrate on the task at hand – namely getting the boat off the start line and out to the Needles. As they left the harbour Paul Hebblethwaite needed three attempts to rig the yankee sheets correctly. 'He'd forgotten everything he'd learnt and no one was watching what anyone else was doing,' James recalled, exasperated at the way everything he'd taught them during the past few months seemed to have gone with the wind. Invariably nervous tension had a detrimental effect on performance, although the *Time & Tide* crew were no different from any other crew in this respect.

As *Time & Tide* motored towards the start line, the wind was already gusting into a powerful force eight gale and driving rain was shortening visibility. For the next few hours all the yachts hung around in a circle while the crew waited, practised manoeuvres, made themselves a brew and tried to settle into a routine. James and Chris put their heads together and decided on a sail plan for the day: they would head towards the start line with only the number three headsail and reefed main, and afterwards drive on with the staysail.

All the yachts had to place themselves alongside the start ferry, which had the Princess Royal and Chay Blyth on board. Luckily James found a bit of shelter from the wind behind the ferry where he could kill the engine and get the crew to hoist the main.

All too quickly, it seemed, the start gun was upon them. *Global Teamwork*, in their haste to get ahead, went over the line seconds early – early enough to be designated a 'blatant premature start' and penalized by being forced to wait at the Needles for an hour. Luckily James, who had seen them heading straight for *Time & Tide*, called for an immediate ease on the sheets, thus depowering the boat and avoiding collision. But then, just as they managed to bear away underneath *Global Teamwork* and round up to come over the start line, James noticed the rest of the fleet powering in behind them.

In the howling September south-westerlies as the boats pounded and crashed their way across the start line, it was chaos on board *Time & Tide*; and what with the din of the helicopters above them and the roar of the wind around them, it became quite impossible to hear instructions being yelled across the deck. As James called for his Southern Ocean sailing goggles to be passed up to him on account of the ferocious spray, his mobile phone suddenly went off. The sight of *Time & Tide*'s skipper with a mobile phone in his hand was to become a recurrent image at the start of every leg – symptomatic of the demands made on a skipper in command not only of a crew but of a charity as well.

'Are you busy?' came a barely audible voice down a hissing line. 'Well, just a little tied up right now,' replied James abruptly. Even though it was a friend from Ipswich calling to wish him bon voyage, it was no time for niceties and he promptly put the phone down. A few minutes later, as James later recorded in his report to Race HQ, 'Things actually got better. My phone, the bane of my life for the last six months of sailing and Trust business, got wet and died. It was going to be a good day after all.'

As *Time & Tide* passed Cowes on a port tack, a ferry of supporters cut across her bow, causing James to slam the boat over in a crash tack and forcing him to give urgent instructions to Greg and Richard to haul in the line on the primary winches.

A few minutes later *Time & Tide*'s own supporter craft passed close by, with friends, relatives and sponsors shouting and waving their final farewells. While Chris was too busy to look for his wife and daughters, Dave was desperately searching out the faces of his sons. 'But it was like looking for someone in a football crowd and I didn't see them. I got very emotional after that.'

On the *Time & Tide* supporter boat, while the children were relishing the stormy weather, wives, friends, mothers and fathers watched with emotionless faces as the fleet headed out through the Needles into the wild, grey sea that lay ahead.

By 3.30 p.m. that afternoon, as the last helicopter disappeared over the horizon, *Time & Tide* pushed out to windward with the seas sending spray high over the bow. By now some of the crew were being seasick; all were exhausted, nervous and soaked. Half an hour later Lesley Bowden was presented with her first casualty.

'We went through this enormous wave,' recalled James. 'There was no back to it and as we slammed down I was bracing myself on the wheel, but it spun out of control and I fell over, trapping my hand between the steering wheel and the wooden struts of the step, which cut into my hand. I had to turn the wheel gently back to get my hand out and when I looked at it there was a big dent and lots of skin torn off. At the same moment someone else, who had been eating sandwiches and drinking tea, was sick over the side and it came flying into my face. It was really the pits, but luckily we then went through another big sea, which rinsed me off.'

Lesley realized immediately that James had broken his hand. She put it in a splint and told him to rest it, but on a 5,000-mile race leg what was resting it? At least the injury now

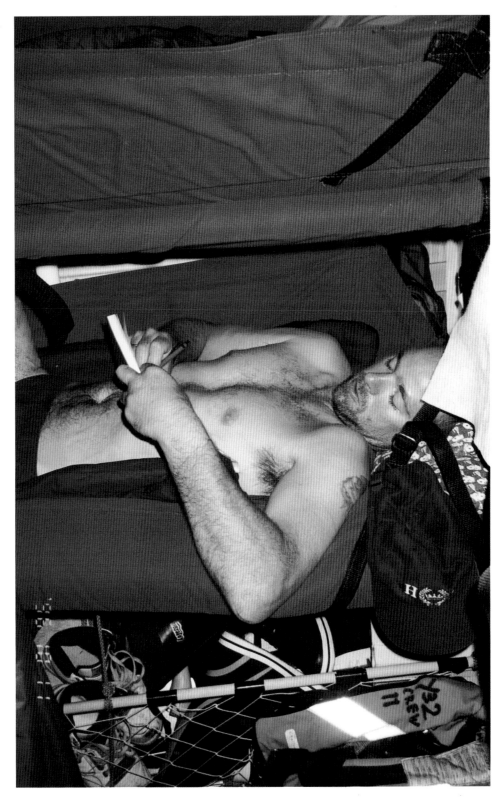

Paul Burns writes his diary. (© John Rich)

Lesley's 'surgery' – first aid on Paul Burns and James.
(© John Rich)

meant he was forced to delegate. Greg took over on the helm and James divided the crew into two watches of six-hour shifts. As night approached there was a subdued atmosphere on board and the next few hours consisted of quiet, sober and robotic sailing as the crew watched the rest of the fleet disperse and realized that there was no turning back.

As seasickness began to take its toll, the watches got smaller and smaller, until for a while there was no watch system at all. For the first time Dave found himself suffering from acute seasickness and was confined to his cabin. Now he understood what experienced sailors meant when they described being seasick as the worst feeling in the world. First you think you're going to die; then you wish you had. Being sick didn't seem to relieve the nausea – it only debilitated you further, until you were too weak, too tired and too hungry to do anything but collapse in a wet and weary heap in your bunk.

Every skipper knew that crew who were violently seasick were better off in their bunks than up on deck trying to help but being totally ineffectual. So Dave and others were laid low for a day or so in their designated bunks waiting for the nausea to pass. A person's bunk very soon became the one and only place they could call their own – as John Rich noted in his log, 'like one's own small world'; retreating to it was effectively a crew member's only means of privacy. The crew were thankful that the Challenge yachts had been designed with comfort as well as safety in mind.

The steel cutter-rigged yachts were purpose-built for Southern Ocean conditions, all 67-foot long with l8-foot beam and 42-ton displacement. Steel was an unusual material to use, considering that a precondition of racing yachts was usually lightness, but Chay had insisted that if he was sending people down to the Southern Ocean, he wanted the boats to be as near impregnable as possible. There was a written system for sailing these yachts that had been devised specifically for inexperienced crews and the whole boat had been designed around one piece of equipment – the winches, which were purposely underwinched to prevent the crew from overwinding the rigging. Although still relatively powerful, the winches were not as powerful as in the de luxe racing yachts, where the job of hoisting and setting sails could be done in double-quick time. For an amateur crew too much power could be extremely dangerous.

All the boats on the Challenge fleet were identical, since the whole point of the race was to give everyone an equal chance, pitting crew against crew rather than boat against boat. A central companionway led forward to a heads and shower port and starboard, and to two 3-person and two 2-person berths with canvas bunks. Heading aft was the galley, with a four-ring gas hob, a small oven and a table with cushioned bench seating. Beyond that were the two remaining twin cabins.

Each yacht carried 12 sails: 4 spinnakers, 2 staysails, 4 headsails, a trysail and a mainsail; all were stored forward, just behind the collision bulkhead. Throughout the yacht food supplies were stored for more than 2,000 individual meals for this longest leg of the race. Near to the chart table were the means to communicate with home, including a radio telephone and e-mail. Navigation equipment included two global-positioning satellite systems, a notebook PC to receive mail and weather faxes, a Raytheon radar system and, in case all else failed, a sextant, which all skippers were required to have with them. The boats were also equipped with three liferafts and an EPIRB (Emergency Position-Indicating Radio Beacon), which could identify the vessel and position it to within two miles, the signal being picked up by passing satellites and relayed to land-based rescue co-ordination centres.

The strict rules for the one-design fleet meant that sponsors with the biggest budgets were forbidden from fitting up their boats with the most expensive equipment. Above all, the boats were designed to be safe, seaworthy 'sailing lifeboats', capable of bringing every crew member home alive – as long as they were clipped on. The designer, David Thomas, described the boats as 'well mannered, easily driven and without excesses of anything, including stability'. Avoiding an excess of stability may seem a contradiction in terms if you're intending to design a boat with safety as your number one design brief, but Thomas explained that this was a safety valve, because if the boat heeled readily, there would be less damage to gear. Thus crew volunteers were protected from the very worst situations. As it turned out, the boats could be and were driven harder than anyone had ever envisaged.

1 October 1996: First Mate's Log: 47°34.5' N 05°33.8' W

Good day's sailing, had three boats behind us, made us feel good. Had great race with Heath Insured II. *Had to trim and drive the boat to get through the tide gate. Sorted the watches out – our problems with crew are not over. It is hard on James and myself as we are the ones pushing.*

Already, two days into the race, it was becoming apparent that the only two people racing the boat were James and Chris. During the night *Heath Insured II* had neared *Time & Tide* through the Passage du Fromveur, hoisted their kite and then steamed effortlessly and gracefully away. By now James was feeling frustrated at their slow progress. 'But there was no way my crew were ready to hoist the powerful kite during a night run, so I had to let *Heath* go. The problem was that no one was trimming to alter the set of sails. Their attitude seemed to be, we've paid, you race.'

Although James knew that the kite should have been hoisted by now, he left it off for most of the next day as well, since people's body clocks had not yet adjusted to the watch system and they were all too wet, hyper and exhausted to be able to handle strong-wind sailing.

Fast Eddie, *Time & Tide*'s sailing mentor, had always maintained that the essential secret for successful racing is to 'trim, trim and trim'. In a report on 2 October to Race HQ Nigel indicated that some of the crew were at least aware of this and were now ready to tweak the sails to catch the wind:

> *We have discovered that now our big problem is speed of mobility. We can do the job but it takes us longer than, we assume, the other yachts. James keeps encouraging us to just concentrate on doing it right first time and is constantly driving home to us about the trim and speed and the speed we trim. Late last night James had us changing sail patterns. (Why not? He has managed to totally change our sleep patterns.) Off watch we are still working on developing life beyond eating and sleeping. Nowhere are you safe from the harsh reality of off-shore yacht racing. Not even the high tog value of my sleeping bag can protect me from the penetrating cries of 'On deck, sail change' – words that will haunt me long after my bank balance has recovered from the bashing I gave it for the pleasure of being here.*

That wasn't the only bashing Nigel received that day. James later reported to Race HQ:

> *Late this afternoon crew volunteer Nigel Smith broke his right leg just above the knee joint, exposing the joint. Lesley Bowden, the medic, cleaned the wound and gave it a squirt of WD40. Paul Burns and David Tait, the sail repair team, were asked for their opinions. It was decided to sicaflex the inner scar tissue to give a firm base for the sail repair thread to bind into, then Duct tape the whole thing till we get to Rio. Nigel tells me that these legs he is currently using keep breaking. (P.S. Nigel is one of our amputees.)*

Just north of Cape Finisterre *Time & Tide* was becalmed while the rest of the fleet caught up with better weather and stormed ahead. The poll of boats that picked up the positions of the yachts every six hours now showed *Time & Tide* to be lagging well behind. James couldn't contain his frustration, knowing that they should have been powering away downwind like the rest of the yachts but instead were rushing nowhere in a sloppy swell at little more than one knot.

If their disability was an excuse, James wouldn't have any of it, although he later admitted, 'On any other boat you can push the ship and retrieve the situation by sending six beefy people to the foredeck. I can't.'

Luckily after twelve hours they picked up light trade winds and for the first time hoisted their spinnaker. At last now they felt they were racing the boat and making progress – even if everyone else was doing just the same.

4 October 1996: First Mate's Log: 40°15.53' N 09°11.29' W

> *Progress slow, now 100 miles behind lead boat. Morale low this morning. Paul up the mast – loose screws. Did some jobs and tidy-up. All hell broke out when the watch on deck did not call for help and had no life jackets on. The wind just built from nowhere. Boat almost broached. We stuffed the kite, reefed the main, changed sail and got the poles in – worked well. Spent two hours on the foredeck doing this. Finally got to bed about 5.30 a.m. Had been up twenty hours. Hard day!*

While the crew were at least getting some sleep, albeit in short bursts, James and Chris were in effect on twenty-four-hour call and becoming increasingly exhausted as a result. In fact,

Becalmed off Cape Finisterre. A tired and frustrated skipper. (© Stuart Boreham)

during the whole of this 5,300-mile leg to Rio James never once got into his sleeping bag. Paul Burns's log entry for 9 October described the effects:

> I stuck my head into the nav station. James was there – I thought awake … I asked for his opinion on the sail trim. He came on foredeck, gave it and went down again. After that he made coffee with mashed potato mix instead of milk powder. I didn't realize it, but he was just about walking in his sleep.

There was literally no opportunity for James to switch off or relax. When *Time & Tide* was heading down the Portuguese coast, and James was trying to catch a rare nap in his bunk, he suddenly felt the boat rock uncomfortably too far to one side. Immediately he rushed on deck, to find the boat on the point of broaching. 'Lesley was in the cockpit holding the sheet of the spinnaker, too petrified to move. Her face looked frozen in time. Greg was fighting the wheel big time. As the helm, he should have been bearing away downwind, giving Lesley orders to let go of the main, but for some reason he hadn't. So I yelled at Lesley, "Let go of the main"; she obviously hadn't grasped that to save the situation you don't just ease it off a bit – you have to throw the main sheet off the winch until it goes flying.'

For the next twelve hours James took over at the helm to show the crew that the way the boat could safely do good speeds was by harnessing the spinnaker for fast downwind sailing and driving her hard. Clearly many of the crew were still frightened of the power of the boat, believing that when things got tough the spinnaker should come down. They had had a choice: either they could take down the kite and go more slowly, maintaining *Time & Tide's* 400-mile gap with the leading yacht, or else they could drive the boat hard, anticipating wind position and putting corrections in before they were forced into a death roll. James chose the second option.

There followed a period of exhilarating sailing. Buffeted by winds of force eight, sailing downwind in a largish swell, they covered forty miles in just three hours, and for the first time the crew's confidence grew. But having been battling with the wheel for twelve hours to keep it steady, James's hands were by now covered in blisters, so he asked Greg to take over at the helm and went below deck to see how the crew were doing. 'To say they were relaxed would be an understatement – they were busy playing Monopoly! They were obviously very confident in the boat indeed.'

The messages received by Race HQ from *Time & Tide* occasionally painted a more positive picture of life at sea during that first leg than was actually the case: 'Well, here on *Time & Tide* we are having a great time. We haven't seen a corporate guest for a couple of weeks,' wrote James, with his tongue firmly in his cheek. But other reports were more reflective, describing moments that captured the very essence of *Time & Tide* – such as James's report written after Greg nearly broached the boat:

> There is something special about watching a true artist at work. Let's take Richard Horton-Fawkes as an example. His blindness is progressive, yet nature seems to bless him with gifts. Three such gifts were on display late yesterday. I handed the helm over to him and away he took us, charging out into the Atlantic from the Powergen Corridor and grabbing the extra speed. Freely available for those with the skill, for the ten-foot seas that were building, his sense of balance, interpretation of the sea's pattern and feel of the breeze on his face give him a greater vision of his environment than many sighted folk. This ability was confirmed later when the breeze had continued to fill and had gone unnoticed by the sighted watch and helm. The skipper

*was first on deck, having been woken by the change in the motion of the yacht, closely
followed by Richard. The broach was in full development. The main was smoked by
James as he passed the winch on his way to the helm. Richard instinctively positioned
himself at the mast, ready to snuff the kite. There on a wildly angled deck he stood
totally together, ready to do a job, with just inner vision – he had no need of sight.
So why, then, when he was serving up supper from the galley through the hatch last
night did he end up wearing it? He hadn't seen the hatch was shut!*

However, within ten days of the leg to Rio, known by the entire fleet as the 'learning leg', it
became clear that *Time & Tide* was not a happy ship. Lesley, whose fiftieth birthday party
had been one of the high points of the week, with cake, party poppers and balloons in the
mess, promptly topped it off with a spectacular fall across the cockpit when a mean sea sent
the boat lurching and her flying. Having cracked a rib and chipped her tibia, she was confined
to her bunk with a splint on her right leg. At least James now had a chance to put into practice
the expensive medical training The Challenge Business had put him through, and, as the Trust
office noted in a message to the boat, 'Even Lesley's plight – the medic being administered to
medically – has something quirkily *Time & Tide* to it.'

Stuart Boreham, whose job it was to repair the heads – in other words fix the lavatories
when they blocked or broke down – had been busy doing just that, when he wasn't being
seasick. But apart from maintenance he was also doing what he considered to be more than
his fair share of galley duties. By the end of the first leg he worked out that he'd been ship's
cook every second day of the voyage.

At the same time there were problems with several other members of the crew. Just a few
days out of Southampton, Dave took James aside to tell him that he wouldn't be continuing
after Rio. The main reason he gave was seasickness: he couldn't envisage going into the
Southern Ocean feeling this lousy. 'But was he seasick or just sick of the sea?' wondered one
crew member who, while fully sympathizing with the way Dave felt, maintained that the
primary reason for him getting off was that he missed his family.

It was certainly true that Dave missed Jane and his three children more than he'd ever
imagined. Whenever he managed to speak to them, he found himself fighting back tears
and longing to get home. Also, whereas he'd imagined he would love ocean racing, he now
found himself longing for the more leisurely pace of blue-water sailing. As he spotted the
Spanish lights on the port side he found himself wishing this was only a cruise and he could
get off. A *Boy's Own* lust for sailing the stormy seas was soon replaced by the realization that
while the highs on this voyage would be memorable, they would be few and far between in
the long, hard slog that lay ahead.

The problem was that back home Dave was used to doing whatever he wanted when he
wanted, so not surprisingly he felt trapped on board *Time & Tide*. Unlike some of the others,
he wasn't escaping from a boring job, or indeed from a highly stressful job, or even from no
job at all. Nor did he have anything to prove to anyone else. And so, within days (perhaps even
hours) of being at sea, he realized that he didn't want to be there at all. He later remarked, 'Our
philosophy at home is that if you don't have a laugh every day, then it's been a waste of a
day. I'm not a serious person but *Time & Tide* was a very serious ship.' He also complained that
during the radio chat shows that linked all the boats on a twice-daily basis, the atmosphere
among some of the other crews seemed a lot more upbeat.

It was true that compared to some of the other yachts there weren't many laughs on board
Time & Tide. Whether this was simply a personality issue or due to the fact that a disabled
crew, who had fought so hard for independence, found social intercourse harder than most

As the miles and days went by the crew's confidence grew. (© Nigel Smith)

is hard to say. But certainly the lack of fun aboard *Time & Tide* was a common complaint voiced by several crew members at various times throughout the ten-month voyage.

James was not altogether surprised at Dave's announcement. He had been impressed by his stoical attitude towards his seasickness and noted that 'up until the equator he worked like a trooper, but then once we were over the equator he went into demob mode.' As far as Dave was concerned, as the weeks progressed it became more difficult to stay involved with the race, as he was no longer privy to decisions being made by James and Chris who, understandably, were more eager to help train up those who would be sailing on with them into the Southern Ocean.

In the meantime, Greg, who could not adjust to James's style of leadership, came in for adverse criticism from some members of the crew. Just five days into the voyage Lesley noted in her log, 'Greg seems to have lost total interest in the boat and its well being. He seems to long to get off at Rio.' A day or two later Carolyn Davies noted in her log, 'Greg has shown no real enthusiasm for the boat to do well and when he is helming it is very erratic – almost as if he wants us to do badly.' James feared that Greg was spreading dissent, but the reality was that he had mentally retired from the race and consequently distanced himself from the crew – some of whom were fast losing respect for him, while others, feeling for his predicament, sympathized but kept out of the way.

Richard Horton-Fawkes had also been showing signs of strain from the outset. Almost immediately James noted how quiet he had become and sympathized that 'it must have been very difficult being so full of doubts.' Already on 3 October Carolyn noted in her log, 'Richard has seemed moody today – perhaps he finds it difficult with so many others around him, when he copes well enough by himself at home.'

Richard was one of the more experienced of the *Time & Tide* crew. He was an instinctive helmsman who had taught himself to sail by the feel of the wind on his face and by the use of an audio compass which beeped when the boat was coming off course. His experience at sea also meant that he was aware of everything that could go wrong. 'It doesn't pay to have an imagination,' he once said, and he admitted to feeling distinctly nervous when less experienced crew members had their turn at helm.

After about three weeks at sea Richard made the decision that he too would be getting off at Rio. James complained later that he had been 'chipping away relentlessly at morale', but most of the crew disagreed with this interpretation of events, though they all acknowledged that Richard had been unhappy about the way some things had been going.

Richard's main complaint was that James was too weak on communication and management skills to keep his crew motivated and united. He also maintained that of all the boats he'd ever sailed on, *Time & Tide* was the least safety conscious. While there was certainly some validity in what he had to say about James's leadership abilities (and James would have been the first to admit this) to accuse him of putting his crew's lives in danger was neither true nor fair. Not one other crew member throughout the ten months ahead was ever to level this criticism at their skipper – all to a man agreed that he was an excellent sailor for whom safety was the main priority. Occasionally James despaired at his crew's failure to take responsibility for themselves and their actions, and he was distressed by the way Richard always seemed to see the negative side of things.

The fact that Richard later spoke out about the safety factor was not, as some thought, a malicious act on the part of a disgruntled crew member, but rather an indication of how genuinely unsafe he felt on board *Time & Tide*. The reason for this may have been that he was more afraid than he cared to admit, but it was more probably due to the fact that out of all the disabilities on board, blindness was the most isolating and arguably therefore the most frightening. While those who were deaf or unsteady on their feet could always see what lay ahead, Richard's perspective was as colourless and unpredictable as the capricious seas.

He was also becoming increasingly disillusioned by the whole concept of a disabled crew sailing in the BT Global Challenge race and he strongly objected to being patronized by the press, frequently referred to as one of *Time & Tide*'s brave and magnificent crippled heroes.

During the leg to Rio Richard would occasionally remonstrate with James, accusing him of failing to train the crew or clarify instructions. He maintained that the crew often didn't understand what he was talking about, 'because he was constantly mixing his sailing metaphors, which you can't do with an inexperienced crew since they don't understand the vocabulary'. Not surprisingly James felt his position was being undermined.

By 16 October rumours about dissent on board *Time & Tide* and the possibility that they were pulling out of the race altogether had somehow reached Southampton. James swiftly faxed a message to Race HQ saying, 'Excellent trip so far so why would we want to consider cutting it short?' He then set out the reasons why Richard, Greg and Dave were leaving the boat at Rio, finishing off with the words, 'My crew have all fought the toughest challenge, which is their lives. Now we are on the biggest adventure of our lives. Rumour has it that some of us shouldn't be alive. We stopped listening to rumour long ago ... may I suggest others do likewise.'

James was still frustrated at the way spinnaker changes, which should have been taking five minutes, lasted up to four hours. Repairs to the boat were never-ending – just as one thing was fixed, something else would break. While Stuart was in charge of repairs to the heads, Chris was a wizard when it came to anything mechanical. Accidents were frequent, though seldom serious, and by the end of the leg Lesley was holding a daily surgery in the galley every morning.

In retrospect some of the incidents seemed comical, though they weren't at the time. In his log on 12 October, Chris noted that while changing a reef, 'The job went pear-shaped, people forgot how do it and it took for ever. During the reef Nigel cut his face when I accidentally gybed the boat – Nigel had clipped on to the boom and gone flying! I felt bad at the time but was pleased to hear that he was OK.' Nigel, whose log was full of terse comment, simply noted that the day, 'Started off with a bang. We put a reef in. I was hanging on the boom. The preventer wasn't on. It went one way, then back. I head-butted the boom. Loads of blood.'

That same day the spinnaker split down both edges and dropped into the sea. All hands were needed in a frantic race to haul it aboard before it disappeared under the hull. Much of the next few days were monopolized by sail repairs as the sewing gang took over in sweltering heat below decks, crouched along the companionway stitching the kite together. David Tait and Paul Burns were the driving force behind the 337-man hours of sail repair, assisted by a loyal gang of workers who literally sweated buckets to get the job done. Needles kept breaking, fingers got sore and, with all the hatches locked tight, the atmosphere grew heavy with the amalgamated smell of sticky bodies and wet sails.

For the main part, the crew were able to forget their disabilities once at sea, though it was easier for some than others. On deck in daylight Carolyn's hearing impediment did not prevent her from understanding as much or as little as any other crew member – only at night was it more difficult to lip read. Paul Hebblethwaite, on the other hand, who had no problem taking instructions before the task was under way, had to rely on Carolyn or on hand signals from the rest of the crew for updates or alterations. If there was a sudden change of plan it was very important that Paul was told immediately and not left to work away diligently in his own silent world on a task that was no longer applicable.

From the start Paul had been feeling particularly isolated by his deafness and, as before the race, frustrated at the way people were neglecting to explain things to him. There were times when he couldn't see people clearly enough to know what they were talking about and other times when he couldn't make himself understood. On 7 October he recorded in his log, 'On duty I was getting tired 'cos it is so boring in the dark. It's very difficult to talk in the dark, as no one likes the torch shining in their faces so that I can see their lips.'

On 24 October he wrote:

> Very frustrating for me 'cos Nigel our watch leader made a mistake on foredeck, just like Paul Burns, and they wouldn't listen to me. After that Nigel said he didn't understand me. So why didn't he listen to me properly in the first place? So I wasn't in a good mood at all, and spent all day being quiet on my own. I asked Lesley for a fag. She kindly gave me one and I shared it with Dave H. I'm going to miss Dave after this leg as he has decided to retire to be with his own family, which I understand. He is a nice, calm, cool man.

James was well aware of Paul's difficulties, particularly with regard to steering. He had written the helming instructions down and explained them to him, but he was concerned about him gybing the main – in other words putting the boat's stern through the wind – and Paul's

Some sunshine
at last.
(© John Rich)

inability to hear the sails luffing, which would indicate sailing close to the wind. Sometimes he would ask Richard to sit by the wheel and give it a tug to leeward if the gybe sounded close, and this seemed to work well. He noticed on one occasion, 'As I was leaving the deck I saw Richard telling Paul the gybe was too close and tugging on the wheel and as he did so Paul released the wheel until he felt the yacht respond. Paul then resumed control and gave Richard a thumbs-up. Both were working in harmony, treating each other as if their disability did not exist.'

The best day for morale was 13 October, the day that *Time & Tide* overtook *Courtaulds*. Champagne was opened and there was a genuine feeling that they were still within grasp of clawing their way back up the pack. Five days later, however, *Courtaulds* caught up and passed *Time & Tide*. It was part of an on-going race between the two yachts that was to continue until Rio. But the crew admitted to finding it hard to get into racing mode on this leg, claiming it was very difficult to build up the motivation when you so rarely saw your opposition.

As *Time & Tide* headed towards the equator, time became blurred, with one day merging into the next and days turning into weeks. It was now slower sailing in fine air conditions, and the crew glimpsed for the first time glorious sunsets, whales, dolphins, flying fish, albatrosses and a few tired swallows who found sanctuary on board. It was noticed by James that the crew responded quicker to the cry 'whale' than they did to 'sail change'.

A day savoured by all the crew was the one on which they crossed the equator and entered the southern hemisphere. For those crossing the line for the first time, the traditionally lighthearted and degrading ceremony to honour King Neptune got under way at 3.05 a.m. on 19 October. Chris was in charge of making the necessary initiating mixture, consisting of porridge, the previous night's Chicken Supreme leftovers, peas, mash, porridge, custard

*Repairing the
sails.
(© Nigel Smith)*

powder, tabasco and blackcurrant squash. James presided over the ceremony at the helm wearing a crown and a trident made out of tin foil and cardboard, while Richard liberally dolloped everyone with the foul concoction and the crew toasted Neptune with champagne for their safe passage. Paul Hebblethwaite, who had shaved off his moustache for the occasion, appeared wearing a Viking helmet (in honour of his nickname) and reckoned it was the best day of the leg so far – though with his long blond hair he was ribbed that his nickname should change from Viking to Vicky!

One major cause of complaint during this first leg was that meals were insufficient, repetitive and often nutritionally inadequate. With breakfast at 6.00 a.m. consisting of porridge, lunch at 2.00 p.m. consisting of soup and a scone and an evening meal at 8.00 p.m. consisting of freeze-dried meat with pasta or rice, almost all the male crew members complained that they were hungry for most of the thirty days at sea. Part of the problem was that those in charge of quantity had left extra supplies in a container in Southampton, having vastly underestimated the amounts required. By the time they neared Rio they were therefore seriously short of basics such as rice and pasta. Paul Burns recorded in his log on 20 October: '8.30 p.m. main meal instant mash and dried crap. No rice. No pasta. Crew very miserable about food.'

David felt that lack of food was giving him a rapacious appetite, which he found disagreeable and debasing. Lesley, whose appetite was meagre by comparison, noted how

*Crossing the equator.
(© Time & Tide/BT)*

David would sit next to her at mealtimes waiting for her to finish: 'If there was some left over I'd ask David if he wanted it and the next moment it was gone.' Of course David could have demanded larger portions from the cooks or made a fuss to James, but he felt there were more important things to make a fuss about. 'Food was the kind of minutia that shouldn't have concerned James, so you had to raise yourself above it – otherwise you'd tie yourself up into little knots and never get through the day,' he said.

James understood the significance of food on a voyage like this and entries in all the crew's logs refer to the particularly appetizing meals he would occasionally cook them. At first, however, some had difficulty appreciating that the evening meal was the main attraction of the day. One evening James had a blazing row with Liz over some custard she'd made, which looked more like yellow water. 'It's only custard,' declared Liz defensively. 'It's not only custard,' barked James, 'it's something I've been looking forward to all day.'

Undoubtedly hunger didn't add to *Time & Tide*'s fortunes on this first leg. With energy levels running low, tempers were short and the general morale of the crew therefore further undermined. Later James was to place the responsibility back with the crew: 'Why couldn't they just broaden their minds and simply make more food?' he asked. 'We had enough bread mix for Africa on board but were still being told by those who prepared the food that there was only a slice and a half of bread for each person. The crew have got to get more demanding of each other.'

John was also getting agitated over food. Having had his stomach and spleen removed following his cancer operation, he now had to eat little and often, but there seemed to be an implicit ban on snacking and those who raided the larder did so surreptitiously and only when others weren't looking.

James had been concerned about John for some time. The man whose leadership qualities had so impressed him during the Fastnet race seemed to be fast retreating into his shell. In a fax to Susan on 13 October James wrote, 'Worried about John Rich. Become a recluse and not the man I first met. No energy.' John's problem with food and the fact that he had initially missed taking a vital Vitamin B12 injection may have partially accounted for this, but also disillusionment had set in. Already on 7 October he had recorded in his log:

> It looks like I will not do a lot of steering on this trip and this is the sad part of the voyage if it doesn't change ... I'm not doing a lot on board, mostly because I'm told that someone else has been trained to do so. Consequently I don't know any more than before the Challenge about systems on board. I hope this will improve ... Have I made a mistake by signing for the Challenge? I don't think so. I still think that the whole experience will make me a more complete person.

Lesley also noticed that John had become a different person. 'He called us his family,' she said, 'but he set himself apart and seemed on the edge. One of the problems was that he had a different sense of humour so we didn't always understand him and he didn't always understand us.' John's expectations had been so high and his willingness to learn so keen that his hopes were almost bound to end in disappointment. But of everyone on board he certainly had the capacity to appreciate the simple pleasures of being stuck out on the ocean 2,500 miles from anywhere. On 16 October he recorded in his log:

> About 6.00 p.m. we entered into rain clouds of squalls. Speed picked up to four and a half knots. I went on deck in my swimmers and had a good rain washdown for some ten minutes until skipper sent me down to put some clothes on. It felt fantastic

standing on deck in the middle of the ocean being washed by fresh water pouring down out of the sky.

Both John and Liz felt they gained far less in the way of knowledge and experience from this voyage than they'd expected. The problem for Liz was that she was a highly intelligent girl who was easily bored. While she would spend time reading the sail-trim manual and never complained about being 'galley slave', she was frustrated by being restricted to the cockpit and forbidden to helm.

John accused James of being a teacher who wasn't willing to pass on his knowledge, but James insisted that Challenge skippers were not hired to be teachers, and sailing with an amateur crew in such hazardous conditions presented him with neither the time nor opportunity.

Although Chay claimed that, unlike in the days of Captain Bligh, £18,750 bought you a seat at the table, entitling each crew member to voice their opinion on planning and navigation, he acknowledged that at the end of the day the skipper had carte blanche on interpretation. He also maintained that whereas The Challenge Business could train the crew up to a certain standard before the race, it was then up to the skipper to select the watch leaders and do what was in the yacht's best interests in the quest to win. Chay realized that some people would return to England after ten months at sea still unable to sail, some would be happy to have just got round and others would be hell-bent on winning. 'But it should all be done by consensus,' he insisted. 'If the entire crew want to have a go at doing

Paul 'Viking' Hebblethwaite. (© Stuart Boreham)

everything and not use their best men for the job it is up to the skipper to allow them to do that.' Chay also said he would have something very harsh to say if one person had paid £18,750 to sail round the world and the only thing they'd ended up doing was cooking or working in the galley.

The problem was that there were too many different agendas on board *Time & Tide*, with some crew members wanting to win at the same time as having a hand at everything. Also, it was perfectly true that some were just too weak to do certain jobs well or safely, and this was often hard to accept.

Stuart, who was allowed to complete only the first, fifth and sixth legs of the race on account of the weakness in his lower limbs, found the trip to Rio extremely hard at times. Not only did he feel he was having to do more than his fair share of galley work; he also felt he was often taking more than his fair share of flak from the skipper and mate, as well as some of the other crew, for all the things that were going wrong on board. Fortunately Stuart had what Richard described as 'incredible resilience and a will of iron, which meant he kept bouncing back'.

While Stuart acknowledged that he hadn't always handled things in the right way, he felt that overall he had been made to carry the can for things that hadn't been his fault. If this amounted to a mild form of bullying, management trainer Peter Mackie was certain that much the same thing was happening on board all the yachts, where personalities were competing for dominance within an artificially fixed and confined space. 'In times of stress we become pack animals,' he explained. 'And it's then that we occasionally pick on the weakest person and verbally eat them.'

If James was at times overly tough and disparaging towards his crew it was only because of the tremendous responsibility placed on his shoulders. Of all the single-handed sailing he'd done he claimed never to have felt so alone as he did on this transatlantic crossing. Later he joked, 'As an ex-heart patient the crew thinks that description of me isn't far wrong – one of them glibly remarked, "And they forgot to put it back last time they opened you up!"'

Not everyone was responding well to Chris's manner, either. As one of the crew said, 'It was as if we were being led by loners. James would never tell us what he was thinking and if you didn't like Chris's style of management you got out of the way.' He added, though, 'He had an abrupt, abrasive manner but you respected him because he'd tell you what he thought. The decision to make him mate was the best thing that could have happened as far as getting the boat to go.' Paul Hebblethwaite also felt indebted to Chris for taking the time and trouble to explain things to him. In his log he wrote, 'He always stays balanced and on the same level. It's good to have a first mate like Chris.'

In many ways Chris's role on *Time & Tide* was the least enviable. Unpopular for having to relay James's instructions, his common refrain would be 'Don't shoot the messenger', as he was frequently on the receiving end of people's gripes and complaints. His log on 15 October gives an impression of the incessant problems he was up against:

15 October 1996: First Mate's Log: 09° 03' N 25° 26' W
> Got up at 1.00 a.m. Could not stay awake. Fell asleep at chart table. Went back to bed at 2.30 a.m., got up at 5.00 a.m. Welcome to the doldrums. Got soaked in rainstorm but was dry again inside one hour. Did lots of sail changes just to keep boat moving. It was very hot – tempers short. Put Richard's rattle back in his pram and tried to stop Liz winding James up. Tried to call home – no go. Got bollocked for going through a squall without calling James. James was uncomfortable with the fact he bollocked me (no prob). It needed to be said and it's hard to find a private place to chat.

*Stuart in the
galley again!
(© John Rich)*

Paul Burns started out by using the leg to Rio to prove to everyone, including himself, that he could do everything. He enjoyed the challenge and responsibility of being one of the two watch leaders, responsible for organizing half the crew during their periods on duty, but as the weeks wore on he became more and more exhausted and in the end couldn't help resenting that he was one of the few being made to do most of the work while others, less able or less willing, hung back. 'If this was a job I'd have left by now', he recorded in his log on 20 October. Eventually a week before Rio, with an abscess on his right knee and his foot black from heel to toe, he put himself on light duties and Nigel took over as watch leader. In his log, for the benefit of his wife, he wrote, 'You know me – I've overdone it again. Here I am, foot up with an ice pack on it. Stump sore, big bruise on side of foot. I just don't know when to stop.'

One of the problems *Time & Tide* had, which none of the other crews faced to the same degree, was the conspicuous disparity between the very fit and the very weak. David and Paul Hebblethwaite had the greatest muscle power, Nigel and Paul Burns the greatest staying power; but others had neither the strength nor, in some cases, the willpower to push themselves forward. At times this led to resentment, with the stronger ones in the team invariably being called on to do most of the hard work.

Almost there – John Rich as Time & Tide approaches Rio. (© John Rich)

David appeared to be one of the toughest on board and the crew respected him as the other watch leader for his guts and ability – even if they didn't always like the candid way in which he addressed them. Accustomed to existing in a highly competitive corporate culture, he was used to people getting yelled at when things went wrong and was only too aware of the insurmountable problems caused when a group lost momentum. But he admitted to finding the trip to Rio at times unremittingly tough. While boarding school had equipped him to live at subsistence level, he missed his girlfriend, Carol, more than he'd imagined and during the voyage to Rio realized he wanted to marry her.

James had particular admiration for those who never complained but just got on with the job. Nigel, who had initially appeared a rather mild, reticent sort of person, had quickly gained confidence, and the more responsibility he was given, the more he took on. He was patient with everyone, disliked by no one and never questioned the skipper's judgement. 'My expectations of Nigel were totally fulfilled,' said James. 'He was one of the few who was absolutely committed to driving the boat fast.' Perhaps Nigel was lucky also for having no expectations of the race. 'I never thought this is how it should be, or that I would come back an expert – I just thought this is how it is, so get on with it.'

From time to time Nigel couldn't help thinking about his colleagues back home, marooned by their nine-to-five jobs in surroundings that never changed. 'If they could only see me now' was the thought that kept coming to his mind. The contrast between the dull routine he'd been used to was so marked that it constantly gave him a thrill and he knew that when he'd achieved his dream of sailing around the world his mates would look at him in a different light. 'If you live on your own you become a bit of a slouch because there's no one behind you and no one to discuss things with,' he once said. 'But with sailing there's always something to do and, what's more, always somebody there to make sure you do it.'

Richard also thought Nigel demonstrated hidden talents and strengths on this first leg and considered him to be one of the few who would make an excellent seaman. 'He had the right temperament and right level of learning capacity, and wasn't too imaginative,' he said.

By contrast, at the end of the four weeks at sea Lesley had come to the conclusion that she would never make a sailor. Whereas she had found training periods exhilarating, now with the pressure to do well sailing brought with it a tension and turned into an endurance test. She also felt in some ways at odds with the whole venture, largely due to her age. 'Except for Richard, who's a different calibre anyway, I was the oldest on board and at times felt part of a different generation,' she explained. 'I definitely didn't absorb things as well as the youngsters, I was no good at anticipating and I'll never understand wind.' Like all the crew, Lesley lost a lot of weight during the thirty days at sea and this didn't make life on board any easier. 'I wasn't strong to start with, but having lost a stone and a half, I found it definitely physically harder than I thought it would be.'

By the end of the first leg, most of the thirteen crew volunteers had mixed feelings. In his log on 23 October Paul Burns reflected:

> *This leg has had its ups and downs. A big up being watch leader, taking the helm and being in control and responsible for all on board. To helm* Time & Tide *across the Atlantic you feel a part of her – you feel you really are personally racing to Rio. I've been from the top of the mast to the bottom of the bilge, from bow to stern, and I've even swum alongside. I've been alive and bouncing with energy then laid up, my legs having let me down. Rio is just around the corner and with it proper rest, real food, maybe a drink or two – then the race starts for real.*

It had been everyone's worst nightmare that *Time & Tide* would drift in two weeks after everyone else, so coming in just four days after the leaders, *Group 4* and *Toshiba*, and only two hours behind *Courtaulds* was a feat in itself. Four days before they arrived in Rio, Carolyn berated those who were disappointed at being in fourteenth position:

> *To look on the positive side, we have done some excellent mileage recently, being the best in the fleet one day; we are a respectable distance from the next boat, with every chance of overtaking them; and we are also keeping up well, to the surprise of everyone who thought we would be weeks behind – so much for being 'losers'! As James said, we are winners the moment we cross the start line for being able to have the chance to take part, complete the race safely and show the world that we disabled can do it.*

But James was frustrated by their slow progress as they neared the finish line. 'We could have beaten *Courtaulds* on the last day coming into Rio if everyone had pulled together and got trimming the sails, but most of the crew had switched off by then and all hope of getting in that day disappeared with the wind. We were drifting on a glassy sea trying to catch the disparate wind.'

As dawn broke on the morning of 29 October the figure of Christ the Redeemer that dominates the Rio skyline came into sight on the horizon. By now the media had joined their painful finish to record every gesture and action as *Time & Tide* crossed the line at 11.30 a.m. GMT. Carolyn recorded in her log:

> *We cross over, amid whooping and horns, and all at once it seems everyone is trying to pass us some form of alcohol. After a cup of champagne (which was tossed aboard from ITN) I made some porridge, by unanimous agreement. So it was that we breakfasted on champagne and porridge on our first day in Rio! I was more than a little drunk, partly on drink and partly on euphoria.*

Although *Time & Tide* had come last, it was a respectable defeat and the rest of the fleet were on the quayside to greet them. The attitude was much the same as it had been when Tracy Edwards's all-women crew on *Maiden* came in to the first port of call at the start of the 1989 Whitbread – honoured for simply having made it to the start line and got through.

At the *Time & Tide* office back in England, despite concerns over crew changes, Susan Preston Davis had cause to feel more optimistic than she had for a long time. They had now secured the interest of ITN, whose chief foreign correspondent, Michael Nicholson, had been in Rio to welcome the crew and his news pieces went out three times that day to an audience of over fifteen million viewers in the UK. Suddenly, with the yacht's arrival in Rio, *Time & Tide* had made international news and people were beginning to take notice. At last attitudes were changing.

Everyone was heartily relieved to have arrived in Rio, not least because they had been dreaming for days of eating something other than porridge and soup. Paul Hebblethwaite made straight for McDonald's; John, who had been studying Portuguese tapes during the last few days of the leg, put on his media cap and started to network furiously; and Dave took Richard sightseeing.

Everyone took advantage of the carnival atmosphere of Rio and some of the crew disappeared off to explore the countryside for a few days' break. The Iate Clube de Rio de Janeiro, one of the most exclusive sailing clubs in the world, hosted the Challenge and what with numerous parties, corporate hospitality days and the BT Global Challenge prizegiving for the winner of the first leg on 16 November, there was plenty of excitement ashore. In between, of course, the crew had to find time to repair sails and service rigs and equipment, as everyone knew that shortcuts on shore invariably led to failure at sea.

With Richard, Dave and Greg now definitely off the boat, and Stuart not back until Leg Five, *Time & Tide* had lost some valuable experience and muscle power. While one of the new crew members, Mike Austin, might bring some badly needed experience to the boat, neither

Time & Tide *in Rio harbour (© Susan Preston Davis)*

ITN's Michael Nicholson interviews the crew on arrival in Rio. (© Stuart Boreham)

of the other two could boast much upper body strength. It was therefore perfectly justifiable that David Tait felt concerned for his own safety on the next, Southern Ocean leg. 'I too for a while considered not going on,' he admitted. 'But I knew I had to get to Wellington whatever happened. It felt like unfinished business.'

John was also having doubts. Having been given only one and a half hours' steering experience on this leg, he felt he had learnt very little about handling the boat and was understandably frustrated. But after some deliberation he too decided to stick with the project, 'In order', as he said in his log, 'to accomplish my goal to sail around the world against prevailing winds and currents in an organized competition racing for the crown of victory.'

In Rio complaints from Richard and Liz about the skipper led to Chay calling a meeting. Richard, Greg and Dave were excluded from the meeting as they were not continuing, but the

Carolyn having
her first proper
meal on shore
after a month of
rations.
(© Susan
Preston Davis)

intention was to find out what was happening on board *Time & Tide* and to see whether the crew still had enough confidence in their skipper to sail into the Southern Ocean with him.

The meeting served a valuable purpose, as it cleared the air and the crew all emerged a lot lighter in spirit, having given their unanimous support to James. Only Liz, who spoke out against James's handling of his crew, felt unresolved about the whole issue. She was the only person to feel seriously short-changed by both The Challenge Business and by her skipper, who, she complained, hadn't given her more opportunity to learn about handling the boat. Chay convinced her that while she had purchased a difficult product, this didn't mean she had purchased the wrong product and, despite her outspoken criticism of him, James encouraged her to continue. This she eventually agreed to do, though it must be said somewhat reluctantly.

For some of the crew Rio wasn't a particularly happy stopover. In addition to the quelling of the rumbling mutiny, two of the crew were mugged, one witnessed a murder and Peter Vroon from Hood Sailmakers, the company that provided each yacht with its sails, died suddenly from meningitis. He had been a well-known, well-liked and respected man who had been closely involved in both Challenge races and on the day before he died had been on board *Time & Tide* praising the crew for their immaculate sail repairs.

Lesley was still very unsure about whether to continue. As the week continued her crisis of confidence took a grip and on the eve of the race she put in an apologetic call to James, telling him that she was terribly sorry but she wanted to quit. Later that evening he and Chris sat with her for several hours trying to put her mind at ease. To their relief their encouragement and subtle persuasion worked.

Back in England Dave was welcomed home with open arms by his wife and brought breakfast in bed every morning. It was to Dave's credit that, despite losing some face over his decision to leave *Time & Tide*, it never bothered him what others thought. 'I've never tried to impress anybody,' he said, admitting that one or two people at work had wondered if he would feel 'a right Jessie', having said he'd be away for ten months but then returning after five weeks. James was sorry to see Dave go but believed he had made the right decision. 'The guy's got a heart of gold and I'm envious of his strong family ties,' he said, believing it had taken a lot of courage to bow out when he did but certain also that he'd achieved a lot from sailing with *Time & Tide*, not least because it had made him re-evaluate his life.

While James respected Dave for his reasons for getting off, he regretted not having been able to turn the situation around with Greg and Richard. For Richard going home was far harder. He described it as a bereavement and as the most disappointing thing that had happened to him for years. For several weeks after his return he was utterly preoccupied by what had happened, swinging between guilt at letting the crew down and anger at the way he felt he'd been unfairly vilified in the press and by members of the sailing community. Most unfairly of all, he felt, Chay had accused him of disabling the disabled.

But eventually these feelings began to pass, and as *Time & Tide* started to prove to the world that it was capable of competing in this race on equal terms, at times doing even better than its able-bodied opponents, he felt respect and admiration for those members of his crew who'd stuck it out through thick and thin – though he never once regretted his decision to get off.

Leg 1 Final Results

	Team	Arrival time
1	Group 4	25/10/96 14:52
2	Toshiba Wave Warrior	25/10/96 17:01
3	Concert	26/10/96 01:57
4	Save the Children	26/10/96 09:10
5	Commercial Union	26/10/96 18:03
6	3Com	26/10/96 20:39
7	Motorola	27/10/96 01:35
8	Heath Insured II	27/10/96 03:37
9	Ocean Rover	27/10/96 05:34
10	Nuclear Electric	27/10/96 07:35
11	Global Teamwork	28/10/96 06:48
12	Pause to Remember	28/10/96 21:41
13	Courtaulds Int.	29/10/96 08:19
14	Time & Tide	29/10/96 10:45

All times GMT.

Chapter Four

Leg Two:
Rio de Janeiro to Wellington

Departure date 20 November 1996; 6,600 miles down the coast of Brazil, confronting the pivotal challenge of Cape Horn where the Atlantic and Pacific oceans meet. On through the Roaring Forties of the Southern Ocean where mountainous seas with hail, sleet and snow are created by gale force winds blown up from the Antarctic.

A week before the start of the second leg to Wellington, *Time & Tide*'s four new crew members arrived in Rio, fully aware of the difficulties that had gone before them but each resolved to do their utmost to help bolster and enhance *Time & Tide* as a vigorous racing team.

These were: Brendan West, a 36-year-old amputee from Maidenhead, Berkshire; Mike Austin, a 53-year-old British Airways pilot who had recently suffered two bouts of non-Hodgkin's lymphoma; John Anderson, a 58-year-old businessman, doing only the Rio to

Carol Sear (© Mark Pepper/MPP)

Wellington leg; and, the youngest of the four, 35-year-old Carol Sear, an accountant from London.

Carol was one of the least disabled on board *Time & Tide* and, like Dave Hodder, she felt uneasy about the validity of her claim to be part of an all-disabled crew. The Trust, however, felt she had every right to be given a place on the yacht, since she had restricted movement in one arm as a result of a serious elbow injury caused by a motorbike accident at the age of seventeen. It still caused severe rheumatism in cold weather. The other relevant factor was that finding new crew members at such short notice had proved exceedingly difficult – not surprisingly, since few people were prepared to make such an important decision about their lives with so little time to ponder or prepare.

The new boys in Rio: left to right, John Anderson, Brendan West, Mike Austin (© Mark Pepper/MPP)

What Carol lacked in sailing expertise she made up for with her enthusiasm, pluck and willingness, but at least she'd had several sailing days' experience and accumulated some knowledge of how to handle a boat. Brendan, on the other hand, had barely set foot on a boat.

Like Paul Burns and Nigel Smith, Brendan lost his leg before reaching the age of twenty. He had been serving in the Army in Germany when a hit-and-run driver knocked him down; and as if that wasn't enough the car behind then ran him down too. There followed several weeks of intensive care treatment, during which he lay heavily sedated, lost five stone in weight and was unable to move his damaged left leg. It was, he said, a relief when the surgeon came in one day and told him it would have to come off.

While in the Woolwich Military Hospital, Brendan remembered Paul Burns being brought in. 'He was far worse off than me and having to endure endless skin grafts for his terrible burns.' Later the two met up again at Chessington rehabilitation centre but subsequently lost touch until *Time & Tide* brought them to the same crossroads.

After the accident Brendan took an electronics training course and now worked for a controls company, Honeywell, as a computer systems manager. Like other *Time & Tide* crew members, he had been looking for a new sporting challenge when a business associate invited him to Southampton to watch the start of the BT Global Challenge race. As their supporter vessel passed within a whisper of *Time & Tide*, Brendan found himself watching the tenacious crew with extreme admiration, envious of their daring ability and of the adventures that lay ahead. When, the following week, he read an article in the *Sunday Times* highlighting the fact that *Time & Tide* was looking for another crew member, it occurred to him for the first time that perhaps it wasn't beyond the realms of possibility that he might be that person.

His wife, Belinda, though initially supportive, was a little confused by Brendan's sudden desire to take part in a yacht race, when he had never particularly shown any great interest in sailing. 'The truth was I didn't think he stood a chance in hell of being accepted,' she said, 'so I thought, let him dream on, and I helped him fill in the application form.' But Brendan's impulsive (Belinda would say reckless) disposition was entirely in keeping with his character. It was no coincidence that at the time *Time & Tide* came into their lives he had just been offered a flying scholarship from the Douglas Bader Foundation – despite being terrified of flying. The reason he'd applied, he said, was 'to challenge that fear and give me a bit of excitement'.

Despite his inexperience, three days after he'd sent off his application form he heard that he'd been accepted to take part in the race. While he was both surprised and thrilled, Belinda was appalled. For a start she hadn't realized he was applying to take part in the whole race and on top of that she was extremely concerned for his safety. 'Most of all I was worried that he would die and I'd never see him again,' she said. 'Then I was worried he'd volunteer to do something dangerous, because that's the sort of person he is. I was also worried he'd do more injuries to his right leg, which has two steel pins in it anyway, and would end up having to have that one amputated too. And beyond all that I was worried that he would change and never settle down back at home again.'

Initially Belinda persuaded him to take part in one leg of the race only but then, feeling guilty at having blighted his dreams and opportunities, she relented and said he could complete the race. His company had given him an unpaid sabbatical, and sponsorship money for his berth fee had already began to trickle in, mostly from companies associated with his work. He had left Belinda in charge of pulling together the final sums, and now, having arrived in Brazil a week before the start of the second leg, was eager to get going, particularly as in his mind the most frightening part was over – namely the flight to Rio.

Brendan was well aware of his sailing limitations and had great admiration for his fellow crew member, Mike Austin, not only because Mike flew jumbo jets for a living but equally because he had considerable sailing experience. Despite having developed cancer three years previously he had sailed 3,000 miles while still undergoing chemotherapy, including taking part in the 1994 Sydney Hobart race. With a depleted immune system, he said, the ocean seemed like the best place to be because it was free of people and bugs. Apart from his passion for sailing, one major motivation for taking part in the BT Global Challenge was to raise money for Dreamflight, a charity supported by British Airways staff that provided trips for seriously ill children.

Fortunately his employers had agreed to give Mike paid leave to take part in the race, as raising sponsorship for his berth fee was never an option. 'People are hardly going to dig into their pocket for a poor airline pilot,' he rightly surmised.

With Richard Horton-Fawkes now off the boat, the oldest *Time & Tide* crew member was John Anderson, who qualified to sail because of a hip replacement operation that had taken place in November 1995. He arrived in Rio two days before the start of the second leg, having first applied to take part in the race only two weeks prior to that. A short feature in the *Sunday Times* declaring that *Time & Tide* would probably have to sail with a crew member short had alerted him to the possibility of becoming a BT 'one legger' and he'd put in an immediate call to the Trust office who were still desperately searching for crew volunteers willing to fly to Rio at a few days' notice.

John Anderson (© Mark Pepper/MPP)

Brendan West
(© Time &
Tide/BT)

Like Brendan, John never believed for a second that he stood any real chance of being accepted on the race, even though he had ample sailing experience. On the other hand his wife, Harriet, was convinced it was going to happen as soon as he'd asked her permission to go. In the event she was proved right, but from the moment John passed his telephone interview with Chay, he began to panic. 'I thought to myself, I've done it now. Do I really want to spend forty days at sea in the middle of nowhere?' Momentary doubts, however, were quickly dispelled by Harriet, who urged him to grab the opportunity and take up the challenge. 'You've always wanted to do ocean racing,' she said, 'so now's your chance. You have to do it.'

The prospect of entering the Southern Ocean on this pivotal second leg to Wellington had been preoccupying the entire fleet ever since their arrival in Rio three weeks earlier, and particularly the skipper and crew of *Time & Tide*, who knew that if they were to be judged as equal contenders they would have to show their true mettle. With the eyes of the world on them, they couldn't afford to fail, especially as a growing number of people were beginning to voice their concern at the thought of a disabled crew being sent to wrestle with their fate in the treacherous Southern seas. A reader in the letters page of *Yachting World* asked:

> *'Is it wise to send these brave disabled crew members, who without a doubt are first-rate sailors, around the world's oceans where there is simply no support for victims of accident or illness? ... I feel in this politically correct world that we have endangered the lives of the whole crew of* Time & Tide *and those involved in any rescue attempt. As sensible human beings, and experienced and increasingly safety-conscious sailors, we have failed in our duty to speak out when we feel that the line has been crossed and an error of great magnitude has been made.'*

Predictably, the crew dismissed their critics as either cautious or condescending and on the morning of 20 November, with the boat well supplied and the new crew settled in, *Time & Tide* pulled away from Rio's Copacabana beach, to complete a circuit of the Bay before heading south in fighting mood, ready for the challenge of the Southern Ocean. But it was another poor start for *Time & Tide*, which hung back to avoid a start fight and was consequently the last across the line. 'However, after three-quarters of a mile we found breeze and began to make ground,' recalled James. 'Everyone else was by now in dirty air getting the wind off the boats in front of them and falling down to leeward. By contrast we were climbing up to windward and by the first mark were sixth.' Many of the crew remembered the look on Chay Blyth's face as his boat drew up alongside them to relay the good news. He was clearly delighted.

After a brief consultation with Chris, James decided to leave the pack behind and stick close to the shore instead, progressing down the eastern seaboard of South America's relatively protected waters. They had nothing to lose by going out on a limb, although, as James remarked in his log, 'When life presents you with the opportunity of a flier, it seems so right and obvious until you do it. Then you begin to wonder what thirteen other determined skippers and their crews have seen and you have missed.'

Fortunately it was a gamble that paid off, as well as the start of a very exciting week.

22 November 1996: First Mate's Log: 28°07' S 46°33' W

Worked with James a lot on strategy, making sure what we were doing was right. We knew no boat would follow us as we were not taken seriously – besides they had to chase the leader. We climbed to second, then at happy hour (we now have a happy hour with booze) we were first and held it all night. James was in really good form. The new people are fine but Brendan's safety is a worry.

From the moment it dawned on the crew that they were leading the fleet there was an immense feeling of euphoria on board, as the crew realized that their critics would now have to find a new line of fire. Not only were they showing the world that they could compete on equal terms; it seemed also that the four new crew members were helping to deliver that essential missing ingredient vital for racing. In her log Carolyn described the emotion she felt at realizing that *Time & Tide* was first:

> *Went up on deck for a little weep as I was so overcome. Even if we come further down the field in Wellington I don't care. I will remember this moment and day and savour it. Imagine what Chay and all the people back home must be thinking and the effect we will have on people – not just the disabled but people like the writer in* Yachting World *who thought we were endangering ourselves going into the Southern Ocean. At least he can see we mean business and are fully aware of the dangers and of the ethos of the Challenge – safety above all.*

Back home the Trust's phones and fax never stopped ringing, with relatives, sponsors, media and well wishers calling to say how delighted they were that *Time & Tide* were leading the fleet. Susan and Guy were over the moon as the effort, struggle and sacrifices of the past four years suddenly seemed to fade away. A fax came from the yacht saying, 'Good morning from a very delighted skipper and crew. Something to savour for a long time.'

While *Time & Tide* didn't maintain their position at the front for more than thirty-six hours, as the race progressed they were still up with the front runners and consequently crew morale remained high. During these first few days of unforeseen success James noted that not one of the other boats commented on *Time & Tide*'s progress. 'Before when we'd been behind, it had been a matter of "Keep on pushing guys, you're doing so well." But now there wasn't a word of congratulation.' The press, however, soon caught on to the fact that the disabled crew were confounding their critics in the world's toughest yacht race. The *Sunday Times* reported that 'In the first two weeks *Time & Tide* have headed the fleet in the BT Global Challenge more than once and consistently taken their place among the lead boats. The crew, who some said couldn't compete after they trailed in the first leg, have achieved more than they thought possible.'

James's report to Race HQ painted a particularly optimistic picture:

> *We are having a great time ... never been so cold, so tired and so wet, and never had so much fun. We have oceans to cross and yachts to chase ... best of all we have already tasted the rich flavour of first against a fleet of very experienced skippers and driven crews. Nobody gave it to us; we fought for it and won. We are hungry for more.*

Within a few days they were punching into their first big sea at thirty-five knots of wind, driving forcefully towards the Horn, and on one day they actually managed to hold the fleet's fastest spinnaker run in twenty-four hours for the Rio to Wellington leg.

Time & Tide could well have maintained its position as one of the leaders of this leg had it not then blown three kites in a matter of hours. As Carolyn recorded in her log on 24 November:

> *Going to bed we had the 'all hands' call: the kite had ripped and both tapes tore from top to bottom. It was the first leg all over again. We could only rush on deck to drag the kite out of the water, with its tapes hanging in mid-air, and dump the whole lot in the lockers. A real sense of frustration and dread.*

Fixing the sail
(© Time &
Tide/BT)

A grey day in the Southern Ocean (© Time & Tide/BT)

The sail repair to the powerful 2.2 kite that had been done in Rio had proved totally inadequate. While everyone was extremely disappointed by this sudden setback, they were also very relieved that it had been James on the helm, rather than one of them, when it blew. The result was that they were now having to use sails designed for upwind sailing when the boat was still having to do downwind gybe angles. Then, a few days later, the generator packed up as a result of bad fuel from Rio blocking the filters. At first The Challenge Business refused to accept this explanation but a couple of weeks later, when *Time & Tide* was attempting to give fuel to *Concert* from its uncontaminated fuel tank, it transpired that many of the other yachts had been unable to assist because they too had filled up with dirty fuel in Rio.

1 December 1996: First Mate's Log: 51°11' S 62°00' W

Got up to find James trying to bleed the generator again. He was in a foul mood. Position was slipping. Weather was poor. Wind was refreshing. After a lot of messing about found a plug of crap in fuel line. Stripping diesel on boat at thirty degrees is not fun with tools flying everywhere ... The watch were asked to put a reef in. It was a mess and took for ever. Took the helm while James put safety lines on. We were now running 30/40 heel. Helming was really hard and I was so cold. We now had fifty kph gusts ... Every large wave washed you away. The angle of heel gave us more problems with

> *the fuel pick up. Had to bleed again. Both James and I were so done in. I had to crash at 9.00 p.m. and got up at midnight. Storm gone. James asleep and the boat was just crawling along. I was shivering it was so cold. Put more clothes on, sorted people out. Put sails up, bled the gen again and put the heating on. Got to bed at 7.30 a.m.*

James felt disappointed by his crew's poor performance while putting in the reef. They had now experienced their first genuinely bad blow and it was a sure taster of things to come. 'I seriously felt like turning into the Falklands. By now we were placed eleventh in the fleet. This was the first realistic wind we'd encountered and they still couldn't put a reef in properly.'

But despite having made what James called 'a pig's ear' of the job, the manner in which he tried to correct the crew had clearly softened. In her log the next day Liz wrote:

> *I can see now why James was concerned. Glad I'm not in his shoes – would not have been so calm. He took it all rather well and waited until the next day to deliver a pep talk and try to ensure we didn't have a repeat of the situation. He really is making an effort and seems completely different to how he was on the last leg.*

Although only ten days into the voyage the sheer force of the weather had taken the crew by surprise, and although they were determined to get ahead of *Courtaulds*, with whom they had been caught in a duel for the last twenty-four hours, panic often got the better of them. Some, however, were already relishing the thrill of being ambushed by the elements. Nigel, who had never yet felt afraid at sea, recorded in his log that day:

> *Mike and I secured the sail and it's at this point that the worst conditions I've encountered on the foredeck completely submerged me and I was left hanging on for dear life. Being lifted off the deck by the sheer force of the waves with the safety harness as a lifeline, I thought I was going to drown. I prayed I wouldn't be tossed over the pulpit. Completely drenched, we returned to the cockpit and finished the watch.*

Paul Hebblethwaite also seemed to be relishing the storms. John reckoned, 'He was a very lucky man because he couldn't hear the building up of the wind and therefore was almost immune to the dangers of the situation. Sometimes I'd be letting out the sail to slow us down and he'd be shouting, "No, no leave it alone – I'm having a great time."'

Two days away from Cape Horn the pressure was mounting, particularly as they were now racing *Heath Insured II* through the La Maire Straits, off Tierra del Fuego. Both yachts were being swept by a current towards the headland, so *Time & Tide* tacked away from its course, leaving *Heath* to pull away and eventually round closer to the Horn. James told the crew that from the moment they rounded this portentous landmark his priority would be to sail the boat safely rather than to race it. He warned that they would soon be experiencing weather that would push each individual to the limit, and that should an accident occur it could have devastating consequences for all. Having given this short but forcible speech, he instructed them to hold a course which would keep them safe, and announced that he was going to bed for the next few hours.

The fact that James was allowing himself more sleep on this leg demonstrated his growing confidence in the crew. Though he was occasionally still frustrated by their incompetence when it came to certain tasks, overall he was beginning to notice a commitment from them that hadn't been evident before. And in the days ahead he was so impressed by the bravery and professionalism of some of them that eventually he had the conviction to declare, 'With guys like these I can sail.' At the same time he was probably right to conclude that 'one or two will never go near a boat again after this.'

The very words 'Cape Horn' conjured up fantasies and nightmares for everyone on board *Time & Tide*. It was, as Eric Newby had written in his epic sea adventure *The Last Grain Race*, 'a memento mori, a skull on the study table'. At fifty-six degrees south it was the most legendary and feared nautical landmark on the globe and the ultimate goal for every yachtsman. It was also a place where storms were capable of ripping masts out of tall ships and sinking small ones in a matter of moments.

For most on board *Time & Tide*, rounding Cape Horn on 4 December was a disappointing experience. With more bad weather anticipated James had decided to stay further off shore in deep water to avoid the breaking waves nearer land and therefore, with Cape Horn out of sight, the crew had little sense of their awesome location.

David injured his back that day when he was washed against the baby stay and though James felt he was capable of carrying on with light duties, Lesley insisted on bed rest for three days. This meant that the crew had lost one of their most valuable assets. With John Rich also off duty with a chest infection and other unconnected symptoms, the strain was beginning to tell on the rest of the crew, who were nonetheless still holding their own under this ever-increasing workload.

The watch leaders for this leg were Nigel and David, as on the final days of the previous leg. Both were competent sailors, tough on themselves and determined to push the crew to their maximum abilities. As watch leaders they were expected to have an eye on the safety and performance of the boat, to transmit the skipper's instructions to the rest of the crew, to liaise with the other watch leader and to organize the general maintenance of the boat. Nigel, who took his duties very seriously, wrote in his log: 'I must concentrate harder on giving people jobs and tidying up. Everyone gets so complacent. The hardest thing is to motivate people into the idea that we're racing.' He also recognized the difficulties and frustrations of the skipper. 'Sometimes when we're on deck James will spot something that we should have seen. He's such a good sailor it's instinctive with him but I'm sure he thinks that after all this time he shouldn't have to do all this. He gets a bit frustrated with us all and I don't blame him.'

John Anderson, a novice to the whole experience of ocean racing, felt in awe of his skipper's ability to take control and work from instinct when things were starting to go badly wrong. On one occasion he recalled, 'All the watch were out in the cockpit. It was so bad they were just hanging on, but James took the helm and to me seemed seven foot tall. Then, from the point of seeming out of control, he gradually brought the boat back into control. He is a fantastic sailor and it was amazing to watch.'

Inevitably the complexities of a sail change in heavy weather could create pandemonium on board, as Carol recorded in her log on 5 December, when Paul Burns sailed the boat too close to the wind and accidentally went into a crash tack:

> *James came up on deck, ranting and shouting at everyone. 'Complete fuck-up in the cockpit', I think the expression was. He moved Paul B. off the wheel, shouting for people to get on deck 'now'. Several people came up on deck and started to bring on the new runner. James shouted at me to let go of the runner outhaul and once it was free shouted for it to go forward. I grabbed it and started forward. It got caught round the boom, so he said to leave it, which I did. I then went to man the staysail. All around me was action. People pulling sheets and winding winches combined with the noise of the wind and the breaking seas. It's hard to stay calm. At least James could see the whole picture, to organize people just out of their bunks, still half asleep. It's very confusing.*

Turning right at the Horn, the fleet were faced with the full force of the westerly winds that swirl continually around the bottom of the planet. At this point it was important to escape the continental shelf where the sea floor climbs dramatically from two miles to 600 feet deep, thus

Wet again!
(© Time &
Tide/BT)

putting the yachts in waters which, though comparatively shallow, are capable of sudden ferocity. As Chay said, 'Basically it is a case of going like hell for thirty-six hours to minimize the risks by reaching the deeper swell of the Southern Ocean. The 500-mile wide Drake's Channel between Antarctica and South America has the effect of funnelling the Southern Ocean rollers and winds which sweep around the globe unchecked for thousands of miles.'

Although everyone had been warned of icebergs and growlers, very few were actually sighted – an event that was met with a mixture of relief and disappointment, especially as Mike Golding on *Group 4* had reported seeing an iceberg the size of Sydney Opera House. But on 9 December, a beautiful clear day with good visibility, the crew did spot across the rising and tumbling crystal blue seas a massive white iceberg, which, from four miles away, still managed to look remarkably impressive. It was accordingly named after Carolyn, who was celebrating her thirty-fourth birthday that day.

7 December 1996: First Mate's Log: 59°30' S 82°21' W

The wind started to build. Got call to go on deck to help put third reef in. Got washed down the deck and had to brace myself between the pole to do the reef. This was the first time I really questioned my ability to do the job in hand. I just did not have the strength needed. Went on the helm in a very confused sea. Crew below very wet and cold. Heater in rear of boat had packed up. Spent two hours trying to sort it out. Eventually went to bed. Did not bother with food, was so done in. Lesley was very low.

Lesley was indeed low. By now she knew for certain that ocean racing was not for her. During the worst of the storms fear had begun to take hold and she was glad to have the excuse of being taken out of the watch system whenever there was an injury to attend to.

Inevitably as in every walk of life the toughest characters survived and even thrived, while those who found it difficult to adjust to the dangers and discomforts of life at sea struggled to stay the course. Lesley was well aware that while her skills as a nurse may have been invaluable she was not much use when it came to sailing the boat and this at times would lead to feelings of inadequacy. James had accused her of mollycoddling the crew and pointed out that some medics on the other boats put the pills on the table and, with the attitude 'If you wouldn't bother your GP don't bother me', let the crew help themselves. But as a nurse this approach was not good enough for Lesley, who wanted to look after everyone and make them better. Sometimes she was also concerned that her experience did not extend far enough and wondered if they would have been better off having a doctor on board.

The further south-west it went, the more *Time & Tide* felt like a tiny insignificant speck in the vast expanse of the Southern Ocean. The nearest land was 2,000 miles away and to the south there was nothing but the Antarctic ice and darkness. They were now running before seas that were being generated in the greatest expanse of open ocean, of a power and volume unparalleled because there was no obstruction to them as they drove eastwards round the world. Sometimes the storms were inspiring. As Carol recorded in her log, 'Even a storm in the Southern Ocean can be beautiful. We have had many sunny days with big, navy blue seas and turquoise skies. There have also been days when everything is grey and apart from the yellow sail it would be easy to believe that the world had turned monochrome.' She had imagined waves crashing down over her all the time but was pleased to note that 'in reality we climb each one and slide gracefully (most of the time) down the other side, though occasionally we get to the top of a wave and crash (belly-flop) with a loud bang into the trough below.'

Chay Blyth, who had a great deal of experience of the Southern Ocean, wrote this warning in an article for the *Daily Telegraph* at the start of the second leg:

> *When you settle into the rhythm of life down south you can't help but be overawed by the sheer scale of the environment. You tend to be overwhelmed by your own insignificance. I can't stress with sufficient force the need to adapt to circumstances. I've been struck by the competitiveness in this race, which has consumed both the professional skippers and their amateur crews. It's not necessarily a good thing, if it is unchecked by reason. The problem is that our 67-foot steel boats are so good that they give you almost too much confidence. You feel you could come through a typhoon and still be safe. The boats are engineered to rigorous standards, but if those limits are exceeded damage will occur.*

By the time they'd been at sea for three weeks the conditions were beginning to wear the crew down. The days were shorter, gloomier and colder but despite being faced with squall after squall they still hadn't suffered any protracted blows, and the vicious weather usually subsided within a day or two; but all the same boredom, frustration and extreme discomfort were beginning to take hold. Clothes remained permanently damp – only Chris had worked out a system whereby he had vacuum-packed various clothes so that he was able to treat himself to a dry set every few days. The cold weather dampened enthusiasm and the relentless hard work and seemingly unending miles ahead could at times make it all seem like a godforsaken and thankless task.

The crew had to crowbar themselves around the deck by hanging on to the boat and propelling themselves forward, and if they missed a handhold they risked being catapulted across the hull. Whatever they did below deck – whether eating, sleeping, or going to the toilet – required maximum effort and was consistently draining. Even the normally stoical Chris recorded in his log on 11 December: 'For the first time I really questioned why I was stuck out here. The thought of twenty more days was hard!' Carol was amazed when she sat down with Nigel and Mike one evening at the end of their watch to hear them admit to buckling under the strain. 'It was an eye opener,' she said. 'I was sure Mike and Nigel were loving every moment.' It was the same throughout the fleet, with race fatigue beginning to set in. This was nothing unexpected, and most Challenge crew volunteers knew it would happen; only those few who had harboured the fantasy that it would be an action-packed joyride were daunted and disappointed.

For some there were moments of real despair. In his log on 13 December Paul Burns wrote:

> No real rest for more than two or three hours at a time, cold, and everything damp – sleeping bag, pillow, etc. The clothes you wear on deck are drenched by waves and rain. It is very difficult for me to get my boot off my left leg, so I'll leave it until Wellington I suppose. The noise is loud and constant – wind and seas, and the crash as we fall from a wave is indescribable. I use ear plugs and eye patches to help me sleep but am so run down would probably sleep anyway. There is heating but it's not very good. One cabin is like a sauna; the rest cold and damp. I feel so fed up I could cry. I wish I was home with the family. I'm in the middle of the biggest wilderness on earth and not coping very well.

Mike, too, had moments of reflection, wondering why he was there. 'This is the hardest thing I've ever done in my life. Can I make it?' he wrote in his log. And then, as if to bolster himself up, he added, 'I've set myself a challenge; others are supporting me and life is all about setting challenges and seeing them through – good or bad. I just hope I'm a better yachtsman and am a better person at the end of it all.'

At the same time David was suffering from lack of mental stimulation and finding the responsibility of watch leader tough. It was up to him to tell other members of the crew what to do and he was capable of giving those in his watch a hard time if they didn't perform well. But despite his tough stance, most liked and respected him. Carolyn may at first have found him to be 'an overbearing, self-opinionated yuppy type' but she soon came to appreciate his humour and his ability to motivate people. 'He was', she said, 'one of the great assets on the boat.'

David clearly had little tolerance for John Rich, who was too sick to be of much use on deck, and had intimated on more than one occasion that 'We don't carry passengers.' It may have seemed a callous comment, particularly about someone who was genuinely sick, but it's easy to see how, when everyone was being pushed to the very limits of their strength and capabilities, those who did very little were quickly resented. Paul Burns, on the other hand, who was always ready to see the best in people, had come up with what John Rich described as very sound advice – namely to 'look busy'.

One thing almost all the crew agreed on was that although Liz didn't have the physical strength to do any useful heavy work, she was a totally committed member of the crew who would do anything you asked of her without complaining. She was an excellent organizer, brilliant at paperwork and good at keeping check of stores and provisions. 'I've got a great deal of respect for her because of her guts and raw courage,' said James, although admitting that he wasn't wild about her asking questions the whole time. 'I think she was born with "Why?" on her lips,' he lamented.

She was happier now, too, because Mike, who was on the same watch as her, was extremely encouraging and supportive of everything she did. Also, with Carol now on board, for the first time there was someone of her own sex who she felt was on the same wavelength and with whom she was able to have a laugh.

However, she was still very frustrated, and determined that if she stayed on as a *Time & Tide* crew member she would have to learn more, particularly in the area of helming, which she wasn't allowed to do because she was considered too weak to guarantee the safety of the boat and the rest of the crew. She was adamant that she had paid her money to develop a skill and not to make dumpling scone mix and clean the heads.

In her log on 29 November she wrote, 'This was the day Chris chose to try to talk me into being realistic. He obviously doesn't know me very well yet. Again he tried in the nicest possible way to explain that I had to come to terms with my limitations and would basically never be able to sail. The more he talked the more determined I became to sail solo.'

Brendan was similarly ill-equipped to deal with the heavier manual tasks of ocean racing. According to Nigel, from the first few days at sea he looked 'permanently shagged out'. Initially he had suffered from persistent nausea and suffered dreadfully from the cold, with the wind seeming to drill though all his layers no matter how many clothes he had on. Lack of food had compounded the problem of cold and exhaustion and for the first seven days of the race he admitted to having spent a lot of time carefully planning his resignation speech to James. But as time wore on Brendan slowly grew accustomed to life on board and even began to appreciate the physical and emotional highs and lows of ocean sailing. He got used to the permanent discomfort, the feeling of damp clothes on his skin and the fact that showers were as scarce as the midday sun.

While hygiene was taken very seriously in all areas of the galley, where germs could spread rapidly with so many people crammed into such a small area, personal cleanliness often went by the board – usually with no dire consequences, other than offending another crew member. Towards the end of the leg David wrote in his log:

> *Nigel commented on my socks yesterday, saying that they honked – and sure enough they were beginning to get to me as well. It's hardly a surprise after almost thirty-seven days' constant wear. So at lunchtime today I changed my socks, washed my feet and put on a new clean dry pair. These should last until New Zealand. I also cleaned my teeth. Maybe one more shave this side of NZ.*

Food was still an issue on this second leg: although now there was a happy hour, and the night watches were supplied with a tuck box of chocolate and sweets, complaints about the quality and quantity of food continued. There was also the on-going question of whether or not the crew were allowed to help themselves to food in the galley, which made David remark that he was looking forward to getting to Wellington, where he could eat something without thinking he was eating someone else's portion. Carol blamed this on the 'food police': the people who kept stock of provisions and rationed portions, and ultimately were responsible for the boat arriving in Wellington with thirteen days' spare supplies. One particularly irksome day she recorded in her log: 'At 2.00 p.m. we were told we had to catch up on local time, so ship time was going back four hours. We then had to wait another four hours for lunch. About seven of us descended on the Ryvita (seems to be the only food that's freely available), jam and peanut butter in a feeding frenzy.' Once again by the end of the leg many of the men had lost a considerable amount of weight. Even as early as 5 December Nigel was recording in his log: 'I'm permanently hungry now – I think because it's cold and we're exerting a lot more energy. I could really pig out and all I think about is ham, egg and chips and chocolate.'

With complaints about food being one of the few areas of dissent left on *Time & Tide*, there was now more time for humour. On 11 December James sent this message back to Race HQ:

> *When I heard that I was going to have the pleasure of one of BA's more senior pilots as crew I decided to extend to him the same courtesy that I'm sure he would extend to me if he knew I was on his flight – heck, I even helped put his baggage on board. Since he holds similar rank I figured he qualified to share the skipper's cabin, which is a compact two-berth afterthought with just enough room for a kit bag and an ego. Its unique ventilation system ensures constant cold and colder running condensation and a floor that was designed to conform to the curve of the hull at the port stern quarter – ideal for someone with one leg shorter than the other, which on* Time & Tide *is a reality. The other reason he got to share with me was because the rest of the crew had got the good bunks.*
>
> *Mike likes to wear these rubber dry suits for on-deck tasks but unfortunately his leaked. So being a reasonable sort of guy I lent him my brand-new Goretex breathable dry suit. We are talking top-of-the-range. Now the other thing I've noticed about Mike is that he does like his food and we do go to great lengths to make the freeze-dried food as tasty as possible. However, it does have the unfortunate disadvantage of giving you wind, and, in Mike's case, if you are wearing a dry suit, occasionally looking a tad Blimp like! So he comes to see me the other day and complains that the suit is leaking. We discover on inspection that both feet sections are coming away from the leggings ... the phrase 'blow your socks off' springs to mind. We are now checking the sides of his sea boots for stretch marks.*

For those who had sailed from Southampton it was noticeable that the atmosphere during this second leg was considerably happier and more relaxed. Even after just two days at sea Nigel noted in his log, 'I think we'll have some fun this leg if everyone keeps their peckers up.' And it was true that even after three weeks together, most of the crew got on well and a camaraderie was beginning to develop. Carol was surprised to notice that there was no gender issue on board, as she was used to working in offices where there were at least 'a couple of letches'. This was not the case on *Time & Tide*, where for the most part people seemed to respect one another.

Also the crew were becoming more appreciative of their skipper. Carol described him as 'mainly laid back, friendly, funny, quite lovable and despite his quick temper not unapproachable'. Carolyn had also noticed that he was trying especially hard to keep morale high. 'He looks after us all by making tea on the night watches and sending anyone to bed early if they look exhausted. Even having three kites damaged hasn't upset him as much as I thought it would,' she wrote in her log.

Just as James's appreciation for Liz had grown, so too had her respect of him, and for the first time she noticed and appreciated that 'James watches for us all the time.' On one occasion she recalled, 'There were two people fighting on the boat and I was impressed because James just told them to walk away from it, adding "I've had to change so you can too."' On another she acknowledged that while she still felt he didn't conduct himself well in a group, in a one-to-one situation he was brilliant and she looked up to him 'as a kind of mentor and leader figure'.

But despite his endeavours to be more caring of his crew James was still basically a loner and would go for days without talking, often eating his meals separately. 'I've never been a

Even on the roughest days there could be rainbows (© Time & Tide/BT)

great team player,' he admitted. 'When I finish my day I want to be left alone, but I try to be as much of a crew player as any of the others.' He was also aware that under pressure he had a tendency to lose his temper; 'but I don't get personal,' he insisted. 'I apologize and explain that I'm angry at the task not the person. We're all suffering from lack of sleep and exhaustion and if I were to put things more subtly they just wouldn't get it. I go in for constructive, rather than destructive, criticism and constructive sailing. I have to bear in mind that these people paid a lot of money to be here.'

To those who accused James of losing his temper too often or distancing himself from the rest of the crew, John Anderson was robust in his skipper's defence. 'You'd have to be a saint in those conditions not to blow your top occasionally and you have to realize that a boss of any firm can't be one of the boys as well. Those who complain should look to themselves first and remember that round-the-world sailors have got to be a special kind of person. It's a huge responsibility. James might never be a saint but he's one hell of a bloody good sailor.'

Towards the end of December the number of crew off sick had risen to alarming proportions. Mike had been put on restricted helming duties, because of an old knee injury which had been aggravated three days after leaving Rio. John Rich had a high temperature and, according to Nigel, 'looked like death warmed up'. For the most part he was out of action or on galley duties: 'I have learnt to judge our speed by hearing the sound of water moving alongside the hull as I lie in my bunk,' he wrote in his log. Even John Anderson, who as Chris noted, 'should have been ideal muscle power for us, having no wasting disease or missing limb', got his big toe badly infected when Brendan stood on it with his false leg, and he had to take a course of antibiotics. 'The saddest thing was that from then on there were only three people who didn't stand on it,' said John laconically.

It looked as if Paul Burns might have to be out for the rest of the leg because of an abscess on his foot and sores on his stump, and he was feeling extremely low. Having the stubbornness of a survivor, he wouldn't admit to being in trouble, though, because he hated feeling like a passenger. He was also worried that he might get dropped from the team because his legs just weren't up to it. David described Paul as a 'rock-hard human being who had to be pushed back on to his bunk even when he was in excruciating pain'. But although he had the mental strength to cut off from all the discomfort, pain and cold around him, at times it got the better of him. On 22 December he wrote in his log: 'The strap on the back of my knee broke yesterday so I can't control it very well. Not one good leg!' Later, reflecting on the whole voyage, he admitted, 'My legs would drain me of energy. My false leg was never comfortable and my foot always ached. By the end of it all I was just tired of hurting.'

So many people being off sick put an enormous strain on the fittest of the crew, namely Paul Hebblethwaite and David, who were the muscle behind such tasks as hauling huge, heavy sails down the narrow companionway as well as the pair who were always to be seen on the foredeck humping sails, pulling halyards and standing up to a regular walloping from massive waves. Although each watch was now officially three hours long at night and four hours long during the day, it often didn't work out that way, because whenever those 'on watch' had to do something that required more hands, some of the 'off watch' people would be woken up and called on deck – and invariably it was David and Paul.

Paul, whose strength and fearlessness were a huge asset to the boat, was still unnerved by the sense of isolation he felt at sea because of his deafness. At times he got very emotional and wound up, feeling that no one was explaining things to him. Chris tried to help, being aware that his frustration stemmed from coming to conclusions about things based on the wrong facts. Paul just needed people to take the time to sit down and explain what was going on, but the trouble was there was never enough time. On one occasion he recorded in his log his anxiety at not being listened to when calling for the halyard to be dropped: 'No one bothers to listen to me and it puts me off completely. Very frustrating for me. Also I have been so low 'cos I don't have conversations with anyone except for Carolyn. When the watch was over, I was glad to go to bed.'

Paul also had a low attention span and was easily bored, finding it hard to enter into conversation with others who didn't make allowances for the fact that humour and innuendo were hard for him to grasp. As David remarked, 'There are two golden rules when talking to Paul: keep the subject the same and don't use sarcasm.' But he stressed what a valuable crew member he was, adding, 'If he's standing next to you on the foredeck you've got the best person by your side.'

Nigel was another member of the crew on whom the others relied to get the job done. On 7 December he wrote in his log:

> Cold and tired. My emotions go up and down like the waves. It's definitely more tiring than the first leg! The day starts well, brisk and bright; then the wind gets up. Last reef goes in, then the second and third, until she is blowing forty knots. I'm nearly swept away by the port winch! Next command: down with the staysail. Guess who's up there – moi!

A week later he wrote: 'I find it hard to get motivated just to get on deck. I'm all right when I'm up there – it's just getting there. I also feel weak at times. I wonder if it's the lack of decent food or sleep! Roll on Xmas.'

Although Nigel didn't possess the physical strength of Paul and David, he had amazing dexterity, a cool temperament – which meant he was on friendly terms with everyone – and a quiet way of just getting on with the job. As Carol remarked in her log, 'Nigel amazes me. He's had his leg amputated above the knee but he moves faster and has much more balance than me. When I follow him on deck, by the time I've clipped on and climbed on to the side he's whizzed up to the foredeck.'

On 16 December *Time & Tide*'s most serious accident of the race took place.

16 December 1996: First Mate's Log: 51°14' S 122°35' W

Wind started to build. Carolyn was getting edgy on the helm, so I went over to help. On my way over, she hit a wave and I got thrown into the cockpit, landing on Brendan's leg. I hurt my back, and was a bit winded but OK. Brendan was in real pain. He had to be carried down and put to bed. They cut his clothes off and it turned out I had landed on his good leg.

Unfortunately during a fifty-knot blow Brendan's right knee had been used to cushion the fall of Chris when the waves knocked him off his feet and sent him flying across the cockpit. It was an unpleasant injury given that his right knee had in the past undergone major surgery.

'I was in agony and writhing around all over the place,' recalled Brendan, 'but I can see now that it must have looked quite comical because we were being very British about the whole thing. Chris was apologizing and I was saying, "Really, it's OK – I'm sure I've only twisted it." But then the pain started to build up.'

Moving Brendan was not an easy task, particularly with storm force winds and mountainous seas throwing the crew all over the place, jarring every bone in their bodies as the yacht descended and crashed through yet another wave. But finally, over an hour later, and in excruciating pain, Brendan was slowly and carefully manhandled backwards by David, Mike and Paul Hebblethwaite out of the cockpit and down below, with his right leg now strapped to his false leg. 'Someone held my hand,' he recalled. 'I don't know who but it was a great comfort.' Once he was down on the dog-house floor Brendan's oilskins and thermal gear were cut away to reveal his badly swollen knee. A slide was made out of sails to help move him easily down the companionway steps and into Nigel's bunk in the forward cabin for easy access. All the time Brendan did not complain, other than giving the odd whimper when the boat lurched. His leg was splinted and put into traction by Lesley with a cat's-cradle affair, which James rigged up using pieces of rig and line tied at one end to the splint and at the other to the end of the bed.

A message relayed back to Race HQ briefly stated what had happened and stressed that, unlike the earlier message referring to Nigel breaking his prosthesis, this wasn't a joke.

The question now was what to do with Brendan. An airlift seemed the obvious answer and James adjusted his course to head north towards the Chatham Islands, a little under 2,000 miles away in the direction of Wellington. However, after a few days and much deliberation on the part of The Challenge Business, it became clear that medical insurance would not pay for an airlift, since Brendan's condition was neither deteriorating nor life-threatening. Lesley felt this was the wrong decision as she was concerned that the longer he remained immobile the greater the risk of complications. Besides, when she consulted the Shipmaster's Medical Guide the advice for a broken leg was to evacuate as soon as possible. James was also baffled as to why this information had taken so long to get through, since in the meantime he had been sailing off route and losing valuable racing time.

3Com handed over painkillers for Brendan in exchange for bottles of wine (© John Rich)

There were also only enough painkillers to last for six days and Brendan was clearly in agony every time the boat rolled. Chay Blyth wanted *Time & Tide* to rendezvous with both *3Com* and *Courtaulds* to get extra drugs, even though *3Com* had ample supplies and was by far the closer of the two yachts. James failed to see why Chay was insisting on this, since waiting for *Courtaulds* would have taken six hours of hanging around and what's more brought the trailing boat back into the race. Race rules stipulated that a yacht coming to another yacht's assistance can appeal for redress in the form of time adjustment, whereas the stricken vessel cannot. In the end both *Courtaulds* and *3Com* agreed that it was pointless for *Time & Tide* to wait for *Courtaulds*, and so on 17 December painkillers and bottles of wine were exchanged when *Time & Tide* rendezvoused with *3Com*, which was later allowed five hours on its time for altering its course.

A day later *Concert* broke her mast, 2,000 miles east of Wellington, going to windward in thirty knots of wind, steep seas and snowstorms. After rendezvousing with *Motorola* to take on emergency fuel, *Concert* became detached from the rest of the fleet and altered her course to the Chatham Islands. She was now totally reliant for fuel on the two yachts closest to her in this vast wilderness – *Time & Tide* and *Courtaulds*. It was a particularly anxious time, as rigging problems had been reported in 50 per cent of the fleet and James was nervous that his might go the same way.

Though they were committed to helping *Concert*, it created a massive dilemma, for, as James put it, 'If I proceeded to give all my reserve fuel away to *Concert*, which by now was dependent on us, and then my rigging went, I'd have had it. But at the same time I couldn't just turn round and say you're not having it. So after great deliberation I made the decision to go ahead with our commitment.' The rendezvous took place in thirty knots of wind and building seas on a cold, sunny day shortly before Christmas. James was particularly impressed by the innovative jury, or emergency, rig which *Concert*, with just a third of the mast left, had managed to set up to give the boat some stability while motoring in heavy seas.

The faces on board *Concert* said it all – ashen, grey, lifeless and yet clearly delighted to meet up with their deliverers. Seeing other members of the fleet hundreds of miles from land in the middle of the ocean always created a special bond and kindred spirit between boats. With engines running and the boats kept forty feet apart, *Time & Tide* took on board extra medical supplies and gave away 100 gallons of diesel, which were winched across on a line in five-gallon drums. Carol had made a couple of loaves of bread to send across. It was hard, exacting work, which took three hours to complete but ultimately achieved its purpose without complications. Finally, Christmas greetings were exchanged and as the two yachts broke away the *Concert* crew sang *Time & Tide* a Christmas carol.

On Christmas Eve James received some sad news. An urgent message came from his girlfriend Sarah telling him that her father had died. It was obviously a very difficult time for her and frustrating for James to be at sea and unable to help.

Christmas Day came and went, memorable for being the day when they had to wrestle with what became known as 'the sail change from hell'. The sky was battleship grey, and the sea confused and truculent as it broke over the deck, doing its best to wash the foredeck clean of anyone who stood in its way. Not surprisingly, safety harnesses were tested to the limit that day. But at least the harsh weather outside and the monotony of life inside was broken by the Christmas meal. *Time & Tide* had announced to the rest of the fleet their menu for the day, but a disbelieving *Group 4* had faxed them back asking for confirmation as to whether they were joking. The menu was as follows:

With the boats 40 feet apart, Time & Tide took medical supplies on board and gave 100 gallons of fuel to Concert, which had broken her mast (© Time & Tide/BT)

Hot Toddy
Scottish Smoked Salmon with Smiling Reindeer Bread
Roast Stincotto: Leg of Pork with an Apple, Mushroom, Tomato and Onion Sauce
Steamed Rice with Broccoli and Carrots
Christmas Pudding with Brandy Custard
Fresh-ground Brazilian Coffee and Home-baked Mince Pies
Vintage Port
All served with a selection of the finest Brazilian wines
(£18,750 PER HEAD, SERVICE NOT INCLUDED)

James recorded:

Celebrating Christmas Day (© John Rich)

> *Silly hats were worn, imaginative presents were exchanged and someone even got a pair of boxer shorts ... what Christmas would be complete without a pair of pants? Balloons were blown up and burst, and for half an hour we were anywhere else in the world. The best presents were the ones we opened in silence while the others chatted. They were the gifts we had brought with us from those we had left behind. They were the only presents not held up. They were the presents that reminded us of the people we draw on when we need that extra courage.*

By the end of the day, as James noted, the galley was 'remarkably reminiscent of one of those Christmas parties you wish with hindsight you hadn't had or worse still been to and not gone home from.'

In the days succeeding his accident, everyone was impressed by Brendan's courage. He never complained and at times was even cheery. Lesley recorded in her log on 28 December, 'I know he gets very bored and frustrated, having lain there for what is now twelve days, but Brendan is still a model patient.' However, there was no doubt that someone confined to their bunk for sixteen days on a roller-coaster ride was going to suffer from loneliness and boredom. He was living in semi-darkness and time went very, very slowly. Compressed by the base of the bunk above him, he was unable to raise his head more than a foot, which meant leaning himself out of bed to raise a cup to his lips or a spoon to his mouth. But although Brendan had moments of feeling low and depressed, he also recognized that 'there was no point in being miserable because people wouldn't have come to see me then, and talking to other people was the one thing that really helped.' Paul Burns would regularly come and chat – the two ex-servicemen shared a similar experience along with a similar sense of humour; and Liz, too, would often come and regale Brendan with tales of her previous sailing adventures. 'Basically she was bored,' reckoned Brendan. 'She was an extremely clever girl and the race just wasn't enough for her.'

On 26 December James was just about to tack the boat when, as David reported in his log:

> Lesley screamed 'No!' We were perplexed. Brendan, she explained, was doing number twos and was so precariously balanced that a tack could have caused extreme discomfort and not a little mess. So the crew sat ready at the winches for Brendan's bowel movements. Some minutes passed – everyone looked expectantly at one another, eyebrows were lifted and smiles passed across the faces of the crew. As the minutes ticked by these looks turned to those of concern and anxiety – is he shitting himself to death or was it a job for Anusol? Finally the shout 'He's doing the paperwork' came and we tacked the boat. Brendan's face was a picture of contentment and Time & Tide was back on course.

From the beginning Brendan had seemed remarkably unperturbed about his injury. The only thing that concerned him was how his wife and family were taking it, as there had been a number of conflicting reports about his condition. Nor did he mind too much when James informed him that the airlift had been called off, as he had been disappointed at the thought of having to miss out on the finish.

By now the length of the voyage was beginning to take its toll on others too. Whereas on the second day of the leg Nigel had reported in his log, 'Mike Austin likes to helm; he likes to talk but is very good for the watch and the boat, constantly trimming,' it seemed that now much of Mike's initial enthusiasm and bounce had been quashed by pains in his knee and the hard slog of six weeks at sea.

Nor was John Rich a happy man. Concerned for his health, Lesley had prescribed a course of antibiotics, but was at a loss to know what was wrong. He'd slowed down like a battery, his responses were getting ponderous and his movements sluggish, and he had lost a lot of weight. On 22 December he wrote a lengthy extract in his log 'On the Subject of Food', which included the sentiments:

> I am glad there are only four legs to go, which is only about 105 days at sea, as I cannot afford to loose any more weight. It also will make stopovers more expensive, as I will need to eat well – not just one meal and sandwiches in the hotel room as I've done before. This time I need three full meals all cooked, and this will increase the budget in stopovers very substantially.

By the end of the leg John was unable to pull his weight because he didn't have very much weight left to pull. It must have been enormously hard for him. He'd paid all that money and spent so much energy on making the dream come true, and then the dream had turned into a nightmare. Liz found him hard to fathom: 'For me the Challenge was just an opportunity which I took,' she said, 'but for him it was something he'd been dreaming of for years, and then all of a sudden he just seemed to switch off and let his dream go.'

By 27 December John was having serious doubts about whether he would be able to continue. Writing in his log that evening he expressed his disappointment in the whole venture: 'I think part of it is that our ship lacks a happy "family" atmosphere. I am not sure whether this is because everyone is tired or because we, the crew, never have been a "family" team.'

Carolyn at the helm
(© Time & Tide/BT)

If relationships between the crew didn't go as deep as expected with a group of people holed up together in such hazardous conditions, perhaps it was because, as Paul Burns surmised, 'everyone wanted to hold a part of themselves back.' Or, according to David, because 'people didn't want to pry into other people's fears, knowing that it might open up their own.' Indeed John Anderson thought it was amazing that people gave each other so much room by respecting silence during a watch and not talking too much.

Four days before the end of the leg, with seas that had been described in an official weather forecast as 'phenomenal', Cyclone Fergus came down upon *Time & Tide*, with sixty knots of wind creating a wild frenzy of confused seas. Brendan had to be strapped to his bunk and most of the crew were told to stay below. 'I'm going to listen to music, try not to worry and hope it goes away,' wrote David in his log, also noting what a fickle place the ocean was. The moment James took control of the helm everyone felt more relaxed because they knew he had the ability to take the boat up the wave, rolling over it to make the ride more comfortable. However, with conditions such as these, no one could avoid falling off the back of rollers, when the boat went up the wave and launched itself into the air, at which point gravity took over, crashing the boat back down again. In these conditions helming was not a right: it was a vastly responsible job and James found there were few he trusted enough to hand control to. He felt safe with Nigel, Carolyn, Mike and sometimes Paul Hebblethwaite, as long as he understood the conditions. Although perfectly capable David preferred not to helm in these conditions. Nervous of the responsibility, he had accurately described spinnaker sailing as 'driving on the edge of being out of control'.

On l January Carolyn wrote in her log, 'With wind of sixty-plus knots it meant that only a few could helm, James included. The guys were so tired after each stint they'd fall asleep fully geared up in the sail locker waiting for the next turn on the helm.' Carolyn clearly got a buzz from steering the boat, although she knew her limitations and was only too happy for someone else to take over once she'd 'started to lose it'. On the subject of helming she wrote in her log:

> My body aches from the waist up with the effort of holding the wheel steady against huge waves of fifty or sixty feet and crashing down the other side, the wheel almost wrenching my shoulders out of joint. It is a big responsibility being on the helm, but I am pleased James thinks I am good enough, and I enjoy it, despite the constant soaking, the aches and tiredness, because I feel I am doing something worthwhile. I know that other things that go towards running a boat, such as cleaning, cooking and clearing the bilges, are just as important but I feel more of an understanding for everything being on the helm. I can go back and say 'I sailed that boat' and mean it.

In the midst of Cyclone Fergus, the crew were so tired they'd fall asleep fully geared up in the sail locker (©Time & Tide)

Although *Time & Tide* caught the tail-end winds of Cyclone Fergus, this first leg into the Southern Ocean was proving far less treacherous than many had anticipated. After all, Fergus could have raged for three days instead of just fifteen hours. 'We got away lightly,' said James. 'It was like tiptoeing through a sleeping giant's playground knowing that if he woke up he would throw his teddy bear at us.'

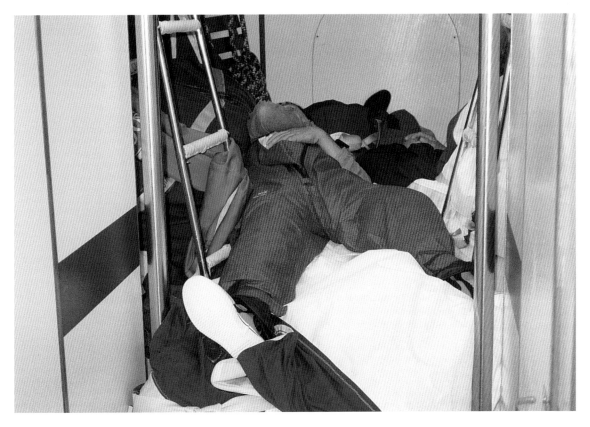

As it neared Wellington *Time & Tide* entered into a fierce battle to the finish with *3Com* and *Courtaulds*, who initially had both been behind them but in the course of one night caught up. By 31 December (the day that *Group 4* arrived in Wellington, winning the second leg) they were pushing hard and though the other two boats were still ahead it was now only by a few miles. The entire crew was up on deck working the sails hard and willing the boat on, Chris Ogg was navigating and James was steering, but the wind was beginning to die. Chris reported in his log, 'We were now eight miles behind *Courtaulds* with no wind. Just sitting 202 miles from NZ. Does it get any more cruel?'

They lost a day crossing the date line and missed out on New Year's Eve, but on the morning of 1 January, Lesley woke the rest of her watch with half a glass of champagne to celebrate the new year. Cyclone Fergus had blown itself out by now, but spirits were low as the wind still failed to materialize.

On New Year's Eve the *Time & Tide* relatives and supporters joined in a BT Global Challenge party at a bar on the Wellington waterfront. For some this was their first chance to meet everyone. John Anderson's wife, Harriet, had arrived in Wellington not knowing a soul, having been pitched into the *Time & Tide* project just a few weeks earlier. Like Belinda West, she had not managed to meet other *Time & Tide* relatives, workers or supporters before she left home. Belinda, who had flown out on Christmas Day, was still frantic with worry about her husband; her worst fear had always been that he might damage his good leg and be forced to have it amputated too. Information regarding his condition, and the situation as far as an airlift was concerned, had been constantly shifting and she still had no idea how serious his injury was. David Tait's girlfriend, Carol, was also eagerly awaiting the arrival of the boat - the couple had got secretly engaged before leaving Rio and she was looking forward to announcing the good news once David arrived in Wellington.

Susan had been unable to go to Wellington but in her stead was Gary Champion, a former TV presenter and a director of Bitcom International, a video production company based in Guildford. Gary had become an ardent *Time & Tide* supporter two years earlier while filming a piece on them for Meridian. Bitcom and the Trust had formed *Time & Tide* Television, an umbrella title under which they were making a documentary of the project. Bitcom were also helping to promote *Time & Tide* by networking with TV stations and providing video clips of the crew. Since he needed to be in Wellington to work on the documentary it was decided that Gary, a gregarious chap and great fun to be with, would be the ideal person to coordinate the plans for the yacht's arrival, assisted by Guy and Stuart.

Even though they would have loved to be sailing on board *Time & Tide* both Guy and Stuart were thrilled by the boat's progress and prayed it wouldn't lose ground at this final, most crucial stage of the leg.

After an agonizing crawl to the finish, *Time & Tide* eventually crossed the line on 2 January at 4.00 p.m., coming in eleventh, their official time for the leg being 42 days, 13 hours and 16 minutes. James had been helming from early that morning and was exhausted, but like the rest of the crew felt elated when the motor boats and helicopters appeared from out of nowhere to welcome them in. First to greet them was Michael Nicholson from ITN, who circled above them in a red helicopter. By now they had left *Courtaulds* well behind, but were unable to beat *3Com* who had arrived just thirty minutes before. It was a respectable defeat, however, particularly as a day earlier they'd been lagging thirty-two miles behind.

Carolyn recorded in her log:

> We were so pleased at the thought of beating Courtaulds, especially after being so close at Rio. Courtaulds' support boat then came out, and they stayed with us for about fifteen minutes cheering us on and yelling encouragement before going to follow Boris (their skipper) in. That made us feel great. Next our support boat arrived with Lesley's son,

Off the New
Zealand coast
the crew
spotted the
supporters' boat
(© Mark
Pepper/MPP)

Simon, having finished his leg on Save the Children; *also David's girlfriend Carol, along with a surprise visitor for me – Dad! When Carol managed to convey to me with frantic waving and pointing that there was someone I knew next to her, I still didn't realize who it was until he took off his cap and sunglasses. Well, that was it then: I was so overwhelmed with emotion, especially after leaving him at Southampton – and here he was at Wellington. I was sobbing on the rail and David was hugging me, so pleased for me. After that I couldn't stop telling everyone, 'There's my Dad over there.'*

As they neared Queen's Wharf a few people could be spotted on the quayside but as they rounded the corner the atmosphere became electric and the welcome *Time & Tide* received was undoubtedly quite the most spectacular of the fleet. With Tina Turner's 'Simply the Best' (which by now had become the crew's theme tune) blasting over the tannoy, dozens of red and yellow helium balloons were released and cannons fired. A crowd of several hundred were there to greet them, waving and cheering madly, including crew from other BT Global Challenge yachts. Later that day Mike achieved his ambition of standing on the quayside and applauding the arrival of the other yachts that came in after *Time & Tide*. And when

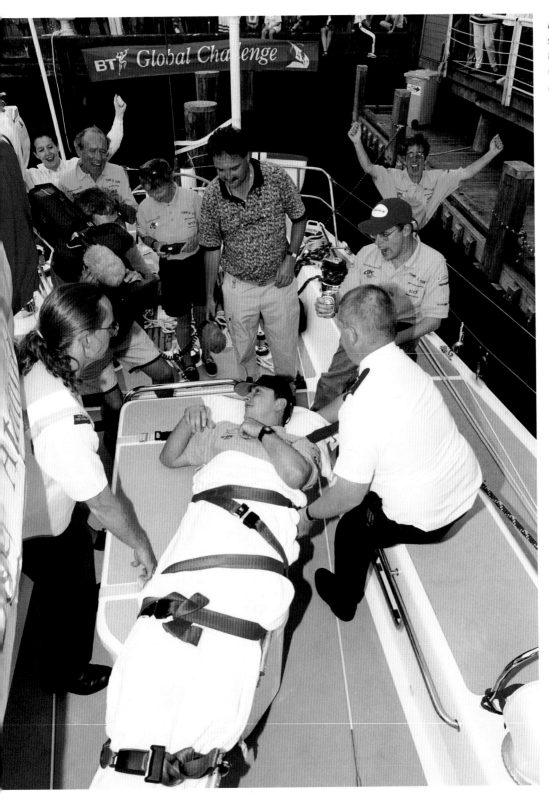

Brendan was stretchered off to hospital (© Mark Pepper/MPP)

Time & Tide received the most spectacular welcome of the fleet (© Mark Pepper/MPP)

Michael Nicholson asked Harriet Anderson how she felt seeing the boat coming in to port, she said: 'It's like getting married all over again.'

While most of the crew stepped from the boat on to dry land, John Rich and Brendan remained below deck to be checked by the fleet doctor. Belinda West was reunited with him in his cabin, and, never having been on board before, was appalled by the damp, cramped conditions he had endured when strapped to his bunk for the last sixteen days. Eventually Brendan was stretchered off, to big cheers, looking slightly stunned and a little embarrassed at having to clutch a bottle of champagne which Paul Hebblethwaite had insisted he take with him. John was also taken to hospital. Having lost fourteen kilos in weight, he stepped gingerly on to the pontoon, helped by Paul Hebblethwaite. He recalled how 'Paul B. stretched out his hand to wish me well. I just shook his hand and said "thank you". I saw David looking on.'

When news of *Time & Tide*'s success reached Britain, relatives of the crew who had spent a concerned Christmas and New Year worrying about storms, icebergs and accidents in the Southern Ocean, were elated and could at last relax and celebrate the crew's stirring victory. Susan, who was in the passenger seat of her husband's car on her way to the London Boat Show when she learnt of *Time & Tide*'s emotional arrival, was ecstatic and immediately rang Paul Hebblethwaite's parents to tell them the exciting news. While Anne and Harold

Hebblethwaite were clearly crying their eyes out on different extensions in their home in Yorkshire, Susan was sitting at the traffic lights at Parliament Square on her mobile phone with mascara streaming down her face, fully aware that other drivers in the rush hour were looking at her strangely.

'All day long at the London Boat Show people kept congratulating us on the success of the crew,' recalled Susan. 'No one could quite believe it. Two years before we had been at the Boat Show with no money, no boat and no crew – and now we had conquered the Southern Ocean and beaten three able-bodied crews. The Chairman of RYA Sailability (the Royal Yachting Association's disabled arm), Geoff Holt, an extremely able and competitive paraplegic sailor, who had been very sceptical about the *Time & Tide* project at the beginning, even came over to congratulate us and tell us that his committee thought *Time & Tide* had done a great deal to change attitudes towards disability. It was an exhilarating day, an enormous high!'

In Wellington each yacht had been adopted by a local bar and soon the crew were off to enjoy their first real food for six weeks. The waitress, not surprisingly, gave them a strange look when they said they didn't mind what they ate, just as long as it was food and came quickly. Later that week *Time & Tide* held a memorable party, to which the entire fleet, including Chay, turned up and which ended with people taking part in a wrestling and beer-drinking competition.

With corrected time *Time & Tide* were officially placed twelfth in the overall race. It was a magnificent achievement, showing once and for all that they were capable of competing on equal terms. Chay was hugely relieved that they'd arrived safely. Now that they'd come through the treacherous Southern Ocean unscathed, he knew they were capable of surviving the next and even more hazardous Southern Ocean leg to Cape Town.

Leg 2 Final Results

	Team	Arrival time
1	Group 4	30/12/96 00:16
2	Save the Children	30/12/96 03:08
3	Motorola	30/12/96 23:06
4	Toshiba Wave Warrior	30/12/96 14:27
5	Global Teamwork	31/12/96 08:05
6	Commercial Union	31/12/96 08:15
7	Pause to Remember	31/12/96 13:23
8	Nuclear Electric	31/12/96 20:50
9	Ocean Rover	01/01/97 16:05
10	Time & Tide	02/01/97 06:16
11	3Com	02/01/97 05:46
12	Courtaulds Int.	02/01/97 06:49
13	Heath Insured II	03/01/97 16:29
14	Concert	10/01/97 06:48

All times GMT.

Strength and fatigue, however, were still an issue. Success at the end of the day boiled down to navigation, weather and sheer brute force and, given that *Time & Tide* was definitely deficient in sheer brute force, the reality was that it was unlikely to end up near the top of the pack. 'We are always going to be slower moving round the boat and have more people off sick than any of the other crew,' explained Chris. 'That's because when the going gets rough we just don't have the strength or people to compete.' But he noted that everyone did the best they could to their own level and that as a group there was tolerance and complete acceptance of each other's capabilities. 'It was only when we were off the boat that disability started to raise its head again.' he observed. 'In an able-bodied group a disabled person will get sympathy whether they want it not, but when we're together on the boat there is no issue of sympathy – it doesn't exist.' David was certain that that was what had made *Time & Tide* gel together as a crew more than any other boat: 'We've learnt to compensate for each other's weaknesses,' he said, 'because whereas all the other crews can bounce up to the foredeck if the boat's tilting, we can't.'

It was hard to say how the other thirteen boats took to *Time & Tide* being placed twelfth. While the feedback was wholly positive and there was genuine admiration for 'Hatfield's heroes', it was also true that no one wanted to be beaten by the so-called 'disabled crew'; and to have had them lag at the end of every leg would have placed the rest of the fleet in a far more comfortable position.

Leg 2 Combined Times

	TEAM	TIME
1	Group 4	065d 11h 03m
2	Toshiba Wave Warrior	066d 03h 23m
3	Save the Children	066d 08h 14m
4	Motorola	067d 11h 38m
5	Commercial Union	067d 22h 14m
6	Nuclear Electric	069d 00h 26m
7	Global Teamwork	069d 10h 49m
8	3Com	069d 17h 17m
9	Ocean Rover	069d 17h 35m
10	Pause to Remember	070d 07h 00m
11	Heath Insured II	071d 16h 01m
12	Time & Tide	072d 06h 23m
13	Courtaulds Int.	072d 09h 10m
14	Concert	077d 04h 40m

All times rounded to the nearest minute.

Chapter Five

Leg Three
Wellington to Sydney

Departure date 9 February 1997; 1,230 miles across the Tasman Sea. Conditions extremely varied, from flat calms to gale force south-westerly winds. Crossings during January and February usually fine settled weather and slight winds from the east.

Shortly after arriving in Wellington James was quoted in the *Sunday Times* describing his crew as 'Different people from the ones who left Southampton. They are stronger, tougher, meaner. They've been through it all without complaint and I take my hat off to every one of them.'

He meant every word of it, but nevertheless the litany of casualties continued. John Rich had been in hospital for several days when investigations revealed a urinary tract infection caused by kidney stones which had developed during the Southern Ocean leg. After two

The crew tried hard to win the beer drinking competition in Wellington (© Carloyn Davies)

operations the doctors strongly recommended that he consider withdrawing from the race and, although bitterly disappointed at not being able to fulfil his dream, he reluctantly accepted their advice. His health had paid heavily for spending forty-two days at sea and he realized he could not afford to put himself through the rigours of another Southern Ocean crossing.

Brendan by now had his leg in plaster, and both he and his wife Belinda were extremely relieved to learn that the break was a relatively simple one with no complications. He was out of hospital within a few days but still too weak to travel and was therefore advised to wait three weeks before flying back to England. Although his and Belinda's plans to go travelling round New Zealand had to be abandoned, they nevertheless had a very enjoyable and unexpectedly sociable time in Wellington. Even on Brendan's second day in hospital Paul Burns managed to persuade the nurses to let him out for the evening so that he and Belinda could join a crew dinner hosted by ITN's Michael Nicholson.

From then on Belinda, who had so reluctantly let Brendan join *Time & Tide* and who still wished he had never been invited to watch the start and never seen the appeal for crew in the *Sunday Times*, became just as caught up in the whole spirit of *Time & Tide*, and just as supportive of its aims and endeavours as her husband. As she came to know and like other members of the crew, she began also to appreciate everything that had been done to take care of Brendan during his sixteen torturous days strapped to a bunk at sea. However, she was still concerned for his health and somewhat daunted when the first thing he asked the medical staff on arriving at hospital was whether he would be fit enough to rejoin the race in Cape Town. She would far rather that he had given up the whole idea of taking part in the BT Global Challenge but she knew her husband too well and did not try to dissuade him. Of course it was too early to say whether the doctors would pass Brendan fit, but as far as he was concerned he was not taking no for an answer.

But while Brendan was eager to get back on to the boat, Liz was once again contemplating getting off, still disenchanted at not having learnt more about sailing and fed up with being told to accept her limitations. Shortly after arriving in Wellington she announced to James that she would be leaving the boat there. After a long chat, James managed to persuade her to stay on board, suggesting she took a short meteorology course while in New Zealand as a means of utilizing her intellectual capabilities.

David was also having his doubts about whether or not to continue. For him the issue was a matter of not enjoying ocean racing enough to justify spending ten months of his life doing it. He also felt strongly that the two extra ports of call included in the 1996–7 BT Global Challenge had made it two months too long, thereby giving people the opportunity to contemplate getting off.

Carolyn and Carol dressed for their first tandem parachute jump (left) *and Lesley trying out a quad bike in Wellington* (© Carolyn Davies)

While Paul Hebblethwaite, having relished the storms of the Roaring Forties, was more positive than he had been in Rio, it still rankled with him that he seemed to have acquired a disproportionate amount of the heavy duty work. However, since his ambition was eventually to charter private yachts round the world, and since he needed all the experience he could get in order to do this, leaving the boat was never an option. Also, given the huge amount of support he'd received from his family and friends in Yorkshire, it would have seemed like a churlish and cowardly thing to do. Occasionally he felt very homesick and the idea of not seeing his parents for several more months caused him much sorrow. For this reason he was extremely grateful when BT set up an audio-visual link between Wellington and England, allowing him to see and talk to his parents for the first time since leaving Southampton. It was one of the highlights of the trip for both him and his mother – even though they spent the entire time trying to hold back tears.

Wellington was a particularly enjoyable stopover for the crew, all of whom felt immediately at home in this attractive, thinly populated city known for the warmth and generosity of its people. On 5 January there was a civic reception hosted by the Mayor of Wellington Town at which a Scots band greeted the fleet by playing the bagpipes – no doubt an entertainment put on for Chay's benefit! Later the Governor General welcomed all the crews to the prize-giving ceremony at Government House. Here the crew received jointly with *Group 4* the prize for the most number of miles sailed in twenty-four hours – 230 miles. This was a great triumph as it meant winning a prize alongside the leading boat for having achieved an equally impressive day's sailing on one of the toughest legs.

There were also a crew sports day, several hospitality sails and many days devoted to the maintenance and overhaul of the yachts. It had always been planned to take the yachts out of the water at the newly developed Queen's Wharf, with its superb dockside and repair facilities, for a minute inspection of their rigs, sails, equipment and keels, but the scale of the work undertaken went further than anyone had anticipated. Rigging failure on so many of the yachts meant that almost all the standing rigging was replaced, at a total cost to The Challenge Business of more than £100,000.

After a week of working on the boat, Paul Burns organized a trip out to the South Island for a crew tandem skydive, at the end of which a few stayed on visiting the local vineyards and sampling the wines. As Carolyn wrote in her log, 'Can you imagine three amputees getting "legless" and trying to get them home in one piece? It has to be seen to be appreciated!' Others went in for quad-biking, tobogganing, walking in the forests and soaking in the volcanic spas.

With the long stopover many relatives had come to join the crew. Liz's parents flew out to see her, Carol's boyfriend Steve was there for a two-week holiday and James's girlfriend Sarah had also come over. Guy Chandler and Gary Champion from the Trust were there too, as was Lesley's son, Simon, who was working with the BT Global Challenge team.

James later paid a visit to an old friend, Jane Hunter of Hunter Wines, who he'd got to know when he was on his single-handed circumnavigation with *British Heart*. She and James organized a wine-tasting and fundraising event at the Blenheim vineyard and some of the crew flew down there to share in the fun. She also presented three cases of wine which were then stored on the boat, to be auctioned in aid of the *Time & Tide* Trust back in England.

Paul Burns and Chris took advantage of the six-week break in New Zealand to fly back to England to spend time with their families. For Chris, predictably, it turned out to be more a matter of catching up with office work, and as a result he arrived back in Wellington exhausted after three weeks away and not altogether sure whether it had been a good idea. Significantly, a crew member on one of the other yachts had cancelled a trip back home knowing that if he went he might never return.

During his time in England Chris wrote in his log:

> Busy three weeks. With the exception of one day, was at work every day and was surprised how easy it was to get back into the issues, although my role was more of a consultant. It did a lot to allay my fear that I wouldn't be able to handle work after sailing round the world. What did surprise me was how Time & Tide was held in such high esteem. I found this very difficult to handle, as everyone wanted to see or talk to me. Just walking in to the Bromsgrove Boaters Club I got a standing ovation. Was under a lot of pressure to see people when all I wanted was my own company.

While Chris was happy to support the *Time & Tide* Trust as much as he could, he was quite clear that he had signed up to do the Challenge for himself and not for the disabled community. Therefore, when people treated him as someone who had sacrificed so much for the good of others, he found it embarrassing and awkward to deal with.

His log continued:

> Time came to return quicker than expected. I felt I hadn't spent enough time with the girls but balancing work made this difficult. Whilst I was really glad to get away from Time & Tide for a few weeks, it made it harder to get back in. What I didn't anticipate was that everyone else's time off was time off – whereas I had worked non-stop for five weeks and come back to the boat too tired.

When he returned to Wellington, *Time & Tide* was still far from ready, compared to most of the other boats, and Chris was annoyed that the crew hadn't returned from their travels in time to meet their commitments. As a result he spent the next few days working from early in the morning until late at night on the boat, trying to get it finished. It was the normal story and the normal chaos: 'chasing jobs, chasing people, getting people to work who didn't want to work, chasing spares that hadn't arrived, chasing the Challenge for jobs and basically trying to push people so that they finished the boat in time.'

With an estimated six to seven days to Sydney, this fourth leg was to be the shortest in the race, devised as one where sponsors and VIPs could take part as honorary crew members on all the boats. Prince Michael of Kent was now in Wellington to join *Ocean Rover* as a one-legger, and on board *Time & Tide* Tony Gledhill, Church's group marketing director, and Malcolm McKeag, a 53-year-old yachting journalist with considerable sailing and racing experience, were acclimatizing themselves to the pre-race routine. Tony had no disability but qualified to take part as a one-legger because he was one of *Time & Tide*'s chief sponsors, whereas Malcolm, who was an old friend of Susan Preston Davis and had known of her efforts to get *Time & Tide* off the ground since the beginning, qualified to take part in the race because he was blind in one eye. So eager had he been to become a competitor that he had even stepped down as chairman of the BT Global Challenge's International Jury (which acted as a protest committee dealing with race matters that needed to go to arbitration). Needless to say, when the crew of *Time & Tide* were asked how many one-leggers they had sailing with them to Sydney the score was immediately doubled to include Paul Burns and Nigel.

Also joining the crew was 36-year-old Geoff Morphew, an Englishman who lived in Wellington with his American-born wife, who was signed up for both the short sprint to Sydney as well as the next much longer leg to Cape Town. Having been an insulin-dependent diabetic for the past six years, he always carried the equipment necessary to ensure his diabetes was kept under control in a pouch around his waist. After the complications with the earlier *Time & Tide* recruit, Julie Ventris, who had become seriously ill during the qualifying Fastnet course and consequently had had to be dropped from the race shortly before the start, James was wary about taking on another diabetic, but agreed to use the Tasman leg as a test run to see how well Geoff managed his condition. Geoff was confident that it wouldn't be a problem. 'The way I've gone about handling this disease,' he explained, 'is to deal with it very logically. I know everything I need to know about diabetes and I put a lot of effort into managing it, to the point even that some people would call it an obsession.'

Malcom McKeag (far left) and Tony Gledhill (centre) joined the crew for leg three (© Geoff Morphew)

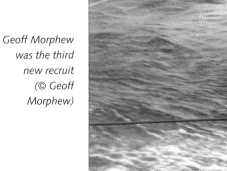

Geoff Morphew was the third new recruit (© Geoff Morphew)

As with so many of the crew, Geoff's experience of sailing was fairly limited. He had started to sail only after moving to Wellington in 1994 and initially had wanted to take part in the Global Challenge 2000, which would have given him ample time to improve his sailing skills as well as raise the necessary funds. But after spotting an article in a local newspaper about *Time & Tide* which included an appeal from James for a new crew recruit to replace John Rich, he decided there was no time like the present and promptly applied. Having passed the interview with both Chay and James, he resigned from his job as an independent data-base consultant, set about contacting major diabetes drug companies for sponsorship, and spent the following three weeks sorting out his life.

Two days before the start, as a way of getting to know the new boys, Carolyn organized a crew go-carting outing. It turned out to be a thoroughly entertaining diversion, with everyone relaxing at the same time as revving themselves up for a more competitive racing mode. As Chris was negotiating a discount with the manager, and Nigel, Paul and the others were heading towards the track with their masks and helmets on, the manager took one look at them and suddenly had second thoughts. 'I'm sorry, sir,' he said, 'but I'm afraid we can't let the cripples have a go.' Luckily, however, it didn't take long for Chris to persuade the manager that tougher obstacles had been fought and won. As Malcolm later said, 'Suffice it to say "the cripples" had a go and were a darn sight faster than most of the others on the track.' For Tony 'tearing around an indoor go-cart track with Chris Ogg in front of me and Stuart Boreham, who has already had many an accident as a racing driver, in spite of his disabilities, behind me was a fairly hair-raising experience.'

Sunday 9 February was reminiscent of the start in Southampton – cloudy, raining, with winds gusting thirty knots. James took the conservative position and once again crossed the start line at the back of the fleet: a deliberate tactic to avoid a start fight, which he now knew served *Time & Tide* no favours. They soon made up ground, however, and by the second mark had pulled up to ninth place.

Within a few hours of the start two of the new crew members were already being badly seasick, as indeed was Chris who, for the first time, had to take to his bunk. While for Tony it was simply a matter of lying down and waiting for the nausea to pass, for Geoff it was far more problematic, as dehydration was likely to cause his blood sugar levels to go haywire.

Before very long Geoff understood exactly why it was said that for the first half hour of being seasick you were afraid you might die and for next half hour you were afraid you might not. He was feeling so ill that he couldn't get his foul-weather gear off and even a drop of water on his tongue made him retch dreadfully. In fact his condition was so bad he knew there was no way he would survive another five days at sea if he didn't improve. Thankfully, however, after eight hours of being violently sick he was able to take his first teaspoon of water and after ten hours ate his first cracker.

But the crisis wasn't over yet, as Geoff still hadn't been able to stabilize his insulin intake and both he and Lesley were well aware that the combination of high blood sugar, lack of insulin and dehydration was potentially life-threatening. 'It was extremely awkward injecting my abdomen in rough seas,' said Geoff, 'but at least I managed to keep my blood sugar levels from going excessively high by doing hourly blood tests and giving myself regular shots of insulin based on the results. The only time I was really worried was when I developed ketones in my urine, which are a sign that things aren't going well, but luckily I managed to eradicate them after four days.'

While Geoff may have been satisfied that his diabetes was under control, James and Lesley were far from convinced that he would make it on to the Southern Ocean. What Geoff didn't realize was that the crew's previous experience with Julie Ventris during the trial Fastnet race had meant stopping the boat in the middle of the race for twenty-four hours to ease the motion, thereby reducing her seasickness and allowing her to take in fluids. Like Geoff, Julie's seasickness had made her go hypo on more than one occasion, and James was alarmed by the possibility of Geoff's diabetes spiralling out of control. It would take only a seemingly small thing like this to trip up the system and effectively put *Time & Tide* out of the race altogether. Only for the final three days of the leg did Geoff recover sufficiently to be a fully active crew member, but he found it all rather daunting. By the end of the leg he had realized that ocean racing would never be his first passion and was seriously considering getting off. He found the size of the sails intimidating and the physical exertion required of him greater than he had anticipated. 'A lot of glamorous things are associated with this race but the harsh reality at sea is that there is no glamour, just the cold, the wet and a lot of hard work,' he said. Nor was he prepared for the long periods of monotony. 'Some of the night watches seemed as if they would never end, especially when there was nothing to do but look over the side at the inky black sea below.'

For most of the short sprint to Sydney the fleet enjoyed good sailing conditions with a steady breeze pushing them along at between eight and nine knots. Spirits were high on board *Time & Tide*; the success of the Southern Ocean leg had raised their sights and now with Malcolm's considerable racing experience they were confident that they could do even better. For the first few days they were running tenth or eleventh in the fleet poll, but James was satisfied with his crew's performance as he knew there was no way they could have pushed the boat harder. There was also no question this time of them forgetting that they were right in the middle of a fierce fight to the finish, as there was always at least one other yacht within sight. As Malcolm said, 'On one night there were three boats in front of us but we blew them all away because we were sailing faster and better.'

The newcomers were impressed by the guts and stamina they witnessed among the more seasoned crew members. Tony reported in his log:

> It was only after sitting on one or two watches with Paul Burns and Paul Hebblethwaite and watching the routine settle in that a true insight into the courage and bravery of this crew is brought to the fore. As one comes out of a very cramped cabin, one is confronted by Paul Burns swinging himself on his remaining leg with his stump trailing behind him, and you realize that ordinary people have got it pretty simple. As it takes twenty minutes at least every time you dress and undress at the beginning and at the end of a watch you can imagine how much effort goes into a day's work on board *Time & Tide* for the amputees.

Similarly Malcolm recorded:

> Time & Tide *loses out because of mobility around the deck. Although the Challenge Business trains all the crews to work slowly and safely, some of the other skippers have by now got their crew to work swiftly and safely. But if James were to try to take any short cuts there would be huge problems.*

From the outset Malcolm had been sensitive about his position on board *Time & Tide*. 'I knew that I had to be very careful when I came on the boat not to upset the hierarchy and pecking order,' he said. Initially James had been concerned that Malcolm's presence on board might destabilize his own position. 'My initial reluctance,' he explained, 'was that I didn't want a rock star on board. I wanted someone with a whole wealth of knowledge who was prepared to share it and equally someone with whom I could bounce ideas off, so that between us we could feed a hungry crew.' But he soon came to value his knowledge and expertise and by the end of the leg was taking full advantage of it.

Having Malcolm on board was undoubtedly a great asset to the boat and it was noted by almost everyone how he significantly changed the dynamics of the crew. Not only was he an extremely affable and approachable sort of person, but he was also willing to pass on information and explain aspects of sailing that were still causing problems. Although Lesley was initially wary of his sharp wit and constant banter, she soon warmed to him 'because he was such a good teacher and such a nice man'. Liz, who regarded the entire eight days at sea as 'a lot of fun and almost like a holiday', put her good mood down to being entertained from beginning to end by Malcolm, who she found 'perceptive, helpful and naturally funny'. Like many of the crew she regretted he wasn't continuing on with them to the Southern Ocean.

For the first few days during this third leg to Sydney the weather conditions favoured *Time & Tide*, with good winds gusting up to thirty-five knots. All was going according to plan until 12 February, when an 'all hands on deck' call at two in the morning alerted the crew to the fact that their powerful heavy-weather spinnaker was ripped to shreds and lying in the sea. At this time of night there had simply not been enough crew on deck to take the necessary action to save the kite. Once again the seams, which had been badly repaired, had blown apart in the wind as if they were tissue paper. For the next hour and a half in rising winds and rolling seas, six members of the crew worked on the foredeck under riding lights, clearing the debris of the shredded spinnaker. A lighter kite was then hoisted, but almost immediately that too ripped and had to be brought down. By now the winds had died, but the sail changes had cost the boat valuable time and James knew that it would take more than just hard work and a little luck to regain their former position.

With *3Com*'s riding lights no longer visible on the horizon, *Time & Tide* was now alone in an empty sea. Tony wrote in his log that night, 'The only other living soul around is a beautiful osprey lazily winging its way along just behind, looking hopefully for the remains of James's bacon sandwich.'

Once both kites had blown, it was, as Malcolm put it, 'like racing with one arm tied behind our backs, because we didn't dare bust any of the others.' By now it was Thursday and the lead between the first and last boat had widened to ninety miles. With little option but to make a bold move and take a flyer, James worked out a navigational tactic which he now felt was their only chance of getting back in the race. The decision was to break away from the rest of the pack and head north. There was only one scenario in which this wouldn't work, namely with the build-up of south-westerly winds, but both James and Malcolm considered this a risk worth taking. Unfortunately it wasn't long before they realized that luck wasn't on their side and they were indeed now faced with their worst scenario.

Chris recorded in his log on 17 February:

> *We finally established that the northerly position had not paid off. The weather did not move round and it looked as though we would come in last. This was really disappointing, considering how hard we have driven the boat. The final finish was very tense, navigating a new port at night under race conditions. Crossed the finish line very unspectacularly. Eventually came alongside the quay after all the formalities had been completed. Everyone clearly disappointed having worked so hard to have still come last.*

Tony Gledhill, marketing director of Church's, joined the yacht for the 'Chairman's Leg' between Wellington and Sydney

It was another frustrating finish. After seven and a half days at sea *Time & Tide* was becalmed about a hundred miles out of Sydney and in the space of eight hours managed just two miles, finally picking up wind mid-morning on Sunday to cross the finish line shortly after midnight.

Although there was a distinct air of despondency on board, it was nevertheless an honourable defeat, given that *Save the Children*, which came in first, had arrived in Sydney Harbour just five hours earlier, and the gap between the first and last boat had dropped to just twenty-six miles. *Save the Children* had beaten *Group 4*, whose skipper, Mike Golding, had been determined to add a third consecutive victory to his tally by being first in Sydney Harbour and was visibly displeased by coming in second.

James was gutted about being last again and felt he'd let the whole crew down by taking a gamble that hadn't paid off. Malcolm also felt responsible. For most of the race they had been operating a restricted helmsman system, allowing only the best helmsmen to steer the boat – namely James, Malcolm, Carolyn and Nigel, each doing two-hour shifts at a time. Malcolm now wondered whether the decision to deny people like Paul Burns and Chris the opportunity to helm had been kind or indeed prudent, when they had nonetheless failed to deliver and still come in last. 'If the crew felt pissed off that a rock star had been given the top job and then sure enough we still came in fourteenth, I wouldn't blame them,' he said.

It was true that the crew felt disappointed, as expectations had been high. Lesley said, 'When my son Simon came to say goodbye in Wellington, his parting words to me were, "You're going to do well." It was such a short leg, the boats were expected to stay close together and I don't think he was the only one to think we would improve on our position.'

All this only added to James's sense of frustration and disappointment – though the crew did their utmost to reassure him that they didn't hold him responsible. As far as James was concerned, only the crew could make him feel better: 'They reassured me that it was a logical decision to make. We went the right way but it didn't work. We took the same strategy out of Rio and that paid off, whereas this time it didn't. Everyone knows that you win some, you lose some.'

Shortly after their arrival in Sydney Carol recorded in her log, 'James blamed himself for the tactical decision which didn't pay off. I said it had been a very good theory and later he thanked me for my vote of confidence.' Like all the crew she was disappointed at coming in last but it didn't alter her overall positive feelings about *Time & Tide*. She went on to write, 'I am still very happy with the yacht, the crew and the skipper.'

Coming into harbour *Time & Tide* was greeted by Michael Nicholson and an ITN camera crew, who insisted they raise the mainsail again so that this time they could film it being lowered, before they proceeded under escort from customs to Darling Harbour. Here, even though it was now the early hours of Monday morning, there was a huge crowd waiting to welcome them in, once again to the strains of 'Simply the Best'. The other thirteen yachts were lined up along the quayside, with many of the crew standing on deck applauding *Time & Tide* as it edged towards the pontoon.

It was impossible not to be moved by the fleet's genuine admiration for *Time & Tide*'s achievement, but for many this was a hollow victory, and being applauded so generously seemed once again to spotlight the very thing the crew were trying to forget, namely that they were different from the other boats.

Malcolm admitted to feeling what others had often felt before: 'We came into Sydney and there were all these other crews standing on their decks shouting, cheering and congratulating us,' he said. 'It was very special and very moving and yet for a moment I felt a tiny tinge of angry resentment that somehow I was being patronized.'

James knew exactly what he meant and observed that while the rest of the fleet undoubtedly had great respect for *Time & Tide* – particularly since everyone had initially expected them to come in a day or two late – 'they were also cheering because thankfully it wasn't them coming in last and they hadn't been beaten by the disabled crew.' He knew there was absolutely no reason why *Time & Tide* shouldn't have come in ahead of some of the other boats and was determined that next time they would do better. 'I didn't join up to run the sympathy boat; my crew don't deserve this,' he said emphatically.

Although the attention given to *Time & Tide* by the public and the media was altogether welcomed by the Trust office and The Challenge Business, some of the crew who were determined not to be viewed as heroes or special cases were still finding it hard to accept. But they appreciated people's support and the feeling of goodwill the project generated, even finding the media's continuing fascination with false limbs highly amusing. As far as Paul Burns was concerned there were no hard feelings when a television camera crew saw a leg sticking out of his kit bag and made him do several takes to ensure that this amazing sight was recorded for posterity.

After the customary celebrations on arrival, the crew headed for the luxury Ritz–Carlton Hotel, a late and very welcome sponsor of the project, where they were to spend a few days

before moving into apartments by the Australian National Maritime Museum in Darling Harbour. Carol wrote in her log a few days later:

> The staff at the Ritz–Carlton are great – really friendly and not stuffy at all. When I apologized to the doorman for looking scruffy (crew shirt and shorts because of working on the boat all day) he said, 'You're not scruffy, I'm just sorry I'm so smart!'

Susan Preston Davis, who had not seen the crew for three months, had come to Sydney with her husband and daughter to co-ordinate the two-week stopover. She had spent the last few weeks sorting out the Ritz–Carlton deal but it had still meant renting apartments for half of the stopover at a cost to the Trust of almost £5,000. The money was raised back in England, helped by John Anderson, who contacted all his business associates asking them to give a donation.

Later when the crew occupied the apartments just a short stroll from where the boats were moored, there was much time for socializing between crews and many a late night was spent in the local pub. Also, several family members were visiting Sydney, including Nigel's brother and his family, who lived in Australia, Carol's mother and her friend, who had come out on holiday, and James's sister Mary, who travelled to be with him for the start of the next leg. Also, Stuart was there running the BT Global Challenge information bureau for BT from the dockside. For almost all of *Time & Tide*'s crew and their families it was their first visit to Sydney and they were determined to make the most of it, but as usual, what with working on the boat to prepare it for the next crossing in the Southern Ocean and the busy itinerary laid out by the Trust and The Challenge Business, there was hardly a moment to breathe.

There was a welcome party at the Cruising Yacht Club of Australia in Rushcutters Bay; the prizegiving ceremony took place on 22 February at Darling Harbour, combining the formal trophy presentation with some customary down-under hospitality in the form of a barbecue; and BT invited the crews of *Time & Tide* and *Concert* for a meal at a quayside restaurant. As a resident of the city, John Rich, who was now almost fully recovered and who had been at Darling Harbour to welcome the crew in, offered to take his former shipmates on sightseeing trips of the area. One particularly nice surprise was that four members of the Zurich Insurance corporate communications department, including Wendy May and Frances Pilcher, had shown their appreciation of the boat they were sponsoring by using their own money to fly over and spend a week with the crew. Feeling themselves to be so much a part of the *Time & Tide* family, they were determined to be more involved than just through the office electronic noticeboard, which gave staff daily bulletins of the yacht's progress. They arrived in Sydney just in time to join the crew dinner, which was held at the famous Doyles Fish Restaurant at Watson's Bay.

Predictably, as soon as James stepped foot on dry land, he donned his trustee hat and with mobile phone in hand once again he set about attempting to generate interest in *Time & Tide* – still the most poorly funded yacht in the fleet. For him the Sydney stopover was a busy, enjoyable but at times stressful two weeks. Not only were there the usual corporate days and Challenge Business matters to deal with, but crew problems continued. One comfort, perhaps, was that after talking to other skippers, at least he now felt reassured that his boat was no different from any of the others in that respect.

Some of the crew were still having doubts or problems. Just forty hours before coming into Sydney David had come up to him to say that he was considering getting off because ocean racing just wasn't his cup of tea. 'I told him I thought he should get off if he wasn't happy because the next leg would be pretty brutal, but on the other hand I said he needed to think about six months of hell for a lifetime of achievement. He promised to talk it over with his girlfriend as soon as he got to Sydney.' In the end, after much deliberation and discussion with Carol, David decided to stay on board 'because of vanity and in order to say I've done it'. He also believed in *Time & Tide* as a concept and was concerned about letting down the countless asthmatic children who had written in praising him for his efforts. While he stressed he was no hero, he knew too how bad it would look if he gave up now.

Paul Hebblethwaite, who had shown enormous progress in terms of developing his sailing and social skills during the last three legs, was still frustrated by feeling alienated from the rest of the crew. Tony commented in his log:

> *Paul is probably the most interesting and complex person on the crew; as he is profoundly deaf, it is almost impossible to communicate with him and of course you cannot on watch at night. He has an innate ability to helm the boat and obviously his other senses are heightened by his lack of hearing ability.*

Paul Burns had also taken a knock during this last leg and felt he had been underused and undervalued, though James insisted he had been trying to give him an easy ride so that he could build up his strength and fitness for the more rigorous Southern Ocean leg ahead. 'But what's the point of being out there on the ocean if you can't participate?' Paul protested. Like Chris, he had felt disorientated coming back to the boat after a two-week break with his family in England and had never fully readjusted to the boat's stringent regime. Also, the fact that he hadn't been allowed to helm the boat for the entire leg had affected his confidence. James maintained that with Paul having to sit down for most of the time while helming it wasn't a position best suited to him, but Paul disagreed. While he acknowledged that 'the brain was willing but the body was weak' he was certain that given half a chance he could do the job as well as anyone else. He still loved sailing and got a thrill from being part of the Challenge event, but his health had taken a battering and his morale was sliding. 'It's magical being on deck and so close to the ocean, even in bad weather,' he declared, but at the same time he admitted that lately he'd found himself 'beginning to wish the time away, which in a way is like wishing my life away.' His flagging spirits weren't helped by the fact that he had chipped a bone in his elbow during the previous leg and needed to keep his arm in a sling. This meant he now had only one uninjured limb left.

For Chris this had also been the most onerous leg so far. Although he never complained about his health, the Southern Ocean had taken its toll and he was beginning to feel a numbness in his left hand and pains in his knees which hadn't been there before. While he didn't deny that occasionally he had moments of despair, he was determined not to harbour such feelings or give in to what he called negative emotion. He had also underestimated how exhausting returning to England would be and found it difficult to readjust to the boat on his return. As a result, for the first time he began to question whether he wanted to be there at all. His wife Maureen joined him for the Sydney stopover and although he spent much of the two weeks on the boat she was able to take some of the pressure off him.

Maureen knew her husband well enough not to expect him to take time off for sightseeing or shopping trips, so she wasn't surprised that he was so tied up with the boat. She had learnt the art of flexibility, realizing that meetings and briefings were constantly called and then changed, and although this didn't stop her from sometimes feeling irritated, she thoroughly appreciated the few relaxing evenings she spent with her husband away from Challenge business. She even enjoyed accompanying Chris and Carolyn on the crew shopping trip to stock up on provisions for the next leg, which included an early morning visit to the fruit and vegetable market followed by breakfast at McDonald's at 7.00 a.m.

Chris had also found the complexities of his job as mate even more demanding on this last leg. While one of the main attractions of being mate was that you didn't have time to get bored, it could also be an extremely solitary position. If James was unavailable the crew would turn to him as a substitute, but often he felt inadequately briefed and therefore unable to answer their questions. He was determined that they shouldn't take advantage of him, and declared,

Start of Leg Four
from Sydney to
Cape Town
(© Susan
Preston Davis)

'I categorically refuse to be their messenger or their spokesman, because there will always be twelve different versions of what they want to see happen.'

Despite continuing difficulties with the crew, Peter Mackie from MaST, who was out in Sydney to visit members of the fleet, was heartened by the change of attitude he witnessed on board *Time & Tide*, especially since with the race now well on its way it was too late for helping with team-building or even for giving much moral support. He knew now that skipper and crew would have to cope on their own and while some dissatisfaction and backbiting was inevitable with a group of people who had lived and worked together for so long, he sensed a far happier crew. As Humphrey Walters, chief executive of MaST, who was sailing as a crew member on *Ocean Rover*, had said, 'Leadership is not a gift, it is learned, and the skippers know that if they are to do well they have to develop their crew. That means they have to be happy and feel safe.'

Also it was becoming obvious as the voyage continued that James was progressively becoming more aware of his shortcomings and more prepared to talk about them. Equally, there was an increasing acceptance from the crew of what James was and wasn't good at. Paul

Burns, for instance, had come to understand and accept that 'James wasn't the big brother figure I thought he would be.' They were also realizing that moaning about their skipper was a pointless task, as the only person they upset by doing so was themselves. 'They've had to learn to find the hugs themselves,' noted Mackie. 'What they're not getting from Chris Ogg or James as far as praise and strokes are concerned they're now looking for in themselves.'

James felt it was fine to praise as long as you were allowed to criticize too, but he considered that too many of the crew were looking for strokes even if they'd got something wrong. 'The trouble is,' he said, 'they're not prepared to take responsibility if something goes wrong.' But wherever possible he tried to give praise where praise was due. Chris, on the other hand, was less inclined to give praise, as he believed people should be able to do things for themselves. 'I'm not into giving insincere praise just because that's what's expected of me,' he remarked. 'I think feedback is important but I'm not going to hand out any medals. At work I don't give strokes because I don't see why one should keep on saying thank you to someone when they're employed to do a job.' But that was the whole point – here on the Challenge boats people weren't employed, they'd actually paid to be there, and many of them expected something back in return, even if just a small pat on the back.

But those who received praise from other crew members appreciated it. For instance, John Rich wrote in his log during the second leg:

> *Finally I think I'm getting the hang of the mast work. Even David T. has noticed my improvements. It is nice for people to notice these personal improvements. I think that praise for a job well done is important and I am greatly appreciative of it, making sure that I constantly try to do a better job.*

Carol and Liz also expressed their gratitude to Mike for having continually told them how invaluable they were and both agreed it had done a lot to boost their confidence.

Perhaps it was inevitable that someone as pragmatic as Chris, who kept such a tight reign on his emotions, would find it hard to tolerate other people's weaknesses, expecting higher standards than often the crew were able to give. However, Lesley insisted that 'the weak are not always weak, they just appear to be so and it's important to remember they have their own hidden strengths too – it's just a matter of having time to find them.'

But that harsh words may have been spoken didn't mean the boat was cruel and when tempers were short it was usually because those working hardest resented those who didn't seem to be pulling their weight. This was an issue of attitude rather than ability and although black humour about 'deaf gits' or 'limbless cretins' were part of the boat's culture, among the crew there was never anything but total acceptance of each other's disabilities. As Malcolm noted, 'On board *Time & Tide* no one has a problem with their problem; it's only outside, among the able-bodied, that problems exist.'

For James, Sydney was the time when a lot of crew complaints got voiced, discussed with both him and Susan, and finally laid to rest. But at times he felt no one fully appreciated the constant pressure he was under, not only to deliver the boat safely to shore but also to keep The Challenge Business informed of crew developments and the sponsors involved and satisfied. 'I feel my failings get highlighted in bloody great neon lights,' he once complained.

At times the demands on James seemed all-consuming. At sea as well as on shore he seemed to be expected to carry the can for everything. 'They want me to teach them, support them and nanny them, and there's not a skipper in the race who won't tell you the same,' he said. Sometimes he felt like a dispensary – handing out knowledge, sympathy and hotel rooms, often with little thanks. And yet at the same time he had great admiration and respect for his crew and felt responsible for them. 'It's my job to deliver them safely home and I'll do my best for them,' he declared.

It was clear by now which members of *Time & Tide* were really benefiting from the whole experience of the race. For instance, just about everyone remarked on the fact that Nigel was a transformed man since leaving Southampton. Whereas formerly he had been shy and withdrawn, now there seemed to be a real twinkle in his eye. He had come out of his shell, was thoroughly enjoying the sociable side of the stopovers and undoubtedly had become one of the key players on the boat. One friend from England remarked, 'We seem to have seen more of Nigel since he's been gone because he's been on the telly so much.' There was no doubt that for Nigel the Challenge was proving to be the trip of a lifetime.

Carolyn was another member of the crew who had no doubts about the value of her experience on the Challenge. During the voyage from Rio she had written in her log, 'We know why we are doing this – to prove to ourselves and to be able to say to the world, "I did that: it can be done by anyone."'

For Geoff, trying to decide whether to continue was an emotional roller coaster. James had asked him to make a decision within twelve hours of arriving in Sydney and after seriously considering pulling out altogether he decided that while it would certainly be too hazardous to do the Southern Ocean leg he would try to rejoin the boat in Cape Town, from where he hoped to continue to the finish.

A few days before the start of the fourth leg Mike also announced that under doctor's orders he would have to bow out of this next Southern Ocean leg. According to one fellow crew member, 'Mike seemed to have had his spirit drained by the end of the third leg.' A big bust-up with James in the middle of the Tasman Sea hadn't helped. They'd been sailing tight against *3Com* when during the course of one night the trailing boat had caught up and passed them. James was furious with Mike, who was both watch leader and on helm at the time, for not having alerted him to the fact.

Initially in Sydney Mike had had a long chat with Chris and told him that he had doubts about carrying on as he didn't particularly enjoy sailing with either Chris or James. But he then declared that he'd changed his mind and didn't want to get off after all. However a few days later his health had come into play. His knee had caused him trouble in the Southern Ocean and now during the Sydney crossing he had torn a muscle in his chest and ended up with acute tendonitis in his hands, making it difficult and painful to do even the most simple tasks. As far as his career was concerned the implications were extremely serious and doctors in Sydney strongly advised he stayed out of the next leg and only rejoined the boat in Cape Town subject to BA medical staff approval.

Yet again Liz was having doubts about whether to continue. James noted that her meteorological course didn't seem to have been put to much use. 'When she came to see me in Wellington to say she was getting off I spent two hours with her explaining how she could be of great use to the boat. I even arranged for her to go and talk to the met man and get some training, but maybe it didn't interest her or maybe she just wanted the attention because she never put this training to any use.' Although Liz's indomitable spirit and consistent hard work had won her the praise of even Chris, she was disappointed that Mike was getting off and all too aware that the next Southern Ocean leg was likely to be a repetition of the last. However, she would probably have continued on to Cape Town, had she not had a row with James the night before they were due to sail. Susan and James had been upset that Liz, among others, had sent the specially made Ritz–Carlton promotional jackets in their baggage to Cape Town, before a farewell breakfast which was being filmed the next morning for the *Time & Tide* documentary. The argument started off as something fairly trivial but pre-race nerves and tension blew it up out of all proportion and in a fit of anger Liz walked out of the project.

To most of the crew Liz had always seemed a fairly reckless and confused person and though this was by no means unexpected, it was still a bitter blow and they felt disappointed and let down by her actions. They would now have to set sail with three crew members short. Not only were they the least equipped in terms of physical strength to face the next leg, reported to be the most arduous and gruelling of them all, but also they would be sailing with less manpower than any of the other boats in the fleet.

At the *Time & Tide* farewell breakfast held at the Ritz–Carlton Hotel early on that Sunday morning, the crew dealt with their nerves in different ways – some were noisy and giggly while others, mainly those who had been joined by their families, seemed altogether quieter and more pensive. However, when Peter Mackie stood up and gave a heartfelt speech about the consequences and significance of the Challenge, all of them began to reflect on what lay ahead.

Mackie asked them to consider what people back home in England were doing now. He said that during the weekend about ten million would be washing their cars, five million would be having a lunchtime drink in the pub and around twenty million would be watching *Blind Date*. He then went on to talk about people's attitude to work. On Monday morning over twenty million people would go to work, out of which ten million would be dreading it so much they'd be looking forward to retirement.

'But when their grandchildren sit at their feet and ask them what was the greatest thing they achieved in their life what will they say?' asked Mackie. 'For most it will be a new car, a new house or perhaps becoming supervisor of the plant. Not one person in all those statistics will be able to say they've been the first disabled crew to sail round the world against prevailing winds and currents.'

Mackie later wondered whether this was the best speech to give in terms of crew motivation, since many tears were shed that morning with the sheer enormity of what lay ahead beginning to dawn on every one of them.

Leg 3 Final Results

	Team	Arrival time
1	Save the Children	16/02/97 07:32
2	Group 4	16/02/97 09:50
3	Courtaulds Int.	16/02/97 10:51
4	Global Teamwork	16/02/97 11:05
5	Pause to Remember	16/02/97 11:17
6	Concert	16/02/97 11:18
7	3Com	16/02/97 11:19
8	Ocean Rover	16/02/97 11:33
9	Nuclear Electric	16/02/97 11:35
10	Toshiba Wave Warrior	16/02/97 11:39
11	Motorola	16/02/97 11:41
12	Heath Insured II	16/02/97 12:01
13	Commercial Union	16/02/97 12:55
14	Time & Tide	16/02/97 13:13

All times GMT.

Leg 3 Combined Times

	TEAM	TIME
1	Group 4	072d 20h 54m
2	Toshiba Wave Warrior	073d 15h 03m
3	Save the Children	073d 15h 47m
4	Motorola	074d 23h 20m
5	Commercial Union	075d 11h 10m
6	Nuclear Electric	076d 12h 01m
7	Global Teamwork	076d 21h 54m
8	3Com	077d 04h 36m
9	Ocean Rover	077d 05h 09m
10	Pause to Remember	077d 18h 17m
11	Heath Insured II	079d 04h 02m
12	Time & Tide	079d 19h 37m
13	Courtaulds Int.	079d 20h 02m
14	Concert	084d 15h 59m

All times rounded to the nearest minute.

Chapter Six

Leg Four
Sydney to Cape Town

Departure date 2 March 1997; 6,200 miles. ETA 37-40 days. Across Southern Indian Ocean against easterly travelling Southern Ocean current. Around two capes, Cape Leeuwin and Cape of Good Hope ('Cape of Storms'). Sailing into Roaring Forties, going around waypoint north of Kerguélen Island (middle of Southern Indian Ocean). Unpredictable winds in this region. Weather conditions change fast as yachts heading into weather all the time.

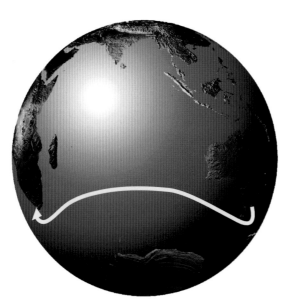

3 March 1997 Fax to Susan Preston Davis at Trust office, England
Here we go again. Tell me why it is I have three guys with only one leg but it's hands I am really short of. Sailed with twelve; now four down with acute seasickness, one banged his head on the mast, one with a chipped elbow which they say will be OK in four to five days' time with rest, one who slid down the deck and had to be prized off the deck cleat before we spent the early hours clearing him up and stitching his bottom.

So, let me see, that adds up to 2.5 people per watch. Still, we have gone from last to eleventh – maybe there's a message there ... Strange how calm my temper is this leg – then I look around and there's no one to shout at!
Hugs, James

Departing Sydney with the new crew (© Time & Tide/BT)

The ebullient tone of this first message to the Trust office, just one day into the race, was a good indication that although this leg had all the potential of being the most demanding yet, James's hopes were riding high and his mood unexpectedly buoyant, considering all the last-minute crew changes in Sydney and the complications that had occurred on board since.

Leaving Sydney had been a successful start for *Time & Tide*, especially since, unlike their departure from Wellington, this time they hadn't been the last boat out: a particularly satisfactory achievement given that so many well-wishers and supporters had come to wave them goodbye. A number of the other yachts put up their kites soon after leaving the Harbour but James resisted the temptation for speed. With two crew members short and three new ones having to learn the ropes, there wasn't the energy or experience yet to race the boat hard.

Grahme Rayner worked hard in the galley (© Time & Tide/BT)

Two of the new crew, 39-year-old Grahme Rayner and 41-year-old Clive Dutton, had been recruited in Australia to replace Mike Austin and Geoff Morphew, while 43-year-old Steven Latter had arrived from England just two days before the restart.

Grahme Rayner, who had lost a leg in a motorbike accident in December 1994, was a recruitment sergeant in the Australian Army and a keen amateur sailor. He was an easy-going, genial sort of chap whose willpower was such that he had returned to work just ten days after his accident, played bowls just five weeks later and at the end of that first year had sailed with a disabled crew in the Sydney–Hobart race. His wife Lauretta, who had been with him on the bike at the time of the accident and broken her ankle as a result, remembered that despite Grahme's leg having been severed at the scene he had kept cheerful throughout, not only giving instructions to passers-by who came to help but joking with the ambulance crew on the way to the hospital.

'That's the sort of person he is,' she said. 'He's always got a positive attitude, but then again he's never been in a position to feel sorry for himself because of the amazing support we've had from everyone – our two teenage children, our friends, colleagues and the Church.' Grahme agreed that he had come to terms with the accident with astonishing ease and acknowledged that some people were still waiting for him to fall off the horse.

As far as sailing in the Challenge was concerned, he was aware that as someone who for the last twenty years had spent his time organizing and allocating jobs to other people, he would find life on board *Time & Tide* very different. But while he knew that this complete role reversal might take some adjusting to, he was convinced it wouldn't be a problem, as for once in his life he was looking forward to being the recruit rather than the trainer. His disability concerned him only in so far as the skin round his stump was still shrinking, which meant he hadn't yet been fitted with a suitable prosthesis. However, he had had a peg leg specially made for the crossing, which he hoped would give him more balance than the regular flex foot and active knee-joint leg which all too often collapsed beneath him.

It was while driving home from holiday with his family and hearing an appeal for disabled sailors on the local radio that Clive Dutton was first alerted to the existence of *Time & Tide*. With 6,000 miles of offshore sailing experience behind him, it was too good an opportunity to pass over and as soon as he got back to his home in New South Wales he contacted the Challenge office in Sydney. His wife, Robin, who ran the pharmacy they jointly owned, supported him all the way, even though it meant that at such short notice they would initially have to dig into their savings to fund the trip.

As a result of a freak accident in 1976 while helping out in a friend's butcher shop, Clive had lost his right hand in a meat mincer. The ambulance men had needed a pneumatic drill to release it and had then had to amputate most of it at the scene of the accident – only his thumb remained, although later surgeons were able to construct a stump-like finger. But like so many of the *Time & Tide* crew who had become disabled through an accident in adulthood, Clive's attitude was laudable: having accepted and come to terms with what had happened to him, he was determined not to let his disability hold him back in any way. Now, twenty years later, the only two things he claimed he regretted not being able to do were counting beyond seven and clapping.

Out of the three new crew recruits Steven Latter, a software consultant from Hampshire in England, was the most experienced sailor. He had become fascinated by the 1992–3 British Steel Global Challenge and had been avidly following the BT Global Challenge on the Internet when he read an article in the *Sunday Times* appealing for new crew members. Immediately it occurred to him that he might be able to help them out. This was just two weeks before the restart in Sydney and although the thought of taking part seemed totally implausible at the time he cleared it with his wife, applied to The Challenge Business and even succeeded in coming up with sponsorship for his berth fee. Steve fulfilled the disability criteria, having had severe atrophy of the upper limbs since 1987 as a consequence of an accident when he fell forty feet on to concrete.

For this fourth leg to Cape Town Paul Hebblethwaite had been selected as one of the two watch leaders and he was looking forward to the responsibility, as well as the challenge, of looking after and communicating with other crew members. However, sadly Paul was never given the chance to prove himself as at 4.30 a.m. on 3 March, just fifteen hours after leaving Sydney, he had an accident which was to leave him incapacitated for much of the next five weeks. With David having just knocked his head on the mast, Paul Burns still suffering from his elbow injury and two crew members down with seasickness, it was rapidly turning into a somewhat luckless start.

Paul had been working on the bow when a colossal wave pushed him down the deck and impaled him on a cleat (a fitting with projecting horns for securing ropes). In agony he made his way below decks, and struggled to get out of his foul-weather gear and drop his trousers to inspect the damage. As James noted, 'He looked like a dog chasing his own back passage.'

Paul wrote in his log:

> *I was on duty at 3.00 a.m. when the wind built up so we got number one down and replaced it with number two. I was sitting on the deck when a wave came over and pushed me forward towards the double cleats near the bow which hit me badly up my rectum. I yelled with pain but couldn't explain how it felt. So I struggled back down to the doghouse, took my foulers off quickly, then took my shorts down and saw the blood. I showed Nigel, who called for Lesley. We moved to the galley where I lay down for an hour on the table waiting for advice from the fleet doctor.*

Steve Latter (© Time & Tide/BT)

Clive Dutton (© Time & Tide/BT)

Lesley could see instantly that Paul had been injured in the perineum (or as Paul preferred to put it 'in front of the back passage and behind the balls') and was immediately nervous about stitching up such a tender area of skin, especially since the boat was rocking violently. Her first thought was to bring in a doctor from one of the other boats, something she'd always been led to believe would be possible in an emergency, but James insisted that would be both dangerous and time-consuming. 'I'm not a midwife,' Lesley explained, 'so I was very wary about sewing him up in that particularly delicate area, but when James volunteered to do it for me I thought he could hold the torch and comfort Paul but I was going to get the anaesthetic in and do the stitching. In the end it took two hours to get just two stitches in but it was better than nothing.'

Both Lesley and James were impressed by Paul's courage. He flinched only occasionally and never complained about the searing pain shooting through his body. For the next few days he was confined to his bunk, bored, restless, uncomfortable but relieved that the weather had calmed, the bleeding had stopped and the wound had not been infected. He was also grateful for the kindness shown by a number of the crew, including James, who brought him a bowl of twisted pasta with cubes of salami, onion and grated cheese on top. 'Fantastic dinner,' he wrote in his log. 'Enjoyed every bit of it. James is a great cook!' In the days ahead, as Paul was restricted first to his bunk and then to light duties in the galley, he started occupying his time with things that normally would have held no interest for him – namely reading and cooking – and started to express appreciation of both.

In a message to Race HQ, giving an up-date of *Time & Tide's* medical difficulties, James mischievously elaborated on the implications of damaging your perineum:

> *Still only another week and our gallant bowman's stitches will be out and he will be able to sit down again. We also have four seapukers who are gradually showing signs of recovery. They still have a problem looking a bacon sandwich in the face but should be recovered in time to see the last of the fresh meat, though our bowman may not be so lucky. It is the concern of the medic, Lesley, and the fleet doctor that strain on the stitches should be avoided at all costs. To this end we have been advised that the bottom line ... pardon the pun ... is that the bowman should be put on a mild course of laxatives. We, the fit and hungry crew, feel that there is only so much bacon and other fresh delights left ... furthermore, why waste good laxatives when we have an abundant supply of freeze-dried food?*

Apart from sailing two crew volunteers short, the fact that there were three novices on board couldn't help but slow things down, particularly since the new crew were on a steep learning curve, having to adjust to the system and methodology of Challenge yachts. However, all three seemed to be fitting in well and it was generally felt to be beneficial to have some new blood on board. On the second day at sea Carol wrote in her log:

> *Although we are short of crew everyone seems more relaxed. We've got biscuits, fruit and chocolate on free issue which helps. The new guys have fitted in really well and seem like they've always been here. Clive has the sort of face which always looks smiley. Steve is helming already and has a great sense of humour and Grahme always seems cheerful, although I know he misses his family a lot. He's got photos of his wife, his children and his motorbike taped around his bunk and when he goes to sleep he says 'g'dnight my darling' (to his wife), 'g'dnight kids', 'g'dnight bike' and 'g'dnight bud' (to me). He's nowhere near as mobile as Paul B. or Nigel but he only lost his leg two years ago. Hope this race will help him. I miss Liz, though, who was always cheerful and helpful on the boat, and will get in touch with her when I get back to England.*

8 March 1997: First Mate's Log: 45°0.8' S 140°12' E

> *Hard day, lot of wind. Boat movement very bad. Chucked about everywhere. People are tired. Moved up the poll to twelfth today. First good news. New people are mixed in what they can do. Grahme's leg is a major problem. Clive will have problems with his hand. Steve seems to be OK – at least his sailing experience is of use to the boat. We now have weather faxes which help us plan. James is different on this leg. We seem to have a better relationship – more balanced. He looks for help and wants to talk issues through!*

It was indeed already obvious to all the old hands that James was far more relaxed on this leg, deliberately operating a more open style of management and discussing tactics with the crew, who now felt they had a say in the running of the boat. This reduced crew conflict to a minimum, as well as making Chris's job far easier. Lesley noted in her log a week after leaving Sydney: 'James seems a changed person this leg – more tolerant of the crew and circumstances.'

Everyone also agreed that while having two less crew put an additional strain on the fittest and most mobile among them, the extra space it created and the ease with which people could now move around the galley made life on board considerably more comfortable than it had been on previous legs. Paul Burns was far happier too, because with less crew vying for jobs everyone was expected to muck in with everything, which meant his anxiety about not being able to helm on this fourth leg proved to be quite unfounded. Consequently for the first time in many weeks he felt indispensable to the boat, which in turn helped lift his spirits.

Generally speaking the spirits of everyone on board *Time & Tide* were high, since the boat was performing well. In addition to having pulled up from last to twelfth position, it had experienced some exciting days kite sailing, including a gybing match with *Courtaulds* and *Ocean Rover*. There was also the psychological factor that now they had rounded the corner, they were halfway through the race and heading for home.

One concern that soon came to light, however, was that the new Australian crew members, while being keen to pull their weight below and above deck, were in fact more limited in their capabilities than anyone had at first realized. Within a day of being at sea it became evident that Grahme's peg leg was going to cause problems for everyone. Nigel's first entry in his log recorded, 'I think Grahme is dangerous and he is also sick as a parrot. Last night he almost went over the side as he attempted to puke over the rail!' Eventually Grahme discarded the peg leg, which had proved to be little more than an effective publicity stunt, and took to sliding around the deck on his bottom; but since that only created painful sores and blisters he finally realized that the only useful place left for him during this crossing was working in the galley. It was not what he had envisaged and for a while he felt quite despondent at the idea of not actually being in a position to do all the things he'd so eagerly anticipated, such as helming, hoisting the sails and heaving in the sheets.

Clive, too, was not finding it easy adjusting to the boat's routine, and for a while couldn't find a useful position for himself on board. Having only one good hand made it impossible for him to steer in heavy weather and with the skin on his other hand prone to blisters, he was also finding it difficult to operate the winches. However, it wasn't long before Clive became very useful helping out with sail changes on the foredeck and by the end of the leg he claimed to be the only person who would quite happily have carried on without pulling in at Cape Town.

Because Steve had had his own forty-foot cutter it didn't take him long to familiarize himself with the systems the crew used and he too soon become a very useful member of the crew, particularly on the helm. Apart from being extremely impressed by the sturdiness of the vessel, he was full of admiration for the methodology used by the crew, which insured minimum damage and injury at all times.

Lesley, who had found the second leg extremely tough and frightening, and had been relieved to be below decks looking after Brendan for much of the time, was already having major anxieties about how she would cope with the kind of intemperate weather known to be a feature of the Southern Ocean. In her log on 8 March she wrote, 'Today Nigel inadvertently tacked at lunchtime and Watch B's scones went all over the galley, dishes flew out of the cupboard and the gash bin spewed all over the galley floor. I just fell apart.'

In a fax sent to Race HQ on 4 March James acknowledged: 'Second to being the skipper the most God-awful job on board a BT Global Challenge yacht must be that of a medic or doctor. They are nearly always tired, wet and cold and yet are expected to show a calm, reassuring and confident manner with excellent judgement calls.' And yet he wished that Lesley would not set herself such impossibly high standards, always trying to implement the best medical practice, when sometimes it would have been better just to do the best you could in the circumstances.

The incident with Paul Hebblethwaite had rattled Lesley's confidence and she was becoming increasingly concerned about Geoff rejoining the boat in Cape Town. Apart from not wanting to repeat the crisis with his diabetes that had occurred during the Wellington to Sydney leg, events of the last few days had shown her that she was being placed, against her better judgement and skill level, in a situation in which she felt out of her depth. In a fax to the Challenge office she explained:

> *I have spoken to James about this and have his full support and backing, as the health issue does effect the safety of the crew and vessel. It also affects the credibility of the*

A rare calm day
in the Southern
Ocean
(© Time &
Tide/*BT*)

project as a whole. He feels that with Stuart and possibly Brendan returning for the Boston leg a strong crew base is important to support the weaker crew members. We have already been told by Mike that he is faced with being crippled if he continues, yet he faxes us to say he will be back in Cape Town and his hands are now fine. I feel it is essential that Mike, Brendan and Geoff should have their medical condition and level of fitness reviewed very carefully in consultation with James and myself, because we are the people with whom the buck stops.

This did not go down well with The Challenge Business, who wanted to know why the decision had been made so late in the day and complained that it put them in an awkward position regarding a crew volunteer who had already been promised a place on the yacht. There was, they said, no excuse for having strung Geoff along for so long, especially since he had already succeeded in raising a considerable sum of money towards his berth fee. James and Lesley argued in turn that the full implications of having Geoff back on board hadn't become apparent until several days into the fourth leg. In the event it was Susan Preston Davis back at the Trust office who was left to pick up the pieces, smooth over the cracks and make the suitable apologies to Geoff, who was now told he would not be sailing in the Boston leg after all.

A little after a week on board, after consulting the weather charts, James made the decision to hold a northerly course, even though the bulk of the fleet were now plunging south. Since *Time & Tide* had been sustaining good speeds up till now and the charts indicated favourable weather conditions if they stayed on course, it seemed prudent to try to out-manoeuvre the rest of the fleet through navigational strategy rather than speed. But, as *Ocean Rover* gybed past them and the only other boat left in the vicinity was now *Heath Insured II*, for a moment James couldn't help wondering whether he was making a grave tactical error. 'I was very optimistic that when the poll came through that evening we'd be well placed,' said James, 'but when it came through we were last and I was gutted. Everything I'd anticipated had gone out of the window and yet the weather still suggested we should stay on course. The next two polls on the following day showed us even further behind and I started getting into a blacker and blacker depression. I just couldn't understand it because I could see *Heath* three miles ahead and they were placed ninth.'

However, by the morning of 10 March the poll showed *Time & Tide* to be in seventh position. 'It was like Christmas Day,' said James, 'and I knew that from then on all we had to do was keep on pushing.'

By now the skies were growing dark, the weather deteriorating rapidly and for the crew the reality of spending another four weeks stuck in the middle of this vast empty ocean was beginning to sink in. Rather surprisingly the sense of isolation was especially apparent at weekends. James wrote in a fax to Race HQ:

> Out here we have a busy week with a constant stream of faxes requesting a whole range of information, the enquiries come in from all sources, newspapers, magazines, Challenge Business, sponsors, even bank managers, but come Saturday morning the fax dies and the reality of the isolation strikes home and the boredom numbs ... A reflective mood seems to set in and crews seem to become quieter and need more coaxing to do sail changes and trim the yacht.

Icebergs were still a rarity but looking for them was a constant preoccupation and on 16 March the monotony was broken when an iceberg a quarter of a mile high and eighteen miles long was spotted. It was equally rare to spot competitors in the huge expanse of the Southern Ocean, but when it occurred there was always great excitement, not only because it revitalized everyone's racing spirit but also because it was an auspicious reminder that life still existed outside their own small 67-foot world. The reality was, in fact, that the Ocean was a fairly crowded place. In order to plot his course James used routing charts which specified the shipping lines considered to be the most cost-effective route between the different ports. Commercial shipping would stick rigidly to these tracks, so James would always steer a route a few miles off to avoid traffic. As a result, for the bulk of the time, *Time & Tide* sailed in fairly isolated waters.

Steve and Nigel (© Time & Tide/BT)

For those who were confronting the Southern Ocean for the second time there was no doubt that this leg was proving far more gruelling and hazardous than the Rio to Wellington leg. Whereas previously storms had abated within a day or two, giving way to finer, calmer weather, during which everyone had time to tidy up, take stock and prepare for the next battering, now the penetrating wind and mountainous seas were more or less continuous. 'It's a bit like living in a washing machine with everything below decks getting damp and being thrown around, including us if we don't hang on tight', was James's evaluation of the scene. And David said, 'It was nothing even close to what we'd experienced before in terms of the intensity, as this time there was absolutely no let up.'

At times the boat felt as if it was positively airborne; at other times it seemed more like a submarine, buried under water. The crew became accustomed to going from deck to bed and bed to deck, falling asleep in a storm and waking up to a storm, always desperately trying to keep control, particularly during the cavernous dark nights when waves seemed to come out of nowhere and ropes were whipped around so violently by the wind that they became as hard as iron bars.

Exhaustion quickly set in and at times James wondered how much more of a battering the boat and his crew could take, especially those who were being constantly woken up to help out if things had gone badly wrong or if crew on the other watch were sick. Some three weeks into the leg David wrote in his log: 'Bloody miserable day: no generator, no electricity, no water, no staysail, no mainsail – apart from that everything fine.'

The reality on deck was that everyone took turns in being washed off their feet by the force of the waves, then thrown across the deck to be rescued only by their harness pulling them up short. With two weeks of Force Ten winds and little respite, even James had to admit that this was the worst sailing weather he'd ever experienced. In hindsight he considered it to have been rather a good thing, 'as you don't want to go all the way down to the Southern Ocean just to have a walk in the park.' In a fax to Race HQ on 14 March James wrote a stirring account of what it meant to be at the mercy of the elements, imagining how relatives at home might feel knowing that their loved ones were caught up in such ferocious storms:

> *You last see them on the dock when you kiss them goodbye and entrust them into the skipper's care. They have all signed the crew declaration form. They all acknowledge it's a dangerous game that they are embarking on, but that's all in the future and in some other boat. When they return to you they will have tales to tell of daring, but I wonder how much will they tell of their own moments …*
>
> *Indeed after our first true Southern Ocean blow each yacht has tales to tell. On* Time & Tide *it was no different – no dispensation for mobility, disability, or even on this leg restricted crew numbers. As the weather deteriorated we reduced sail till we were sitting comfortably in gusts topping sixty knots. The crew were exhausted, this being their longest and most powerful steady blow. As it grew to its peak the huge seas took advantage of the limited experience of our helms – 'limited' bearing in mind they have sailed further than most yachtsmen who have been sailing for ten years and have weathered more gales than those same yachtsmen would face in twenty years. But this race has the amateur's race tag and oh how we are never allowed to forget it.*
>
> *I watched my amateurs in action last night. One sat in the leeward side of the cockpit until a large wall of water fell on him. He went over backwards into the scuppers, where he proceeded to swim like a salmon against the stream as he was swept towards the rail and the awaiting Southern Ocean. He had to come past me. In that microsecond I wondered if I could leave the wheel to grab him. Could I have held him and what of the fate of the others on deck left exposed to the next breaking sea if I'd left the wheel to spin free?*

Fortunately my wayward salmon is brought up short on his safety harness as a second wave tries to finish the task of the first. The salmon lifts himself off his back and coughs and vomits copious amounts of seawater and drags himself back into the cockpit, only to take another wave down his front, but he doesn't care and I am no wiser as to what I would have done. I'm only grateful that he has listened to one thing I have said: clip on. It's already a past issue. The need is to concentrate on what's happening now on deck, who is where and where is the next wave and its angle to us. They are trying to secure the main down when we rise up a massive sea and plunge down into the trough to see a wall of white water breaking on board. I yell a warning to the deck. My world goes white and the wind is knocked from my body. Water forces its way down my oilskins, up my nose and down my throat. A terrific force is trying to wrench me from the wheel. I feel a panic build inside. How many of my crew are still on deck? As things clear I look to where I last saw people ... one ... two ... three ... four.... Four has moved somewhat and is going to be sore in the morning, and so in a matter of seconds I sweep the deck following the destructive path of that wall of water. The rig man ... Where is he? The shroud is empty – the last picture in my mind has him squatting there. I turn my head to leeward and astern, searching for him in the water. I'm yelling his name to the rest of the deck ... Where is he? No one seems to respond. Shit, it's happened ... I've lost a man overboard ... I'm still yelling. Someone by the mast points down and the familiar face grins up from the other side of the mast.

Much of James's time was spent nursing his crew's confidence. Grahme and Clive seemed to find it difficult to cope physically when the sea got too rough, Paul Hebblethwaite, who had been the most fearless of all, now approached jobs with caution, afraid of ripping his stitches, and Lesley was too petrified to venture up on deck in blows over thirty knots. Once or twice James found her fully dressed, ready to go up on deck but crying her eyes out and bolt rigid with terror. On Easter Day, 30 March, she wrote in her log, 'I am almost sure I will get off in Cape Town. I have found this voyage so difficult. I have been very unsettled and feel out of kilter with what it's all about.'

Carol, who had written in her log after one of the first blows, 'I quite enjoy being on deck when the sea is really wild and the boat heeling so much that most of one side is in the water', now wasn't so sure, particularly as she was suffering from acute pain in her right hand. In Sydney she had been diagnosed with Carpal Tunnel Syndrome, caused by pressure on the median nerve, and now whenever she did anything with her hands – writing, holding a cup, stirring porridge or simply grabbing hold of something – they became a mass of pins and needles. However, since she was an extremely plucky and adventurous young woman, no amount of pain and numbness in her hands was going to prevent her from doing what she wanted, including going up the mast. On 16 March she recorded in her log her attempt to put in a new staysail halyard:

I'd volunteered to go up the mast during the last Southern Ocean leg but James wouldn't let me. So now was my chance. The new halyard had to be fed into the mast from the top. Showing nerves of steel (but inside quivering like a jelly!) I climbed in the harness amid jokes of chastity belts etc. James finished doing it up for me (because I looked so clueless). Then it was straight to the mast (gulp). Nigel tied the spinnaker halyard on to the harness and hooked on a safety line and the new staysail halyard. James took the helm and the idea was that Steve and Grahme would 'sweat' me up the mast (i.e. pull the rope instead of winching). I went up about fifteen feet that way but it involved shooting up two feet then dropping down a foot, up again then down, which was pretty unnerving. They finally decided to winch me up but went too fast so it was

difficult to get out of the way of sticking out mast lumps etc. By the time I got to the first spreaders I was having second thoughts. As I was contemplating how on earth I was going to get past the spreaders without swinging wildly about, James yelled, 'Are you happy? If not, don't worry – I'll do it.' I'm afraid I wimped out and accepted the offer. The guys were all really kind but I still feel like a wimp. It was lucky I did wimp out, though, because James had awful trouble trying to get the halyard into the mast and was up there for ages.

Above and opposite: *stormy weather* (© Time & Tide/*BT*)

Carolyn also felt real fear for the first time during this second Southern Ocean crossing, intensified by the fact that for the first time she had the added responsibility of being watch leader. In her log she wrote:

I came down from a particularly gruelling session on the helm during a storm, and burst into tears, caused partly by tiredness and also by fear of being unable to handle the steering any more. James and I spoke about fear and how everyone has their own. He told me he feared dropping a position in the race, or, worse, losing one of us over the side when we make our way to the foredeck. He also spoke about the fears he had during his solo circumnavigation when he thought he would die at one stage, with the realization that he had no one else to rely on if the going got tough.

Even David had moments of feeling out of control on the helm. According to Clive, on one occasion Steve's harness got stuck, 'and David freaked out when he realized that he and I had been unclipped by Steve while he'd been trying to loosen it. His confidence was so shaken that about half an hour after that he unintentionally tacked the boat.' The incident was recorded also by Nigel, who wrote in his log, 'I can remember falling out of bed and a lot of shouting going on. It's 4.30 a.m. and Dave has put in an inadvertent tack.'

James's way of instilling confidence in his crew was to make everything appear as easy and effortless as possible. Once, in an attempt to prevent the boat being caught broadside to the huge waves and subsequently rolling over, the normally self-composed Nigel was starting to panic and consequently over-steering. James, having sheeted the main to ensure that it was better trimmed to hold the boat to windward, grabbed the wheel and quickly got the boat back in groove. Then, to show Nigel that there was no cause for alarm, he took his hands off the wheel, folded his arms and said, 'See, you can go to sleep with this one.' Then he handed the wheel back to Nigel and went below.

On another occasion Nigel recorded in his log:

> *I got credited with the biggest bang so far and it was a big one. As the wave crested in front of me the bow went down and a huge wall of water landed on me. Carol was sent flying and the cockpit was awash. A few comments were passed when I came down, especially by James, who got soaked by the kettle!*

Carol, who was riding shotgun with Nigel at the time, admitted it was the first time she'd been dumped on by a wave in the cockpit and not surfaced grinning or even laughing. She wrote in her log:

> *For the first time I felt scared. When I got below I dreaded going back up again, although I didn't say anything. I felt sick and couldn't even eat a chocolate bar! I think it was the fact that Nigel wasn't happy that made me nervous – he's usually (or at least seems to be) in control. When the time came to go back on deck I swallowed hard and got*

on with it. The sea had calmed a bit but there were still a few dodgy moments. By the end of the watch I was able to move around the cockpit untangling lines etc. rather than just clinging on.

James's biggest fear was losing someone over the side
(© Time & Tide/BT)

Sail changes in these turbulent conditions were down to a minimum. As David put it, 'In over fifty knots of breeze you put up the smallest rags of sail, and just sit back hoping for the best with your fingers crossed.' At the same time you couldn't afford only to use little sails, as that would slow the boat down, and maintaining good speed was essential for safe steerage. 'Most of us feared the sail changes,' admitted Carolyn, 'but often we had no choice but to go forwards and retrieve the sail before the wind tore it apart – it was that bad.'

One of the more challenging moments was when from his position at the helm Nigel spotted the lacerated leech of the staysail. With the boat rolling violently and those on the foredeck floating on each wave, it was eventually brought down to reveal that in a wind that had suddenly risen from thirty-five to seventy-five knots more than half the sail had been completely shredded, producing what James described as 'one brutally murdered sail'. Shortly after this the batten cars, which had been causing problems for a few days, gave way and the main had to be dropped in fifty knots of wind. The batten then had to be rebuilt with glue, steel rulers and fibre washes, but there was too much wind to get the main back up for several hours. This was sailing to survive, not sailing to race. Chris later pointed out, 'I don't think any of them realized how dangerous the situation was, because basically if you get it wrong with the mainsail off the boat's in jeopardy.'

During the following night, with winds now light and variable, the running backstay broke under load with a loud bang. Had it happened thirty hours earlier during the storm they would have lost the mast. Luckily James, Chris and Nigel were able to devise a jury rig which held all the way to Cape Town.

Compared to the appalling conditions on the foredeck, life in the galley was generally more congenial. Occasionally the crew found time to play games, listen to music and generally relax. Showers, however, were an infrequent luxury, not only because they were restricted when the generator broke but because they seemed like an unnecessary inconvenience. Carol noted in her diary on 17 March, 'There's a rumour that Paul H. and I are using all the water on showers. Considering I've only had two or three I must smell better than I thought!' Life was so much about discomfort and endurance that small pleasures such as the warmth of your bunk became the most treasured aspect of the day. For Paul Hebblethwaite 28 March was one day much like any other:

> The sea was rough. My feet always cold due to wet boots. Up at 1.30 p.m. – the conditions still just as rough so we didn't have proper lunch. Back on duty the seas were still very high. By midnight the barometer started to rise. Up at 3.00 a.m. So tired I wished I could stay in bed where it's so comfortable and warm. Felt so chilled when out of bed because of the damp conditions in the cabin, these wet floors and having to get dressed in damp clothes.

There was notably much more fun on this leg, with some unexpected treats and moments of light relief. For instance, the day Steve decided to boost morale by making mulled wine for the crew was infinitely preferable to the time he made tea in the dark accidentally using custard powder instead of milk powder. 'There were a few complaints,' he observed, 'but the funny thing is everyone drank it.' There was also the time Clive played a rather sick April Fool's trick on Carol by pretending to be dead in his bunk when she tried to wake him up.

There was the minimum of complaint about food on this leg. For once there was ample and the odd bottle of spirits was brought out after a particularly stressful episode on deck, helping everyone to relax. Grahme, having struggled to find out where he fitted in on the boat and initially having felt like extra baggage, had found a useful niche for himself in the galley and felt far happier as a result. 'I loved it,' he said. 'I would get up at daylight, wash up, cook people's breakfast, wash up, then make lunch and so on. Like this I was kept busy all day, time went by much faster and I didn't dwell on things. Also I was very impressed by the way the other guys would keep on toiling and seeing their determination kept me going.'

Confined to the galley for so long, Grahme taught himself if not exactly how to cook at least how to prepare meals, which resulted in some interesting creations. The secret of giving the crew a tasty meal, he concluded, was to use plenty of tabasco, not to shy away from chilli sauce, to regard mustard as a welcome addition to soup and even to serve spaghetti bolognese in sandwiches. 'The Pommies thought this was a bit unusual but once they hooked into it they didn't mind', he remarked cavalierly. In truth, though they had eaten it all up because they were hungry and because it was a brave first attempt by a novice cook, they far preferred Grahme's more traditional menus, especially the hot cross buns he made for them on Good Friday.

In time the crew became indebted to Grahme, who, in taking on the role of galley slave, relieved them of the onerous task of cooking. Even Chris, who had been concerned about the mobility issue and annoyed that so often new crew members were less able than had at first seemed apparent, was impressed by the way Grahme came to terms with his limitations and made himself useful: 'Grahme redeemed himself in the galley because he had such a great attitude,' he said. 'As a result the group didn't get agitated because he was pulling his full weight and fulfilling a very useful role.'

It was the first time since the motorbike accident that Grahme had had to test himself over a long period of time. The thing he found most difficult was the lack of privacy and not being able to get away from other people. 'Even when I was with the Army I could jump on a motorbike and sit in the shrub for a few hours,' he said. 'But here there were people around you all the time and that sometimes got me down.'

After days of storms, even the flag got shredded (© Time & Tide/BT)

For Nigel, in many ways, it was his toughest leg yet. Having replaced Paul Hebblethwaite as watch leader, he felt he had now been doing the job for too long and was fed up with running around telling people what to do. On top of this, tension was building between the two watches and the pressure was starting to weigh on him. He was also concerned about his leg as he kept bruising and damaging it. In his log on 16 March for the first time there is evidence of real race fatigue: 'I feel tired and unhappy. Just can't get into the swing of it,' he wrote. It didn't help when he discovered that twenty-four Mars bars he'd been storing for himself in a bag on top of the fresh-water tank had somehow got lost in the bilge. The ritual of a reward every day therefore shifted to a reward every Thursday when he treated himself to a cup of Earl Grey tea, a Mars bar and ten minutes' peace and quiet in the galley.

Carolyn found the job of watch leader much more demanding than she'd imagined. She knew it would be a responsible position but hadn't quite realized just how much it would put her on the spot and make her accountable for her actions. 'In hindsight I could have done better and behaved better,' she admitted.

With days and nights now blending into one, the endless and unremitting nature of the storms was beginning to get to everyone. While the crew had been reasonably prepared for the repetitive nature of the wave fronts, they were totally ill-prepared for their frequency, as it was an atypical weather pattern for this time of the year. Steve raised a snigger from his fellow crew when he described the BT Global Challenge as the sailing equivalent to sodomy. 'Why go this very unnatural route against the prevailing winds and currents,' he wondered, 'when there's a perfectly good passage the other way?'

Niggling between the watches continued, whether it was Watch B complaining about not being relieved from duty on time or Watch A complaining about not receiving enough help with difficult sail changes. Even the normally even-tempered Carol found herself affected once or twice by the sour mood of the boat, particularly when David seemed to lose his rag and criticize her with little justification. Clive, who was still getting used to people's idiosyncrasies, was somewhat surprised by David's level of sarcasm. 'When you ask him to do something and he doesn't want to he'll just say "No" up front and carry on reading,' he noted with a mixture of awe and indignation.

However, despite a dip in crew morale, everyone realized that this kind of bickering was unavoidable under such stressful conditions and was also undoubtedly taking place on every other boat in the fleet. Most importantly they also realized that these low patches were an inevitable part of ocean racing and quickly forgotten once the weather and the mood changed. Nigel wrote in his log towards the end of the leg, 'Feeling a lot happier. I think it's the respite in the weather, which gives everyone a breather.'

On 20 March Carol wrote an expressive account of the crew's frame of mind after nearly three weeks at sea:

> It is bad enough battling against the weather without battling with our fellow crew members as well. But as luck would have it David woke me up with a 'Come on, love, time to get up!' I was still upset (feeling very wimpy) and said, 'How can you call me "love" when you've been a bastard all day?' He then took the mickey a bit (not nastily) so I told him him to piss off. When I got up David came to chat to me. He was very sweet actually and I felt like a real drip. I told him the problem and he said, 'We're all going through shit and have different ways of dealing with it. I grizzle, everyone knows I grizzle, but you know me well enough to tell me to fuck off.'

For Paul Hebblethwaite this was not turning out to be a very successful leg. Not only had his accident denied him the possibility of being watch leader, he had been confined to his bunk before being put back on deck and expected to provide the same kind of muscular strength for which the crew had now come to rely on him. But much of what he had formerly taken for granted now made him nervous and putting renewed pressure on his still fresh wound was making him increasingly agitated. On 20 March Paul wrote in his log, simply:

> *Nightmare!*
> *Wet and freezing cold.*
> *Tired.*
> *Short of sleep.*
> *Sore arse!*

Given that communication with Paul was so difficult, it didn't take long for him to feel that no one really cared about his problems and concerns. On the other hand, it was also true to say that if people tended to let him get on with things it was because he gave the impression of being an enormously resourceful young man whose fierce independence had created a tougher exterior than was actually the case. David saw this second Southern Ocean leg as 'a voyage of discovery for Paul because he was quite shocked to discover that the boat could run without him.' The truth was, however, that the isolation Paul felt on board *Time & Tide*, which had been so heightened during these last few weeks, was making him increasingly frustrated, moody and short-tempered. 'If I make a fuss because I don't know what's going on they accuse me of being oversensitive,' he complained.

James and Chris rebuilding part of the generator (© Time & Tide/BT)

Chris, on the other hand, was finding this leg far more satisfying. Contemplating the highs and the lows of the trip he concluded:

> It's very hard to see the highs, but I guess that having done the trip, after the event, it will become a major achievement and this becomes the high as the bad stuff fades away. The passage has been a lot better than expected in terms of the way James and I worked and that really helped pass time. Also I've got more sleep because of this. Fixing the main and the generator were also major achievements. The only real low was the days of storms. Just day after day – it was so draining.

As usual Chris and James had had to apply themselves to fixing everything that broke. Their greatest challenge took place three weeks into the leg when the generator was declared terminal. Since without it there wasn't enough fuel to run the engine, make water and produce battery power, it became essential to beat the problem. In the end, and eighteen man hours later, they managed to rebuild the generator in a *Blue Peter*-like fashion by using an empty tuna can, glue, cling film and Sikaflex. 'It was a very satisfying thing to do, especially during the full force of a gale,' said James. 'Out in the middle of the ocean the isolation and the weather dictates your life, and yet here we were cocking a snook at it all. In real world terms a mechanic would have told us you're stuffed and yet the whole ethos of *Time & Tide* is not to take things lying down or have our lives dictated for us. We set out to change attitudes and rebuild generators!'

The weather fax had also packed up after a couple of weeks at sea. Ever since leaving Southampton *Time & Tide* had had problems with their weather fax but it wasn't until Sydney that The Challenge Business had finally discovered a cabling fault in the computer and fixed it. However, 2,000 miles from port, *Time & Tide* was once again without weather pictures and therefore racing with an additional handicap. Whether or not this ultimately made any difference to the result was hard to say but Adrian Donovan, the skipper of *Heath Insured II*, said when *Time & Tide* arrived at Wellington, 'If James can sail like this and lead the pack without weather maps, I hate to think what he'd do if he had them.'

For Paul Burns this had been a brilliant leg, even though he had started out with continuing sores on his foot and stump, as well as an additional problem with his elbow which had become inflamed during the Wellington to Sydney leg. The reason he had felt more at ease and in control was that he had thrown himself wholeheartedly into the work and applied himself to everything that needed to be done. Even the thought of nearly having broken his leg when seventy knots of wind threw him across the foredeck to the end of his safety harness and bruised his leg from top to toe didn't seem to daunt him. Instead he just gritted his teeth, let the pain subside and got on with the job.

As far as James was concerned Paul Burns had come up trumps on this leg. 'I gave him a lot of grief before we left and he responded to it well. He needed to wake up and shake up. We demanded a lot from him and he came through it and did very well indeed.' Carolyn reported in her log:

> Paul Burns has worked very hard this leg, never complaining when he is in pain, which is almost all the time, I reckon. He has had to carry out seven or eight sail repairs, staying up off watch to finish the work and coming on deck to helm as well. He is truly brave in that he does as much as everyone else, but in pain and discomfort.

James's good mood also seemed to have lasted for most of the leg. Carol noted in her log on 28 March:

He's a lot more approachable and I feel far more comfortable around him. Apart from the weather and the minor bitching amongst watches this leg is far more pleasant, with people getting on and watching out for each other. Could be that I've got to know people more but I feel there is a bit of pressure off James because he now knows we can cope with the Southern Ocean.

On night watch (© Time & Tide/BT)

Then later on 4 April she wrote: 'James is great 90 per cent of the time. He notices things that the others don't and is interested in things that the others aren't – beautiful sunrises, sunsets, moon, stars, Southern Lights. He's always got time to appreciate and to comment so we can enjoy them too.'

And Grahme, who was used to managing teams of people himself, was impressed by the way James attempted to calm people down when they got frustrated: 'He seems to pause, assess the situation and then come up with a solution. When things get tough he works very hard at being calm and making jokes so as to take people's minds off the tension.'

9 April 1997: First Mate's Log: 36°30' S 24°01' E

The last few days have been very hard. The wind was light. We have been becalmed or slow moving for a period of twelve hours plus. We have just over three hundred miles to go. We are still in tenth place with Nuclear E *breathing down our necks and* 3Com *and* Rover *looking out of sight. James has become very tense and talked to me about shaking the crew up. He is trying very hard to keep his cool. We had a crew briefing to get the message across that we were still racing to the finish.*

It was by now a familiar pattern that towards the end of these long, difficult legs the crew seemed to be overcome by a lack of energy and enthusiasm, stemming partly from boredom, partly restlessness and partly fatigue. It took a great deal of effort and encouragement on the part of Chris and James to motivate the crew at times like these, particularly since the race was by no means over and everything still depended on their determination to get to the finish.

As they came into Cape Town the weather conditions changed to a very light easterly wind, which meant slow, frustrating sailing with lots of sail changes. But finally the heavy weather spinnaker was hoisted and with a good breeze behind it, *Time & Tide* started to fly. 'It was an awesome day. We were pushing the kite way over the limit,' recalled James. 'We were eighty miles from the finish, doing a steady eleven and a half knots and fairly shovelling along. I didn't dare put anyone else on the wheel and had to calculate how badly I wanted to pee and how quickly I wanted to get to Cape Town.'

But it seemed to be *Time & Tide*'s bad luck yet again to be becalmed as they were literally coming into port. 'Nothing can describe how that feels,' observed Nigel. 'You've seen only sea for five weeks, which is so unbelievably monotonous and then you see land, you're so nearly there but the wind dies and you can't move.'

The wind did indeed die about six miles from Cape Town, so that for several hours the boat was moving barely more than 0.4 knots. The supporter boats which had come out to greet them went back in again after a couple of hours, realizing that *Time & Tide* wasn't moving anywhere fast. The crew came to know that coastline, with Table Mountain in the background, very well indeed that day and against a spectacular sunset they tried to cheer themselves up by having an impromptu champagne party on the foredeck to the sounds of Paul Burns's CD of Monty Python songs, including 'Always Look on the Bright Side of Life' which was played over and over again.

Arriving at Cape Town – at midnight (© Carolyn Davies)

They had anticipated coming in by 3.00 p.m. that afternoon but finally arrived just after midnight on Saturday 12 April with four boats still behind them. Even though it came in so late at night there was as usual a vast crowd waiting to welcome *Time & Tide*. 'It was,' said

Clive, who was for the first time experiencing the kind of emotional pull *Time & Tide* seemed to have on people, 'a most humbling experience'. ITN's South African bureau had intended to cover the story but on that particular day were sent off to an uprising in Kinshasa, so Gary Champion had to persuade ITN in London that *Time & Tide* could do the job for them by using a professional camera crew who were working with the *Ocean Rover* project.

Amongst the crowd waiting to greet the crew were Susan Preston Davis and Stuart, who had just flown in from England, Brendan, who felt extremely emotional, having last seen the boat in Wellington, and Chris's wife Maureen and their two daughters. Three friends of Nigel's from England were also there, as was Grahme's wife Lauretta, who had flown in from Australia, and Paul Burns's wife Sheila, who had been waiting anxiously for several days. Having failed to anticipate the boat's late arrival, she had already booked her return flight to England and was due to leave in just a few days' time. Once again David's fiancée, Carol, was also in port to greet him. This was a particularly special stopover for them as, unbeknown to anyone else (and that included Carol's family, who lived in South Africa), the couple had arranged secretly to get married a week before the boat set sail for Boston. Although David maintained that his decision to marry Carol had not been influenced by the Challenge, it seems probable that the timing of the marriage may well have been a consequence of the many weeks spent at sea deprived of her company.

James had always fully endorsed the Challenge's ethos of promoting good seamanship which amounted to 'look after your vessel and your vessel will look after you', and his caution had paid off. Whereas other yachts in the fleet had come in with sails blown or with damage to their rigging and mast, *Time & Tide* was relatively unscathed, proving there was more to ocean racing than just sailing with speed. But as with the other yachts, the Southern Ocean had left its scars: parts of the metal hull had dented above the water line from the sheer force of the waves hitting it.

Time & Tide's performance on this fourth and most arduous leg was by everyone's standards a triumph. Once again *Group 4* won the leg, with *Concert* coming in a close second. *Time & Tide*, by now known as the sentimental favourite of the race, was placed tenth, beating *Courtaulds*, which had come in third at Sydney, and *Nuclear Electric*, the bookies' favourite and the winner of the British Steel Global Challenge. *Nuclear Electric's* skipper, Richard Tudor, didn't appear too happy at the prospect of losing a slot to *Time & Tide*, but the respect the crew won from the fleet was immense.

A mark of how the tide had turned was that Helen Wybrow at the Challenge office, who initially had been so hostile to the idea of *Time & Tide* taking part in the race, sent James and the crew a heartwarming message of congratulations just before they reached Cape Town:

> *As this leg draws to a close and Cape Town becomes tantalizingly closer and closer (and before you all get lost in the jollifications of arrival) I would really like to say an enormous WELL DONE to you all. Your performance on this leg has been outstanding. Not only because of the extra challenges you face but because of the fact that you sailed this, the toughest leg of the race, two crew short. As someone who said that it couldn't be done when* Time & Tide *first proposed it compete in the race, all I can do is admire your achievements. I wish I could be there in Cape Town to welcome you all safely in and crack a few beers with you. You deserve all the plaudits you will receive on arrival.*

The crew's continuing strong performance proved once and for all that their strong performance on the previous Southern Ocean leg had not been merely incidental, and it was a particularly fitting reward for Susan and Lucy Quinlan, who during the past five weeks had been struggling in quite a different way to keep *Time & Tide* afloat. While the crew had been having their worst ever time battling with the storms of the Southern Ocean, the coffers back at the Trust offices had been at an all-time low with only a few donations trickling in.

'This was by far the lowest point of the project for me,' said Susan. 'There was so much to do, so little money coming in and so many bills to pay. We were trying to find crew for leg five, the legal action was taking up a lot of time and draining what little resources we had, and then, to crown it all, an unexpected VAT demand for £16,000 arrived from the Customs & Excise. This was a big blow and threatened to almost wipe us out financially. I despaired and couldn't see a way out of the financial mess unless we found another sponsor but we had so little time and resources to do that. The pressures of juggling the Trust's financial and legal affairs, the worry about the crew who were having an extremely tough time and the endless workload of trying to liaise with the boat, sponsors, relatives, BT and The Challenge Business was overwhelming. Only Lucy and Guy really knew how bad things were. As a trustee James had to know what was going on but during that leg we tried to minimize any problems for him and make our faxes as upbeat as possible.'

By the time Susan left for Cape Town, the Trust's accountants had agreed a payment schedule with the Customs & Excise whereby *Time & Tide* had to pay back a certain amount of money each month, and this eased the impact of this massive demand. It was a welcome reprieve, although no one was under any illusion that this spelt an end to their financial woes.

Time & Tide in Cape Town with Table Mountain in the background (© Lucy Quinlan)

During their stopover in Cape Town the crew stayed in the brand new five-star Table Bay Hotel, owned by Sun International and built on the Victoria and Alfred waterfront. As with so much of the fundraising, the deal with the hotel had been struck at the eleventh hour, with Sun International agreeing to offer free accommodation to the crew for one week on arrival and one week before departure. It was a tremendous relief to Susan that they had secured this prestigious sponsor and in such luxurious surroundings too, since the alternative would have

David and Carol got married in beautiful Stellenbosch
(© David Tait)

meant the crew having to stay on the boat in hot, uncomfortable, noisy conditions while major repair and maintenance work took place.

Staff at the hotel, which had opened its doors only one week before the boat arrived, were at first a little taken aback by the crew's casual dress style and on first sight assumed them to be a scruffy band of yachties. But as ever it didn't take long before the crew had managed to charm the management and staff into becoming enthusiastic *Time & Tide* supporters.

Gary, who was also out in Cape Town and who wanted to film the crew taking time out and enjoying themselves, persuaded the hotel to give spa treatments to the crew on arrival. As a result within a few hours of stepping on shore the crew were relaxing in the open-air spa bath on the roof of the hotel with drinks in hand, relating their tales of peril on the ocean waves. The men had massages while the women had facials and manicures, and in the course of the next few days everyone started to relax, particularly the amputees, who had found the going extremely tough during this gruelling crossing.

As usual most of the crew managed to do some travelling and sightseeing during the stopover. Lesley was extremely happy to see her daughter and son-in-law and took a few days' break with them. Anne Hebblethwaite, who had been desperately anxious about her son during the crossing, had come to Cape Town on an unplanned visit and was reassured that his wound had healed and that he was very much his old self again. After giving a group of deaf children a tour round the boat and telling them about the trip, Paul and his mother hired a car and drove down to the naval base at Simon's Town and then on to Penguin Bay and the Cape of Good Hope.

Other members of the crew hung around Cape Town and spent time in the bars, restaurants and shops. One or two group outings were organized including a visit to a major 'climbing wall'. With the aid of handholds, footholds and pullies Carol and Carolyn managed to get two-thirds of the way up in an attempt to reach the prize Suzuki jeep perched on the top, but Paul Burns had to give up at the halfway point after four attempts. For someone who hated being defeated and who refused to accept his limitations, this was another unfortunate blow. Needless to say for most of the stopover Chris remained in Cape Town, taking a couple of days off to spend with his wife and daughters, but for the most part working hard on the boat.

While Clive and Steve were both sorry to be leaving the crew, it had now been confirmed that Carol and Grahme would be staying on. It had also been confirmed that Mike would not be returning to the boat, which meant that Carol, who originally had only intended to do the three legs from Rio to Cape Town, was now given his place. Grahme had secured his berth until Boston, having raised the necessary $9,000 for the next leg, but as soon as he arrived in Cape Town he set about seeking further sponsorship deals through the South African rotary clubs to finance the final leg to England. During the first two weeks of his time on board

Paul Hebblethwaite with a party of deaf children he'd shown round the yacht (© Carol Sear)

Time & Tide it had been unclear whether Grahme would continue, because his peg leg had left him effectively almost immobile, so a priority on reaching Cape Town was to get some adjustments made, this time to include a rolling knee joint and rotating ankle, as well as to put on some weight, since he had lost two stone during the course of the trip.

Rejoining the boat for the Boston leg were Stuart, whose lack of mobility posed fewer hazards during this next fair-weather crossing, and Brendan, who had been given the all-clear by the doctors, even though his knee was still giving him grief. From South Africa Brendan, who had by now been joined by Belinda, went to Zimbabwe to see the Victoria Falls, and in order to test out his knee decided to have a go at whitewater rafting, which involved an 800-metre descent to the water's edge. His knee held up during the long climb down and both he and Belinda got a big buzz from being tossed around in a large rubber craft as massive currents propelled them down the Zambeze River (a sport many considered lethal); but the trouble came when he attempted to climb back up the gorge again. In the end, in order to preserve his knee, Brendan agreed to be strapped on to a door and carried by six of the strongest men up the 1200-metre ascent. It was, according to Brendan, 'probably the most frightening thing I've ever experienced and I certainly did a fair bit of whimpering that day.'

Two new members also joined the crew: John Spence from Preston, who at the age of eleven had had a serious accident when the bike he was riding went under a lorry, resulting in his right leg being amputated below the knee, and Greg Hammond, aged twenty-nine, a mechanical engineer from New South Wales in Australia, who had no lower right arm because of a congenital defect at birth.

Leg 4 Final Results

	Team	Arrival time
1	Group 4	09/04/97 01:35
2	Concert	09/04/97 01:55
3	Toshiba Wave Warrior	09/04/97 05:41
4	Commercial Union	09/04/97 21:19
5	Motorola	10/04/97 05:55
6	Save the Children	10/04/97 09:53
7	3Com	10/04/97 16:13
8	Global Teamwork	10/04/97 16:48
9	Ocean Rover	11/04/97 07:45
10	Time & Tide	11/04/97 22:07
11	Nuclear Electric	12/04/97 08:07
12	Courtaulds Int.	12/04/97 11:43
13	Pause to Remember	12/04/97 12:33
14	Heath Insured II	12/04/97 12:55

All times GMT.

Leg 4 Combined Times

	TEAM	TIME
1	Group 4	110d 20h 00m
2	Toshiba Wave Warrior	111d 18h 15m
3	Save the Children	112d 23h 10m
4	Motorola	114d 02h 45m
5	Commercial Union	114d 05h 59m
6	Global Teamwork	116d 12h 13m
7	3Com	116d 18h 20m
8	Ocean Rover	117d 10h 25m
9	Nuclear Electric	117d 17h 39m
10	Pause to Remember	119d 04h 21m
11	Heath Insured II	120d 14h 28m
12	Time & Tide	120d 15h 14m
13	Courtaulds Int.	121d 05h 15m
14	Concert	122d 15h 24m

All times rounded to the nearest minute.

Chapter Seven

Leg Five
Cape Town to Boston

Departure date 4 May 1997. Longest leg of the race. 7,000 miles of predominantly downwind or off the beam (spinnaker) sailing through the horse latitudes, also known as the variables. The Doldrums around the Equator bring unpredictable and very light winds: the race can be won or lost at this point. Into the northern hemisphere and north Atlantic where the Gulf Stream can run at up to five knots.

A great deal depended on the outcome of this penultimate leg to Boston and James was well aware that *Time & Tide*'s position on arriving in Boston would almost certainly determine its position in the race overall. He also realized that this would be a particularly challenging leg for the crew, who needed to work quickly and effectively together, refamiliarizing themselves with the techniques of downwind sailing, and carrying out sail changes with maximum speed and efficiency.

After a moving ceremony in which Archbishop Desmond Tutu blessed the entire fleet and mentioned *Time & Tide* in particular, *Time & Tide* edged away from the pontoon at Cape Town.

*Greg Hammond
(© Time &
Tide/BT)*

At this point, James and Chris were still trying to get the electronic wind and speed systems to function correctly. Despite all the efforts of technicians during the stopover the equipment was still malfunctioning and it was to fail later, 500 miles south of the Equator. As Carolyn later recorded in her log, it was an all-too-familiar scenario: 'The start was like most others, full of tension, nerves and mistakes due to being out of practice. We had two overriding turns on the main halyard winch and the headsail halyard winch which made us look messy, then as we tried to hoist the sail it got stuck half way up.' Chris was extremely disappointed by their poor performance and observed that just about everything that could have gone wrong did.

*John Spence
(© Time &
Tide/BT)*

According to him, if you couldn't pull off the start line and fight equally up front with everyone else, you put yourself at an immediate disadvantage which could cost you places later on.

But to their relief when the first poll came in *Time & Tide* was placed ninth. By now, like the rest of the fleet, they had their kites up and were heading north-eastwards in good following winds. This fast downwind spinnaker sailing was to set the scene for most of the leg to come.

For once none of the crew was seasick and for several days most of them were in buoyant mood, as there still seemed every chance of keeping up with the rest of the fleet. However, all too soon it became apparent that *Time & Tide*'s main obstacle this leg would be inexperience. Not since Leg Two had the crew done any serious downwind sailing and therefore most had more or less forgotten how to manage testing spinnaker work combined with consistently high boat speeds. From Australia to South Africa they had been beating to windward in very different sailing conditions, but now when the winds were light it required sensitivity and skill to grasp every bit of wind available, and when the winds were heavy it required strength and the ability to steer the boat and hold a steady course as the pressure built. Fortunately James now had Greg Hammond on board: with many years of sailing experience behind him he was able to help James teach the crew how to sail the boat downwind.

'By three days out of Cape Town I'd done the bulk of the helming and I badly needed some sleep,' said James. 'When I went to my bunk *Pause to Remember* were three miles behind us but when I woke up two hours later they were on the horizon with their spinnaker up and we were now six miles behind them. I felt gutted.'

In order to maximize their strengths, James decided to change the watch system, allowing only the best helms on the wheel – namely David, Chris, Nigel, Paul Burns and Greg. These crew members now worked in six-hour shifts, which were intended to give them more time to settle into the pattern of helming.

Although Greg Hammond was one of the most experienced crew members, his disability prevented him from helming in rough weather. Due to a congenital birth defect, Greg's forearm tapered halfway down to a stump, but though this clearly restricted what he could do on board he didn't view it as a disadvantage, claiming that being disabled had opened more doors than it had closed.

Twenty-nine years old and an engineer by trade, Greg had left behind a wife and two small children in New South Wales. He'd first heard about *Time & Tide* when James had flown to Sydney during the Wellington stopover to recruit new crew members. Initially when he approached The Challenge Business there hadn't been any places left, but just three days before *Time & Tide* was due to leave Sydney, out of the blue he'd been offered a place on the Southern Ocean crossing. Much as he would have liked to have gone, he wasn't able to make the necessary arrangements at such short notice but agreed to join the boat in Cape Town instead.

Like Greg, John Spence had arrived in Cape Town just a few days before the start of the fifth leg. John, a 45-year-old from Lancashire who was head of procurement for British Aerospace and had left behind in England a wife and two teenage sons, was a less experienced sailor than Greg but had been fascinated by the BT Global Challenge ever since reading about it in the *Sunday Times* on the day the fleet set sail from Southampton. From then on he'd followed *Time & Tide*'s fortunes avidly and the more he read the more he had become convinced that there might be a place on board for him. When he heard that *Time & Tide* had left Sydney two crew down he made arrangements to do business in South Africa and turned up at the Table Bay Hotel to try to secure a place on the boat.

Of the five amputees now on board, John was probably the least affected by his disability. He comes from what David called 'the world of flat caps and whippets' and is, as Carol described, 'a thoroughly nice guy, always bright and cheerful and willing to help', or as

Paul Burns
working up the
mast
(© James
Hatfield)

*It's a long way
down
(© Paul Burns)*

Brendan wrote in his diary, 'a nice unassuming bloke'. Like so many of the *Time & Tide* crew he has a remarkably sanguine attitude towards his disability, claiming that losing his leg at fourteen had been 'a doddle'. 'When I had the accident at eleven,' he explained, 'the doctors left my leg as it was for another four years so that the damage above the knee could repair itself, but I had callipers and sores and it was nothing but a hindrance. By the time I was fourteen it was actually me who said to them, 'Don't you think it's time this leg came off?' It was very clever of them really, because they'd been priming me to say this for a long time and it made me feel as if it was my idea. It was the best thing that could have happened to me. Within days I was playing football.'

Since neither John nor Greg had any experience of working on a Challenge yacht it was down to the old hands to teach the new boys the correct way of doing things. Much as everyone liked and respected the two new recruits, a hazard of constantly having to train up new volunteers was that it wasted valuable time and inevitably hampered the boat's progress. Chris said, 'Although Greg clearly brought something to the boat we still had two new people who had to be taught about the boat's systems and then there was the mobility problem with Stuart, Brendan and Grahme. Often I'd be running a sail change on the foredeck to find myself with only one other experienced person. In the early days of *Time & Tide*, when we talked about achievement and racing speed, what we never anticipated was the number of changes to the crew we'd have to accommodate.'

John Spence experienced the problem first hand. On his first night on board James asked him to go to the bow and take care of the gybe preventer, a device that stopped the boom involuntarily moving across the boat with a wind shift. 'I didn't really know what he meant but I went all the same and sat next to the gybe preventer, determined not to take my eyes off it. The trouble was that they all assumed I knew more than I did, which meant that even though I was trying to be helpful I think at first I just got in their way.' Like everyone else John was keen to be useful and look busy, so while learning the ropes up on deck he also got stuck into cleaning the bilges, cooking and being a willing dogsbody.

In an e-mail from the boat to disabled students at Boston's Bridgewater State College, James set out an explanation of the boat and his crew.

> It's important you understand we were not a team. We were a bunch of people thrown together and I was told to get them ready. Some of my crew will leave still not being able to remember how to tie a bowline or trim the sails. Everyone on the crew has a different reason for being here. We did not get to select who was on our yacht. Unlike most activities where you do things with your friends, here what you get is as good or bad as it can be. Some want adventure, some want to race, some want to just sail, some actually just can't wait to get off.

Chris and James were all too aware that there were still those for whom doing well seemed less important than simply completing the race, and therefore motivating the crew during this long and trying leg was an ongoing struggle which at times felt like very uphill work indeed. One of James's favourite sayings, which he pinned up on the bulkhead, was, 'Are you involved or are you committed to this race? In a bacon-and-egg breakfast the chicken is just involved ... the pig is committed.'

David saw it as inevitable that not everyone had the same commitment to racing, since people's motivation for joining *Time & Tide* could not be viewed in the same light as that of those joining the rest of the fleet. 'On *Time & Tide* people got involved for all sorts of reasons,' he remarked. 'For some it was because they wanted to race but for others it was because they were disabled and wanted to do something exciting.'

By 13 May *3Com* had overtaken *Time & Tide* and despite averaging good speeds *Time &*

James and Chris try to repair the compass (© Time & Tide/BT)

Tide dropped back to fourteenth position. Everyone felt disheartened. In his log Brendan wrote, 'Can't bring myself to write a sponsor race report because of our poor position.' However, this wasn't the end of their race with *3Com*. One dark clear night after 2,500 miles at sea *3Com*'s lights appeared over the horizon. As they crossed paths within 6 feet, *3Com* headed due west while *Time & Tide* kept on its north-westerly course. But in reality they were never to overtake *3Com* again and although they subsequently tried every tactic possible for the rest of the leg they trailed at the rear of the fleet.

Despite the frustration of not doing well during this fifth leg to Boston, in sailing terms it was a magnificent crossing. With day after day of fast downwind sailing, the crew now experienced the best sailing weather of the trip, and this couldn't fail to have an exhilarating effect on everyone. 'God knows where in the world you'd go to get better spinnaker sailing,' commented James, who, like everyone else, was enjoying keeping dry for a change. The crew themselves were overawed by the sheer power of the boat, the consistently bright sunny days and the clear evenings with spectacular sunsets, meteorite showers and displays of the Southern Lights playing across the sky. They even spotted the space shuttle launch from Cape Canaveral – an awesome sight resembling a massive firework or a back-to-front comet with a fiery tail. 'We really must begin to appreciate this experience and console ourselves with the fact that *Group 4* are probably too busy to enjoy anything!' wrote Carolyn.

But despite the exceptional sailing, *Time & Tide* was having more than its fair share of bad luck. As Chris said, 'We found every bloody hole on offer.' Sails kept ripping, resulting in nine sail repairs, all of which were co-ordinated by Paul Burns, who selected those with the greatest patience and attention span to assist him. Then, to crown it all, the instruments started playing up. The main problem was that the steering compass kept jamming, which meant that while the digital read-out showed the boat to be on course, James could see quite clearly that it wasn't. When after a while the compass freed itself, it would show *Time & Tide* to have sailed thirty or forty minutes in the wrong direction. In this way the yacht zigged and zagged its way up the Atlantic for days on end. 'All my helms relied heavily on instruments,' explained James, 'and it was too late to go back to basics by checking the wind dial at the top of the mast to see what angle the wind was coming at. The Challenge training is very high tech, for the simple reason that there just isn't the time to teach amateur crews all the necessary theory. For my crew, therefore, it was rather like having been taught to drive on an automatic and then suddenly being handed the keys for a manual. Not surprisingly it completely threw them.'

15 May 1997: First Mate's Log :13° 46' S 06° 46' W

We are now in fourteenth place and have been for days. Despite trying very hard we cannot close the gap. The wind has been very light and whilst we have had the kite up for ten days, other than the odd gybe all the effort is in keeping the boat moving ... Time has dragged at the thought of thirty more days, and the thought of the Doldrums is painful. The race is too long and this leg should go straight to Southampton ... Carolyn and Paul H. are well pissed off that they are not helming but they all agreed that speed was important and the best should helm. Tried phoning home but they were out. Look forward to any news from home. James is very low. He is beating himself up about our poor results. We had a long chat today. Hope it helped. Agreed new course and agreed to go for bust.

On 21 May James faxed the Trust office: 'Just crossed the Equator. Nice to be back in your part of the world. Congrats from all here to all of you. Almost home.'

Crossing the Equator meant once again performing a ceremony in honour of King Neptune. This time the victims were all those who hadn't been on the first leg to Rio. A lethal concoction of leftovers (including a sprinkling of engine oil) was dolloped over the innocent crew. Grahme, fearless as ever, went first – a mistake, perhaps, as he then had to sit in the tropical sun and feel the sludge slowly hardening on his skin, until even his beard developed a crust. Carol described the day's events in her log:

Grahme was first and actually ate some (YUK!), then John, who said he enjoyed it. Then Brendan who got some down his pants and Greg, who almost threw up! They all got a couple of ladles full from a huge pan. Then it was my turn. I got the inevitable dollops down my cleavage followed by the whole of the rest of the contents of the pan (about half) over my head ... I couldn't believe how much of the stuff got stuck inside my swimming costume even after a salt-water dousing. Lumps of ham were falling out at one point!

Three days later on 24 May, exactly one year to the day after the boat had been christened, *Time & Tide* completed its circumnavigation of the globe. This was indeed cause for celebration, although no one felt much like it, since there were still 3,000 miles of the race to go. Carol made some commemorative bread for Lesley, Carolyn, Nigel, Chris, David and the two Pauls – a special round loaf with an arrow going right around and then crossing over; for those of the crew who had only done one leg she made a roll with a very short arrow; and for those who had done two or more she made a roll with an arrow going almost all the way round. Appropriately James's roll had an arrow which went three times round.

Late that day James sent a fax to the Trust. He had in fact written it back in September on the morning of the start of the race from Southampton, intending to send it only if they successfully got round.

Crossing the Equator initiation for those who missed it the first time (© Time & Tide/BT)

Dear Sue

Tick another box, that's the name of the game. It's a horrible morning in Southampton and there's one hell of a job ahead and here am I writing you a letter that I'm not sure when I'm going to send. If I listen to some people it will never be sent. If you and I had listened to others, today would be happening without Time & Tide. *I am really scared at the responsibility that now rests on my shoulders. I hope I don't let the crew or you (or me) down and further hope that in due course you will receive this letter from me. I'm about to deal with box one.*

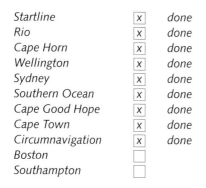

Startline	x	*done*
Rio	x	*done*
Cape Horn	x	*done*
Wellington	x	*done*
Sydney	x	*done*
Southern Ocean	x	*done*
Cape Good Hope	x	*done*
Cape Town	x	*done*
Circumnavigation	x	*done*
Boston		
Southampton		

Just found this in the files and although there are two ports left we have achieved the world.

Hugs and congratulations, love James

Some of the crew were determined to do whatever they could to make the boat run faster. David got his watch to sit on the leeward rail. Carol suggested dumping their surplus water to make the boat lighter, but James pointed out that this wasn't sensible sailing, since they were at the back of the fleet and therefore couldn't rely on boats coming up behind them should they get into trouble. 'But bless her heart,' he recalled, 'she got up and dumped all her magazines over the side instead.'

Everyone observed that James was feeling extremely gloomy about their poor rating in the polls. 'Sometimes, for days on end,' David said, 'we wouldn't hear our position because I don't think he could face telling us, but then he'd suddenly come bouncing up on deck and tell us we'd taken five miles off the boat in front. Great, we thought, until we realized we were still eighty miles behind.'

Once past the Equator *Time & Tide* hit the Doldrums and was becalmed for days on end. The sails hung limply and the boat trickled along looking for every idle puff of wind. Not surprisingly the intensity dropped off and the crew became as listless as the weather, immensely frustrated at having to sit for hours, stuck like a parked car in a lot. In a fax to Race HQ James tried to be light-hearted but his frustration was evident:

It's almost criminal having to do time in the Doldrums. Here we sit, breeze all around us, in the centre of a spotlight of calms, the sea reflecting like the tortured mirrors of a fun fair, distorting the viewer to delusions of grandeur or despair. There isn't a single person on board who wouldn't give their right arm – well we could trade a couple of spare legs – for just one small Southern Ocean blow. It's been exhausting for the crew, as it has for the other yachts, constantly changing sails to suit the precarious mood of the wind. Our course is so random that I'm waiting for a traffic cop to nip out from behind a swell, pull us over and charge us with driving without due care and attention through a high pressure zone, or loitering with intent to sail. You take your life in your hands when you suggest that the trimmer should move a tad faster. With the temperature and humidity as uncomfortable as this, any one of us could be considered armed and dangerous when tooled up with a winch handle. Fortunately the crime rate, like the breeze, is pretty low round these parts. But we would like to get out on bail ... Please.

On Sunday 25 May Brendan wrote in his log:

Still in the Doldrums. We are now 402 miles behind Group 4 *and in last position. The sea looks like an oil slick. We have a lot of cloud cover, which occasionally causes a huge downpour. Everyone's wearing their foulies which all stink because they were hung in a container in Cape Town for three weeks, so putting them on is a deeply unpleasant experience. We have tacked the boat more times than I care to remember and we are still doing only one knot. Everyone is a bit down due to our poor progress and position in the fleet.*

For once the crew didn't need every minute of their free time to recoup on sleep, and so there was plenty of time for talking and relaxing; occasionally the Monopoly or draughts board came out and everyone had a can of beer and tried to unwind. There was also time for the odd prank, such as the picture that was taken of the five amputees all sitting along the rail holding up their spare false legs like trophies.

Stuck in the Doldrums (© Brendan West)

Throughout the Doldrums *Time & Tide* kept losing ground and slipping further and further behind the rest of the fleet. This caused a great deal of frustration and disappointment among the crew, most of whom suffered long periods of boredom. As watch leader, Nigel complained

The five amputees with their spare false legs (© Time & Tide/BT)

to James that he didn't feel he was doing enough. 'Welcome to long-distance ocean racing,' came back the reply.

Ocean sailing has often been described as 90 per cent boredom and 10 per cent panic. The 10 per cent panic is the exciting part and there certainly wasn't a great deal of that on this leg. In the Doldrums especially it was hard to keep motivated, and even Chris realized that 'If you weren't skipper or mate, helming or watch leader, you'd have been bored out of your Christmas tree at times.' There were, however, a few dramatic moments, such as when Carol nearly went over the side. She recorded the incident in her log:

> I was just rerouting the spinnaker sheet and guy around the headsail sheet when the headsail sheet straightened with such force that it flipped me over the side. I ended up dangling upside down from the guardrail still clinging to the headsail sheet. I remember feeling very calm (actually thought it was funny – the sea was so calm) but I did yell, 'Catch me! Catch me I'm not clipped on!' As I went over Paul B. was there in a flash and he grabbed me and I grabbed for him, catching the sleeve of his very stretchy T-shirt. Brendan said he just sat there with his mouth open, unable to move, and Paul H. didn't even notice ... When I got back on deck later I yelled, 'Sorry James!' and he said, 'That's OK', in a resigned (slightly amused/bemused) voice. As I went over I wasn't scared of hitting the water but I would have been annoyed with myself at slowing the boat down even more while I was picked up. James and Chris both in turn gave me a squeeze and said, 'Are you OK?' which was good of them. There have

Nigel adjusting the runner block (© Time & Tide/BT)

been a few jokes about me being so keen to save weight that I threw myself over the side. I can tell it's going to take a while to live this down. I find it incredible that with all the amputees and wobbly people on board it's the able-bodied that have had most of the accidents.

Although most of the crew complained they didn't have enough to do during this crossing, there were some who claimed never to be bored. Lesley, for instance, said boredom just wasn't part of her make up, and David, also a watch leader on this leg, was quite content for once to sit back on the rail mellowing out, just watching the world slip quietly by. And Greg was just too busy keeping an eye on the steering and trim of the sails to get bored. 'The whole of the thirty-nine days was a buzz for me. I took every minute in and time went very fast.'

He recognized, however, that sailing in just one leg was an entirely different experience from sailing the whole way round the world and he fully appreciated why many of the crew wanted nothing more by now than to get home. James observed that already some of the crew were getting nervous about coming home. 'There were plenty of quiet moments on the boat with people thinking about what happens next. We all knew that once we docked in Southampton it would be goodbye and then back to the real world.' On reflection James felt he had become a lot more patient during his time at sea as well as a lot more confident of himself and his ability to look inside each situation and each person.

For others too it was a time for quiet reflection. With the race drawing to a close Carol had often found her mind wandering off elsewhere during this leg. She spent a lot of time in the cockpit or on bow watch 'thinking too much, beginning to worry about the end of the race and knowing that I would miss everyone a lot'.

Because this crossing was not only the longest but also the leg which involved the least physical work, Paul Hebblethwaite's frustration was beginning to show itself in anger, impatience and surliness. James and Chris found this particularly hard to tolerate and wondered whether sometimes Paul's deafness was used as an excuse for his difficulties, when really they should have been put down to attitude. 'On one occasion,' recalled James, 'he was at the wheel but got so frustrated at not being able to grasp the sensitivity of the steering that he just walked off and left the helm unmanned. Later he got upset with me because I wouldn't let him back on the wheel but I explained that leaving the helm unmanned was unacceptable behaviour when you were responsible for everyone on the boat.'

David, who got on well with Paul, was the most sympathetic to his needs. He claimed it was futile shouting at him since he usually had no idea what was being said around him and therefore would become all the more exasperated. He was also aware of just how much of the conversation Paul missed. 'I guess he gets about 3 per cent of it,' he said. 'On one occasion some of us were sitting round the galley table discussing the way the sails are set. We were all laughing and chit-chatting and at the end of it all I turned to Paul and said, "You've got to get the luff spinnaker breaking if you don't want to lose power." Well, he looked at me as if I had two heads, because he knew we'd been talking for half an hour and must have said more than just that. But I couldn't even remember, let alone repeat, all the banter and silly jokes that had been said. After all, how much of any conversation is actually about the subject?'

While Paul wanted to be kept in the picture the whole time, he also recognized that when people came off watch they were usually exhausted and didn't particularly want to go through everything a second time. 'But I'm still part of the crew,' he insisted, 'and they should try and compensate for my deafness because if they're not strong enough to work on the foredeck I have to compensate for their disability by working extra hard.' He was sorry that he'd become a lot more volatile during these last eight months. 'I used to be a nice person before I started out on the race but I've changed,' he said regretfully. 'Now I'm much angrier and much more immature.'

Carolyn sympathized and remembered that she too had once felt isolated by her deafness. 'I used to have a real chip on my shoulder, feeling no one understood me or could be bothered to talk to me. And it was true a lot of the time, but I learnt to accept it and to realize that in order to feel included it was up to me to make twice as much effort as anyone else.'

For Paul Burns this was also proving to be the most difficult leg of the race so far – but for quite different reasons. On arriving in Cape Town his wife had gone back to the hotel room with him and announced that their marriage was over. It came as a devastating blow to Paul, who was eagerly looking forward to getting home and being reunited with his family. Whilst he recognized that their marriage, like most marriages, had its problems, and whilst he was well aware that Sheila had been reluctant to let him join the Challenge in the first place, he had hoped that being away would cement their relationship once and for all, and therefore during much of the voyage he had been contemplating the future, planning how to change things for the better.

'While I was away she realized there was more to life than me and our marriage and she met another man,' he explained. 'My absence gave her the opportunity to stretch herself and become much more independent. I'm not saying it wouldn't have happened without the race but the race certainly brought things to a head.'

In Cape Town Paul had been utterly shattered by the news and when Sheila had returned to England he followed her, hoping they might hammer it out together at home and agree to start piecing their thirteen-year marriage back together again. It proved a futile endeavour, however, and he returned to Cape Town a crushed man.

'I considered pulling out of the race altogether,' he said, 'but I knew that that wasn't a solution because then I would have lost both things – my marriage and my dream of sailing round the world. So I returned to South Africa, drained and brokenhearted, but determined to finish the race.'

The thirty-nine days spent at sea during the Boston leg were torturous for Paul. He was desperate to communicate with Sheila, if only to sort out who would live where and what would happen to the kids, but it wasn't easy having to do so through faxes, which went via Portishead and in effect meant broadcasting his innermost thoughts and private domestic affairs to the world. The faxes that arrived from Sheila were blunt and uncompromising and each one seemed to rip him further apart.

The one reassuring factor was having the support of the crew, many of whom had by now become firm and good friends. And even though his mind was seldom on the job at hand, for the most part James dealt delicately with him, which he appreciated. 'It was a bad trip for Paul,' observed James. 'He was stuck in a situation where there was nothing but thinking to do. Once or twice when a particularly bad fax came through I would sit him down with a brandy and have one myself. I wasn't in a position to censor the mail but I felt it my duty to know what was going on. Even Portishead on one occasion called me back saying Paul had just received a very bad fax and was he all right.' Brendan, who was particularly friendly with Paul, noted in his diary: 'Paul seems quite down. Don't think there is anything I can do to help. Perhaps he will "shout at the page" with his pen when he gets round to writing his diary.'

Paul was shocked by how badly the news had affected him and at times felt exceptionally gloomy and depressed – so much so in fact that at one point James even put the crew on suicide watch. According to David this was totally uncalled for, since Paul was not the suicidal type, but James had never actually meant that Paul would intentionally throw himself over the side; he just knew that if you were incapable of paying attention to the minutiae around you you were at risk. He was also aware that potentially it endangered the rest of the crew and consequently halfway across the Atlantic James took Paul off helm duties and handed the responsibility to Carolyn instead.

Paul Hebblethwaite with a sextant (© Time & Tide/BT)

This pleased Carolyn enormously, as for the first two weeks her relief at not having the responsibility of watch leader, and therefore being able to sit back and 'watch someone else take the flack', had been tinged with disappointment that she hadn't been given the chance to improve on what she'd learnt during the previous leg. Helming was something that seemed to come quite naturally to her and she enjoyed it because it was something she could do without relying on anyone else or having to make the effort to lip read.

For Lesley this was turning out to be a far happier leg. She had found the Southern Ocean a perilous and unpleasant experience, hating the loneliness of being stuck up on deck with just one other person, responsible for the lives of the rest of the crew, with the hatches battened down and nothing but the roar of the waves for companionship. Now that the weather was fine and the sailing – before they reached the Doldrums –exhilarating rather than terrifying she felt much more at ease. She also appreciated the two new crew members; and having always felt a little out on a limb being the oldest on board, she particularly liked having John Spence around, who was closer to her age and with whom she shared common interests and concerns. James understood that she was trying her best and also acknowledged her fear of sailing as being one of the greatest disabilities for any crew member. 'You have to admire her pluck for just sticking it out,' he said.

Lesley noted that Brendan was a little more cautious moving round the boat this time, but he was clearly delighted to be back. Ever since breaking his leg, his knee had been causing him a great deal of pain, even to the extent that as late as Cape Town he had been wondering if he would actually be getting back on the yacht at all. But typically he had chosen not to tell anyone, not even his wife. Now that he was at sea and there was far less walking to do than on land, to his relief his knee was giving him far less trouble. As one of the least mobile on board he spent most of his time if not in the cockpit then in the galley cooking, cleaning or helping with sail repairs. In his view the crew fell into three main categories, though never overtly so, which he described as: '... the management team, the helming people and the underclass. I was one of the underclass, which meant that I did the crappy jobs, and if there was nothing to do I'd sit on the rail for hours waiting for something to come up. I never got mind-bogglingly bored because on the whole people were good conversationalists, but occasionally time passed extremely slowly.'

Like some of the others who never got a chance to helm and spent a lot of time on galley duty, Brendan wished it could be otherwise, whilst at the same time recognizing that the best people should be allocated the best jobs in order to make the boat go faster. He missed Belinda but knew that this time round she was much more relaxed about him being away. Not only had she met most of the crew, some of whom she felt would be friends for life, but also she knew it was only a matter of weeks before Brendan was home.

As for Grahme, Brendan noted in his diary on 9 May: 'He seems a little low. He says this leg is very tough mentally.' It was true that Grahme was affected by the mood of the boat, feeling that with more spare time tempers were getting frazzled and 'some relationships getting rather tattered round the edges'. But he was cheered by the fact that the new prosthesis he'd had made for him in Cape Town was holding up well, making him safer and more mobile on deck. Also, this time round, he wasn't missing his family so much and most days would find solace reading the New Testament in a beautiful new leatherbound edition which the leg maker's wife had given him on departure.

Like Greg, Grahme helped to bring some humour to the boat by not taking himself too seriously. As one crew member remarked, 'He didn't have a great deal of sophistication but there was a lot of warmth and humour about him.' One cause of amusement was Grahme's ever-lengthening beard. He hadn't shaved since Sydney and there was now three inches of growth in which crumbs and bits of food would frequently find a home.

It was Grahme who discovered Stuart's teddy bear and, thinking that the crew needed a diversion 'to stop them contemplating the fluff on their navel', he made Ted the butt of many a crude joke, affectionately naming him 'Ted the Slut'. Carolyn noted in her log that Stuart 'came in for a fair amount of stick, especially when we discovered him asleep clutching a teddy bear'. But even though Ted was photographed in various compromising positions luckily Stuart seemed to take it all in his stride.

As far as Stuart was concerned this was turning out to be a far more successful leg than his previous crossing. He had feared that with the majority of the crew having sailed most of the way round the world together it would be difficult for him to fit back in as part of the team, and was therefore much relieved to find that most people welcomed him back on board with open arms. Overall he noticed that there wasn't nearly so much politics and backbiting as on Leg One and he appreciated having the support of most of the crew. Grahme noted that by the end of the leg 'Stuart had probably grown up more than anyone else on this trip because until this race I don't think he'd ever been exposed to people under pressure.'

The big question now was whether or not Stuart would be allowed to sail in the last leg to Southampton, where the seas were likely to be far rougher and the weather far more unpredictable. While Chris and David felt he was potentially unsafe to have on board and might therefore compromise the safety of the crew, not to mention James's excellent safety record, Susan was adamant that Stuart should be given a fair chance. In a fax to James she wrote:

> I would be very upset if he didn't go on the last leg, even if he has to be strapped into his bunk the whole way ... The trustees know for a fact – no Stu, no Time & Tide. Nobody would have had the opportunity to go on Time & Tide without Stu's loyalty and sitting freezing his arse off on a lawnmower from John O'Groats to Land's End raising money for the Trust, which at the time was the only thing that kept us going. Leg Six is pay-back time. The strongest should support the weakest, since the weakest helped them have a boat to sail on.

By 29 May *Time & Tide* was finally out of the Doldrums. But it was now 550 miles behind the leader of the fleet, *Group 4*, and to all intents and purposes in a different race altogether. By 4 June the outcome of the fifth leg looked set, though there was still the remotest possibility that they could improve on their position.

4 June 1997: First Mate's Log: 28°86' N 53°11' W

> Have been getting good weather maps but position is too final to make much difference. There is however an outside chance that the high over Boston may bunch boats up at the finish. Been talking a lot with James. We seem to be keeping each other going. With very little happening, i.e. no sail changes, people become more intense.

By 6 June the sea resembled a glassy blue-black oil slick, the sky was turning grey and they were now moving from one squall to another but still unable to catch up with the fleet. Not surprisingly the frustration was beginning to get to everyone. On 8 June Nigel wrote in his log:

> Well, one thing's for sure: what I've found out about myself is that my patience with and tolerance of other people has gone right down. I don't know if I'm just bored or others have just lost interest in what they are doing but no one is motivated any more and haven't been for a long time. I wonder if it's because we've been fourteenth for so long. I'll be glad to see the end of this leg. The windward legs were horrendous but at least you never had time to get bored.

Much of James's frustration came from the fact that the majority of the crew simply did not recognize or understand the huge amount of effort that he and Chris were putting into driving the boat forward, and at times he felt they were blaming him for the boat's poor position. He also felt let down when after nearly five legs at sea some of the crew still failed to grasp that they too were responsible for sailing and pushing the boat on. And he was amazed that they so seldom appreciated just how quickly and seriously things could go wrong.

Chris put it down to a basic naivety. 'I think they forget that legally if anything happens to them James and I carry the can. They think James is hard on them but they have no appreciation of the responsibility he takes on. Of course we have to shout because if you're at the helm and you see something potentially dangerous about to happen you're quite helpless to do anything about it except shout. Half the time the crew have no idea of the risk they're putting themselves in.'

Greg was one of the few who fully appreciated the constant pressure James was under: 'It's a big task taking thirteen people on a charter round the world (which in effect is what he's doing) and keeping them motivated all the time. He has incredible drive and determination and often the only way he can get the rest of the crew going is by cracking the whips.'

Just a few days outside Boston *Time & Tide* hit its first real blow. The weather turned bitterly cold and T-shirts and shorts were exchanged for winter woollies and foul-weather gear. This was a great relief and of much excitement to John Spence, who had been complaining that he hadn't yet experienced a real storm and therefore couldn't really say that he'd been ocean racing. Unfortunately just before the blow *Time & Tide* lost the whole of her brand new 1.5 spinnaker. The sail ripped up the side and along the bottom and ended up in the sea like a picture cut from its picture frame. It was essential to retrieve it as they didn't want to incur a penalty, so James turned round, operated a man overboard procedure, and rescued the sail which, with so few days left at sea, wasn't worth repairing.

The finish into Boston was painfully long-drawn-out. Just a few miles outside the harbour *Time & Tide* was becalmed and stuck without a whiff of wind for eight hours. But the crew were much cheered by the sight of their supporters waving and yelling at them from a Boston Police Force launch. On board were Susan and Lucy, as well as James's eighty-year-old mother and his sister, who had come out to Boston for the duration of the stopover. James later observed that his sister had been 'waving the Union Jack as if it had gone out of fashion'. Also on board were Stuart's parents, Carol Tait, Lesley's son Simon and his girlfriend, plus an ITN camera crew and a *Sunday Times* journalist, not to mention a large number of the Boston Police Force. Chay followed in his launch, encouraging them to get to the dock fast, where another 500 people and fifty television stations were waiting to greet them. But for the time being *Time & Tide* could do nothing but helplessly bob up and down in the water waiting for the wind to pick up. Thankfully by the time they eventually drifted into Rowes Wharf the huge crowd were still there, lining the quayside waiting to celebrate the disabled crew's arrival. At the edge of the pontoon were Brendan West's parents, who had only just got off a plane and were standing there, still clutching their suitcases, eager to be reunited with their son.

Carolyn recorded the finish in her log:

> *Press boats were circling us, as were the helicopters above. I felt a bit like 'been here before' with all the attention and was trying to concentrate on the boat, keeping it going, while other boats kept whizzing past, spoiling our wind ... We eventually pulled into Rowes Wharf, where it seemed most of the fleet had waited for us, as well as many Bostonians. What a welcome again! The champagne flowed, interviews were given and burgers demolished by a hungry crew who hadn't eaten nearly all day, before we all went to Sherlock's Bar for a mass reunion with the other crews. Grahme was drunk before we got there, and could hardly walk – his false leg kept buckling under him!*

Grahme, who admitted that he had a rather dopey grin on his face that night `and fell over just about everything in sight, was delighted when he stumbled down to the boat the next morning and James selected him to join half a dozen other members of the fleet to be taken on a sightseeing tour of Boston by the BBC, who wanted to get some extra footage for their documentary.

Although everyone was delighted to have reached Boston, coming in last somewhat dampened the celebratory atmosphere. *Time & Tide* had left Cape Town in twelfth position, a day and a half ahead of *Concert* and half an hour behind *Heath Insured*. Arriving in Boston it was now in fourteenth position and a day behind the boat in front. If James had wanted anything from the race, it was simply not to come last, but that seemed almost impossible now, unless another boat was to run into major problems – and no one would wish that on anyone. Realistically the best James could hope for now was not to come into Southampton at the back of the fleet. Friends, supporters and the media were bound to remember this final leg more than any other, so there was still a great deal to play for.

Lucy and Susan had spent the past six weeks working hard on trying to secure accommodation for the crew in Boston – a task which proved harder than anyone had initially imagined since in a city known to be the most expensive in America there was very little low-priced accommodation available. Since the Trust's coffers had by now nearly run dry, Susan was determined to save as much money as she could to pay the bills at the end of the race and to give the crew a homecoming befitting their enormous achievement. There was always the option of staying on the boat, but after a 7,000-mile ocean leg and with the temperatures in Boston reaching the nineties clearly this would not have been good for crew relationships.

Accommodation was finally arranged through Jeni Graham, a BA purser and keen sailor who had become involved in the project through Stuart and was one of *Time & Tide*'s most effective and loyal supporters, even to the extent that she had managed to arrange her flying schedule to fit in with the crew's arrival in each port of call. Jeni's partner, Mike Russell, had good business contacts in the USA and Jeni had spent hours on the phone networking with various companies and organizations until finally her efforts had produced the results she had been looking for. General Atlantic Partners asked Outdoor Explorations, a Boston group which organized activities for able and disabled people, to find *Time & Tide* various facilities in Boston and they came up with university accommodation at the Massachusetts Institute of Technology in Cambridge, an attractive area near Harvard Square where there were plenty of reasonably priced bars, cafés and shops; they also provided the crew with a minibus and car for the duration of their stay in Boston.

Although as usual there was a lot of work to do on the boat during the stopover, there was also time to relax. Unlike many of the other crews, who split up the moment they reached port, the *Time & Tide* crew seemed to be spending more and more time together. As Susan pointed out, 'By Boston the atmosphere among the crew had entirely changed. It was as if at last they'd really gelled and were enjoying each other's company.'

Crew outings included a visit to the Red Sox baseball match, fixed up by Outdoor Explorations, which, despite the rain and despite the fact that not everyone was a fan of baseball, was one of the high points of the stopover, particularly because at halftime the words 'Congratulations to *Time & Tide* and welcome' were flashed up across the scoreboard in neon lights. It was also a significant stopover for the Challenge as it was here that Chay learnt of his knighthood.

While in Boston Paul Burns, Brendan and Grahme (Nigel was away visiting his sister in San Francisco) went to see a top US prosthesisist in Salem to sort out their legs. Stannah Lifts, one of Paul's personal sponsors, provided transport to take them to and from Salem for their clinic appointments. Not surprisingly, when the transport turned out to be a chauffeur-driven stretch limo, the boys revelled in the five-star treatment.

James with 'Wheels', one of the students from Bridgewater State College in Boston (© Dr Joseph Huber)

Another high point of the stopover was when the crew met the disabled students from Bridgewater State College who they had been e-mailing from sea. After an entertaining and enjoyable dinner hosted by the Palm Restaurant in Boston, the students went sailing with the crew and in a relatively short space of time some became firm friends. Later, Dr Joseph Huber, director of the Children's Physical Developmental Clinic at Bridgewater State College, wrote a letter of thanks to the crew:

> *I do not believe that any other sporting event for the disabled has demanded so much media attention around the world except for possibly the Paralympics. With all that has occurred here in Boston, the crew of* Time & Tide *have accomplished their mission of 'racing the latitudes to change attitudes' and therefore have made a significant contribution to the disabled as well as the able-bodied throughout the world.*

While in Boston the crew were also delighted to meet Steve Spinetto, Boston's Commissioner for Disabilities, who looked after them during their Boston stay and had arranged the police launch boat as they crossed the finish line. Steve was an amputee and by extraordinary coincidence had been run over by a launch and lost his leg thirty years ago to the day that *Time & Tide* arrived in Boston. Every year since then he had spent the anniversary lamenting the loss of his leg. However, seeing the five *Time & Tide* amputees line up along the deck as they came into port had had a powerful effect on him – so much so that the very next day he came down to the boat grinning from ear to ear, explaining that he had been so moved and impressed by the spirit and motivation of the lads that miraculously he no longer missed his leg.

Leg 5 Final Results

	Team	Arrival time
1	Group 4	07/06/97 13:19
2	Motorola	08/06/97 05:42
3	Toshiba Wave Warrior	08/06/97 19:20
4	Courtaulds Int.	09/06/97 00:01
5	Concert	09/06/97 07:04
6	Save the Children	09/06/97 09:03
7	Commercial Union	09/06/97 16:29
8	Nuclear Electric	09/06/97 19:59
9	Global Teamwork	09/06/97 18:46
10	Pause to Remember	10/06/97 00:37
11	Heath Insured II	10/06/97 06:00
13	Ocean Rover	10/06/97 11:28
12	3Com	11/06/97 03:28
14	Time & Tide	11/06/97 23:21

All times GMT.

Leg 5 Combined Times

	TEAM	TIME
1	Group 4	144d 21h 48m
2	Toshiba Wave Warrior	147d 02h 05m
3	Motorola	148d 20h 58m
4	Save the Children	148d 23h 48m
5	Commercial Union	150d 10h 58m
6	Global Teamwork	152d 19h 29m
7	Nuclear Electric	154d 00h 48m
8	3Com	154d 10h 18m
9	Ocean Rover	154d 10h 22m
10	Pause to Remember	155d 17h 28m
11	Courtaulds Int.	156d 17h 46m
12	Heath Insured II	157d 08h 28m
13	Concert	158d 10h 59m
14	Time & Tide	159d 07h 05m

All times rounded to the nearest minute.

Chapter Eight

Leg Six
Boston to Southampton

Departure date 29 June 1997. Relatively short sprint across the Atlantic. Good steady downwind sailing. Conditions nearer to UK are affected by current position of Azores high weather system, making weather predictions difficult. Atlantic lows quite commonplace, bringing strong winds and driving rain.

J ames and Chris's sailing strategy on leaving Boston was to put the crew with the most sailing ability in positions most likely to enhance the performance of the boat. Everyone was desperately keen to do well on this leg but equally everyone knew that the entire fleet would also be giving it their all. So despite *Time & Tide*'s determination not to come in last, in reality the crew knew that there was only the slightest chance of being able to improve on its position.

Colin Tabor
(© Grahme
Rayner)

Two new leggers had arrived in Boston just a week before the start of the race – Colin Tabor, a 42-year-old sports sponsorship manager with very little sailing experience, and Simon Needs, a 37-year-old property developer, who had been sailing for twenty years and taken part in various national and international championships.

Colin had initially heard about *Time & Tide* in press and television reports while languishing in hospital following a double hip replacement in December 1996. However, he hadn't thought a great deal more about it until a few weeks later when he went out to meet some friends at his local pub. As he came hobbling in through the door on crutches, one of them suggested he give Chay a ring and join the disabled yacht. It was a lighthearted remark said in jest, but Colin took the comment to heart and called The Challenge Business.

Like several others on board *Time & Tide*, one of Colin's main motivations for taking part in the race was his thirst for adventure. Chay had always billed the race as an adventure, but by now Chris was beginning to feel that too many people were there for the fun of it and not enough were bringing the high-calibre quality of sailing they desperately needed for racing. While acknowledging that the likes of Colin brought a maturity to the boat that the project had so crucially lacked in the past, he still maintained that in terms of sailing the leggers often brought with them more problems than they solved: even the ones with experience had to be prepared to relearn their base training and start again. Chris cited Greg Hammond as an example of someone who had realized almost immediately that if he tried to change the regime of the boat he'd very quickly come apart.

Simon's motives for joining *Time & Tide* were different from Colin's, in that as someone who had recently undergone a liver transplant he was determined to show others in the same

Simon Needs (© Simon Needs)

position as himself that having the operation didn't necessarily stop you taking part in adventure sports or stretching yourself to the limit.

Both these new crew members arrived in Boston to find a tight-knit crew. Simon particularly felt that as a legger he was treated as an outsider and had to work doubly hard to become valued as a team member. But if the crew and their skipper didn't appear as friendly as he would have liked, it wasn't out of any malevolent feeling towards those coming into the race for the last sprint, nor was it because they were all wallowing in the gloomy prediction of coming last; it was simply because by now they were exhausted and, as David remarked, 'war weary and longing to get home'. Paul Burns got it right when he said, 'The two new guys were full of the enthusiasm that we'd had at the start, but by now we'd calmed down and knew what to expect.'

Both Colin and Simon felt it their duty to bring to the boat renewed determination and enthusiasm which the tired old timers appeared to have lost. They also resolved to try their best to inject some humour into the crew: something which they succeeded in doing admirably – particularly Simon, who joined Grahme in the role of the boat jester.

For James this was one of the best starts. The boats were all bunched together and despite the kite tearing just over the start line (involving five sail changes in sixteen minutes) *Time & Tide* found some sea breeze and powered out of the harbour. However, by six o'clock the yacht was caught in a foul bit of tide and had to watch as the rest of the fleet moved away. 'So in our traditional fourteenth place we head on,' was Nigel's comment in his diary that evening. Things might have turned out better had not the ill-fated powerful 1.5 spinnaker then shredded all the way down the seams just before midnight.

'After that we just waited for the weather to kick in,' explained James, 'but it didn't happen and we were stuck with very light winds for four to five days. It was so frustrating because the boat was busting to be power driven, yet there was no breeze. Then a day after the first kite blew we lost our second 1.5 spinnaker, which in the end cost us many miles because it meant we didn't have the appropriate sail for the weather.'

The repair, lasting several days, was co-ordinated by Paul Burns, with Brendan, Carol and others joining the sewing circle and dedicating most of their watch time to the mammoth task of stitching and gluing 140 feet of sail. 'Paul Burns did a truly excellent job,' said James, 'and if it hadn't blown again just twenty-four hours before the finish we would have stood a very good chance of winning the best sail repair prize.'

Soon James became resigned to the fact that they wouldn't get the strong breeze they needed. There was talk of a tropical storm coming through, but that never materialized and for most of the time it was, as Brendan said, much like 'sailing on a gigantic pond'. Towards the end for a short while they encountered winds of thirty knots, but for those who had experienced the Southern Ocean this was nothing to write home about.

While James for the most part was still controlling sailing procedures with step-by-step instructions, those on the foredeck were managing sail changes with greater precision and alacrity than ever before: both he and Chris noted that the 'A team' were at last performing consistently well under pressure. But what tended to preoccupy people most was the position of the boat in the daily race polls, which one moment gave grounds for optimism and the next plunged the boat into a mood of doom and gloom.

7 July 1997 First Mate's Log 43°N 04°51' W

Well, we got up to eighth, down to last, rounded the waypoint, back up to twelfth and now last again. It's hard to explain to people why. Some of it is just how the positions get calculated. We have been in thick fog for days. The wind is very light and our arrival time is now suspect. Talked to home yesterday. Can't wait now to get home. Had very cold night; yesterday was long day with very little sleep. There's more fun and good humour this leg, and James is doing good job of keeping his cool.

As far as the crew were concerned, James was at his most relaxed. He seemed far less despondent about their position than he had on the previous leg and lost his temper only twice. Brendan recorded a revealing incident in his diary:

James told Simon to stop messing around and get on course. Simon replied, 'I am trying my best and I'm not mucking around.' James: 'Your best isn't good enough.' When Simon came off the helm they proceeded to have a massive row, Simon saying that he didn't 'have to put up with this shit'. They were both out of order, but that is the first time I have seen a crew member stand up to James for the full length of an argument. When the argument subsided and everyone calmed down James came to the wheel and showed Simon how to helm in these difficult conditions. They both seem to be friends again on the surface; James even apologized for shouting.

Simon, who unlike the rest of the crew hadn't become acclimatized to James's outbursts, took exception to being shouted at for something which he felt wasn't his fault, but James insisted that whoever was in control of the wheel took responsibility for what went wrong. 'The trouble with Simon was that he thought he could run the boat,' was James's comment. 'He didn't like being told to get off the wheel. I don't mind people arguing back but I don't like aggression. I've always told the crew that when I lose my temper it's not personal to them and I think they accept that now.'

Frustration at their slow progress affected all the crew, though most were by now resigned to coming in last. Brendan noted, 'The crew seem curiously quiet; they all look very tired and are having some trouble getting used to the watch system.' Carol, normally one of the boat's more ebullient crew members, felt uncharacteristically miserable for the first few days at sea and found herself frequently dissolving into quiet tears. She was unable to work out exactly why, but it was clear to other crew members that she was dreading having to face all the unresolved issues of her work and personal life when she returned. Away from the controlled timetable of the last few months, when practically every moment of her day had been organized and accounted for, the future loomed like a huge great gaping hole.

James noticed that Nigel was looking pensive and was a lot quieter than usual. For him returning home was going to be particularly hard. On the first day of the leg he wrote in his log, 'The reality of being in England in two and a half weeks is daunting, but all good things come to an end.' The company he'd worked for in England had since closed down and with both parents deceased and his brother and sister living at opposite ends of the world he had no family to return to. But already there was talk of a reunion. Brendan noted, 'Everyone is planning to go to Nigel's local, the Little Gem, the smallest pub in Kent, on our return. It's the day before I return to work, so common sense dictates that I don't go ... but common sense never stopped me doing anything before!'

No one, apart from Lesley who had been dishing out painkillers, was aware just how much Brendan's Southern Ocean injury was still affecting him. In his diary he wrote:

> My broken knee took a major bash at the race start and bled quite badly. My stump has also been bleeding, due to the amount of walking I did in the last two days in Boston. Both legs are difficult to stand on. I suppose I could hop from foot to foot ... I feel like I want to sit down, and have a long chat and a hug with Belinda. James still seems remarkably relaxed. The whole crew seem different. The pain in my knee is now stopping me sleeping.

And then later:

> My knee has been so painful that if I move it from the sitting position it causes me to yell out involuntarily. I then have to sit for thirty seconds for the pain to subside and catch my breath. I think it will last until Southampton but I am really concerned for the future.

Four days before they were due to arrive back in Southampton, James's girlfriend Sarah faxed the boat with news of an article in the *Sunday Times* by Margarette Driscoll telling of the highs and lows on board *Time & Tide*. For the first time in a newspaper article some of the reality of ocean racing was being described and Hatfield's heroes appeared more human than heroic. This was a 'warts and all' piece, highlighting only the most dramatic and controversial incidents. As snippets of the article were fed down the line to the crew, the general feeling on board was that while the article might have been too negative in its overall tone, what it described had all been true and therefore should be recorded.

James, however, wasn't at all happy, particularly with the teaser for next week's article, which suggested that he had 'thumped' one of the crew. For a long time he racked his brains trying to think who this could possibly refer to. Finally he started thinking of synonyms for the word 'thumped' – 'hit', 'whacked' and 'assaulted' came to mind – and suddenly he remembered how just off Cape Cod he had had to grab hold of Stuart to get him off the winch. 'Chris had been driving and misread the light, so we'd been heading straight for a fishing vessel. There was no time to make mistakes, so I simply barged Chris off the wheel and yanked Stuart off the winch to crash tack the boat. Afterwards I apologized to both of them. Then I remembered that Stuart had been lying in the scuppers saying, "I've been assaulted, I've been assaulted."'

It was certainly true that at the time Stuart had considered this kind of treatment not only unjustifiable but also in blatant disregard of the ethos of the *Time & Tide* Trust. However, James and almost all the crew believed the action to be perfectly justified, considering that the skipper was acting on impulse to protect the boat. As Brendan, who was present at the time, said, 'Assault is too strong a word to use; manhandled would be more appropriate.' After all, hadn't Stuart chosen to play this rough-and-tough game and shouldn't he therefore expect moments when reason and good behaviour gave way under the intense pressure of living life on a knife edge? Most agreed with James when he said, 'I've been on boats where you get more grief if you don't untie the mooring lines quicker.'

Brendan recorded in his diary:

> *Stuart and James had a very intense talk in the doghouse during our first night watch. Lots of hand-waving and finger-pointing. In the second watch Stuart whispered to me that the* Sunday Times *article alleged that James hit Stuart during the trawler incident. James said that if Stuart did not withdraw the allegation, he would get off the yacht before the finishing line. We would therefore not finish the race. Stuart shrugged: he doesn't know what to do.*

We're back
(© Simon
Townsley)
In the end Stuart did withdraw the allegation by sending a fax to the *Sunday Times* stating that 'James's actions, though hard for me to accept, were vital to protect the safety of the crew and vessel in a critical situation.'

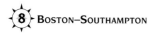

Chris was surprised by Stuart's actions. For someone who had been so loyal and supportive of the project to have been so controversial at the eleventh hour was hardly going to enhance *Time & Tide*'s reputation. Stuart's defence was that he had been assured that the article would not come out until they'd reached port; but some of the crew just couldn't understand why he hadn't waited until well after the race to detonate this time bomb. But Stuart felt he had kept his head down for too long. 'Basically,' he said, 'James was the bus driver and I was one of the paying passengers. If a paid passenger doesn't like the way he's being treated he has a right to get up and complain.'

Despite the bad feeling that the article created, ironically this was Stuart's best leg of the race, both in sailing terms and because he felt James was far less harsh on him. He noticed a change in James's attitudes to his level of ability: 'On legs one and five I felt James was treating me extremely unfairly when I was doing my best to pull my weight. But during the last leg he treated me much more positively. I think he has realized finally that we all have different strengths. If I couldn't do something as well as the next person, it didn't mean I wasn't willing but simply that I wasn't capable.'

James reiterated this point when reflecting on his own behaviour and concluded that one thing the race had taught him was patience. 'I now look at things which in the past would have made me mad because they weren't being done quickly enough or well enough and realize the person is doing their best. It may not be my 100 per cent but it sure enough is their 100 per cent. So when Stuart winds in the winch he's doing it as well as he possibly can.'

On 12 July – five days before the boat arrived in Southampton – Chris wrote in his log, 'Everyone just wants to get in now. The race is over and it's time for us all to move on.' Knowing that the end was in sight and that any grievance they might have would fade in the fullness of time, there was a happy and relaxed atmosphere on board. 'This last week has been enjoyable – everyone looking forward to finishing, jokes being told, lots of leg-pulling,' wrote Carolyn in her diary.

Humour, which had seemed so lacking in the first stages of the race, was now part of the culture of the boat and helped keep everyone amused. David took particular delight in the farting competition between Colin and Grahme, played on deck (and helped along by the freeze-dried food), which kept his watch amused for four entire hours. The score was 32–29 to Colin. Stuart's teddy, whose jacket had been embroidered with the *Time & Tide* logo by his mother, continued to be the butt of jokes. James remarked that 'probably that was a very good thing, as it acted as a focus. If you wanted to think bad thoughts about someone you let them out on Ted.'

James was grateful for Grahme's input on the boat. While he couldn't do much in the way of heavy-duty sail changes he had helped keep the spirits of the crew up and been particularly helpful in providing a listening ear for Stuart. Also, although he worked for the army in a managerial position, he had never once lorded it over others – in fact he seemed to relish being one of the Indians for a change and admired James for handling his role as leader so well. 'I hope that on reflection some of the crew realize that when James was tough with them it was in their best interests. I know for myself that it's nice to stay popular but as leader it's a choice you have to make. I saw James toss for that for himself. He sometimes used humour to calm the situation down and smooth it over. All this touchy-feely stuff that's written about man management is all well and good, but going out and doing the job is quite a different thing.'

In fact Chris had come to regard James as 'a real softy at heart' and like the rest of the crew he noticed that during this leg James was far more laid back and relaxed, seeming rarely to lose his cool. 'Chris doesn't understand how I can be so patient,' said James, realizing part of the reason that he and Chris worked well together was that they created a balanced and united front. 'I couldn't have done the trip without him,' admitted James once it was all over, 'but unfortunately he was more ostracized by the crew than I was. They've grown to accept the fact that I'm the skipper and I go off and do the things that skippers do, but they haven't been so forgiving of Chris, because he had the role of constantly having to cajole them.'

James knew, however, that Chris wouldn't have had it any other way and that he was grateful for having been given the position of first mate, as it had kept him continuously busy. Had he had to suffer the boredom and frustration which some of the other crew members had experienced, the voyage would very soon have become intolerable for him.

On Wednesday 16 July Nigel wrote in his diary, 'We wake up to see England on the port beam.' For everyone it was an amazing feeling and there was quiet calm on the boat. Then in the early hours of Thursday 17 July, just twenty-four hours after *Group 4* had arrived at port and won the race, *Time & Tide* came in sight of Southampton. Carolyn wrote in her log:

> *To think that soon we will be welcomed back into the fold of our normal previous lives ... It will be good to get back to reality, but we have become like a small community on* Time & Tide, *with all our own brand of humour, gossip, arguments, mistakes, etc. which I think we will miss. I'm glad to say I have enjoyed the trip – it is an experience I will carry with me for ever. Not many people can say they have sailed round the world, not to mention on the first yacht with a disabled crew, who proved it can be done, despite prejudice and ignorance.*

There was now great excitement among all the crew, knowing that soon they would step foot on land again and be reunited with their friends and families. Coming in last no longer mattered: they'd done what everyone said couldn't be done – circumnavigated the world – and for most that was success enough. On top of that on two legs they hadn't come in last and as a crew had won more prizes than half the yachts in the fleet.

The supporter ferry with wives, parents, children and sponsors had left the dock at 6.00 a.m., and was heading for a rendezvous with the yacht in the Solent. Michael Nicholson and an ITN camera crew were also nearby on a press boat. Having become very involved with the *Time & Tide* story, Nicholson seemed as excited as everyone else, and was fighting to give the story as much air time as possible.

The arrivals at the previous ports had been emotional, but nothing matched the crew's homecoming to Southampton. Excitement mounted on board the supporter ferry as everybody strained to catch sight of *Time & Tide*'s red spinnaker. Many wives and mothers stood on the upper deck side by side, holding large handmade 'Welcome home' banners and flags. On the deck below everybody lent over the railings, stood on chairs and jumped up and down to catch a glimpse of the crew members they were supporting. 'Land of Hope and Glory' blasted out of the speakers as the yacht approached the ferry and many people wiped away tears; but when 'Simply the Best' started to play everyone sung along with the words at the top of their voices, swaying, waving and clapping in unison to the music: the whole ferry became a *Time & Tide* family with everyone venting their emotions. Even the normally composed Maureen Ogg couldn't hold back the tears. By contrast, Paul Hebblethwaite's mother, known to weep easily and copiously on such occasions, found to her surprise that for once she was dry-eyed. 'I'm just so happy to have him back,' she said. 'There's no need for tears any more.'

Only Lauretta Rayner stood well back out of sight of the yacht. Her husband hadn't been told she was there and she wanted to surprise him on the pontoon. Because the couple had spent the last of their savings on Grahme's new leg, ever since Cape Town Lauretta, in Australia, and Susan, in England, had been trying to get an airline to sponsor her with a ticket to England. Just a few days before the boat was due to arrive in Southampton Ansett and Virgin Atlantic agreed to give her a free flight over. Grahme had always known there was a possibility she might be there. 'I was looking pretty hard at the ferry,' he said, 'just in case she was there, and then I checked it out very thoroughly and thought, well, she isn't there, and

someone else handed me the binoculars to check. I then went to the other side of the boat away from the ferry for a few minutes and once I got a handle on it I came back with the rest of the guys and started to pick up on the excitement they were feeling and waving to the crowd and all of a sudden we went past the oil refineries and the guys that were working there turned their sirens on. It was incredible.'

The supporters' ferry (© Simon Townsley)

Back on the supporter ferry Paul Burns's wife, children and mother, Joan, were impatiently looking out for him. Joan had teamed up with Brendan's mother, whom she hadn't seen since both their sons had been in Woolwich hospital following their amputations in 1980. The two women had shared a room provided by the Red Cross and found a common bond through grief as they willed their disabled sons back to health. Both were clearly devoted to their sons and delighted to be reunited in far more joyous circumstances.

By the time *Time & Tide* made it to the pontoon hundreds of spectators had converged on Ocean Village to welcome home the crew who'd won a place in everyone's hearts. The atmosphere was electric and Susan and Lucy hugged each other, knowing that finally the race had finished. For Susan, particularly, a huge weight had been lifted from her shoulders. There followed another terrific blast from 'Simply the Best', after which the crew were showered with champagne, before being reunited with their wives, girlfriends and families. Supporters and hundreds of wellwishers lining the dockside were also waving, singing and cheering.

For Grahme it was a particularly emotional moment. 'I looked on the dockside and saw a face that brought a tear to my eye: Lauretta. It was great to have someone there to share it with because there was so much emotion in the air, and all my friends were now involved with their families again, that I felt that I had been really missing out. The family of the boat was now breaking up and everyone was going back to their own. I then went down below and packed up all my gear, and for the first time it really hit me that I had spent the last six months with these people and that time was now coming to an end. It felt like I was losing a part of me.'

Sir Chay was also there, announcing to the world his pride and support for the boat he'd initially been so reluctant to let join the race. There were many familiar faces present, too, that morning – for example, Lynn Faulds Wood and her husband John Stapleton had woken at the crack of dawn to get to Southampton in time, as had some of the veterans from former legs such as Dave Hodder, Mike Austin, Malcolm McKeag and Steve Latter.

For James, coming into the Solent was his most memorable homecoming yet:

> *The whole crew were working as one big, beautiful team and I think everyone was aware that no mistakes could be made. The supporter ferry had had to keep well away because of their manoeuvrability, so* Time & Tide *moved across the river and sailed close to the ferry. In fact we came so close that some of the supporters thought that they could almost reach out and touch the mainsail. We then tacked across the river towards the oil refinery, where sirens were going and people were standing by the water's edge waving. Whenever we looked from the boat there were people waving, horns sounding, flags flying, people cheering – it was very emotional and very, very exciting. It was almost as if the boat got swept along on a wave of euphoria rather than the wind and*

Yes! We did it
(© Simon
Townsley)

tide. Then suddenly we were up by the finish line, the police boat cleared a path through the supporting boats and the artillery guns fired a finishing round for us. Then we dropped the headsails, turned and ran back past the guns, who then fired two more rounds in salute. Michael Nicholson was one of the first journalists to greet me. He at least had the presence of mind to push a bottle of champagne towards me rather than a microphone at that moment, but there was so much emotion in his eyes I do not think he could have spoken anyway.

Turning the corner and coming into Ocean Village marina was stunning: the cheering, the noise, the people waving, the flags, the balloons, the sirens going off and people eight deep surrounding the dock. For the last time we edged Time & Tide *into the dock and we had won the race. Sir Chay was there with his magnum of champagne and all I could see was a sea of people cheering and clapping. Somewhere on the pontoon was my mum. The lines went ashore and the boat stopped; the music played on and somewhere I hoped there was a fat lady singing that it was over. It was incredible. The crew were hugging each other and shaking hands and kissing with a lot of backslapping. More journalists came on board – more interviews, and all the hard work and all the fear, courage and determination of the whole crew was repaid.*

So now it was time for reunions and re-establishing relationships. For some, being separated from their partners had enhanced their relationships. During their weeks at sea both Brendan and Grahme had missed their wives far more than they'd expected. Brendan's log was full of touching reminders of his devotion to Belinda. On one occasion, having just spoken to her, he wrote, 'It was lovely to hear Belinda's voice. My spirits are up already and I feel suddenly optimistic. Is this love?' And while reflecting on returning to the humdrum of his old life he wrote, 'It goes without saying that being at home again will be brilliant. Doing this race has made me appreciate it more than ever.'

However, he knew too that his time on *Time & Tide* had given him a thirst for adventure and nothing could restrain him for long. 'I won't hold on to *Time & Tide* in a sentimental way,' he said. 'I'll give most of the T-shirts away, and just keep one for myself. But I know I'll soon get itchy feet and want to do something else. Possibly I'll end up learning to fly, because that's something which still terrifies me.'

Like most of the crew he had built up some special relationships during the voyage. Carol, for example, had become like a sister to him; and a strong bond seemed to have developed between all the amputees. It was easy to see what drew this particular group of people together, as they all came from an Army or Navy background, shared a similar brand of humour, were horrendously intrepid and on top of that all manifested an unusually stoical attitude towards their past injuries.

It was clear, too, that Belinda had also grown from the experience. She had enjoyed the stopovers and although she regretted the fact that Brendan's knee would never be the same again, she realized that the race had been hugely beneficial for both of them. She had gained her independence and knew now that when Brendan got involved in his next adventure she would be more acquiescing, realizing that nothing would separate them for quite so long again. Brendan had even assured her that although he planned to go sailing again, it would never be out of a day's range of a pub, restaurant and her – in that order! In James's eyes their relationship had grown immensely and Belinda had become far more accepting of her husband. 'It's very exciting realizing that when you love someone you love them without controls,' he concluded. 'It's like jumping out of a plane – free fall is terrific.'

The bond between Grahme and his wife had also strengthened. Ever since their shared motorbike accident in 1994 Grahme had been forced to rely more on his wife than perhaps he would have wished but it had brought them closer together; now he realized more than ever just how fortunate he was to have her support, love and loyalty. The voyage had changed him in ways he hadn't expected, as well as allowing him the luxury of time to contemplate his future. Having spent the past six months thinking only about himself he realized that on his return he might be 'a bit of pain to live with', but at least he had discovered during the course of the race that he had a gift for public speaking, and the logical step forward for him now was to get involved in promotions. He had succeeded in starting up a Sailability club in Cape Town and had plans to help promote the Global Challenge 2000 back in Australia.

Chris was one of the happiest to be home. Not only was he delighted to see his wife and daughters again, but he was also eagerly looking forward to going back to work on Monday. As someone who adapted to change easily, he knew that slotting back into the old routine wouldn't present any problems. Although his health had undoubtedly deteriorated and he now had trouble with his elbows and knees, he had no regrets about having taken part in the race. 'I set out to sail round the world and I've done it,' he said impassively. 'I'm disappointed we have to explain away why we've come last, but at the same time we've achieved an awful lot.'

Although Maureen was greatly looking forward to Chris coming home, she knew it would take some adjusting to. She had lightheartedly talked about wondering how far on the Richter scale the aftershocks would go. 'Chris and I are equally strong characters,' she conceded, 'and although I missed him as my partner I got used to coping alone. But I know now that all the things I've been doing for more than a year – such as getting Susan off to her sailing competitions – he'll take charge of again and I'll be largely redundant. I don't mind, but I think things will take time to get back to normal.'

Though no one regretted having sailed in the BT Global Challenge, some of the crew returned with mixed feelings about their experience. David was particularly disillusioned that *Time & Tide* hadn't done better and felt that their disability was no excuse. He had been one of the mainstays of the team and, although his tough, uncompromising attitude hadn't been popular with some, the crew who had worked with him and come to rely on him in all kinds of weather conditions had grown to admire and like him.

But like Chris he was ready to move on. Deutsche Morgan Grenfell had not only been one of the boat's main sponsors but had also given him time off, so he felt an obligation to return to work, though he didn't yet know where he would be posted. Carol, who had given up her home and her life to follow David round the world backpacking, was now keen to find a home and settle down. Always supportive of her man, she too breathed a sigh of relief that the race was over, knowing that although their life would be back to the frenetic pace of the money markets, at least they would have a base together.

Despite relishing the homecoming, Paul Hebblethwaite continued to feel disgruntled by his experience. To the end he objected to Carolyn being classified as deaf, insisting he was the only deaf person on board and she was only hard of hearing. While Paul's hearing loss was certainly far more severe than Carolyn's, some felt that it was a shame that he was the only person on board *Time & Tide* who seemed inclined to divide the crew into a hierarchy of disabilities. James praised Paul for his conduct on this final leg, on which he demonstrated far less impatience than on previous legs; but while Paul greatly appreciated all the sailing experience he'd gained during the past ten months and had enjoyed sampling the sights of the world, he didn't feel the race had changed him in any way other than to make him an angrier and tougher man. He was particularly disappointed at not having been given another chance to be watch leader.

Despite these feelings he was generally liked by the crew, who felt that in time his disgruntlement would pass and he'd see the race in a more positive light. He was thrilled to see again his mother, father and brother, who came to greet the boat at Southampton. Susan had arranged for the crew and their families to stay in a beautiful Lutyens-designed building,

Home at last
(© Simon
Townsley)

the New Place Management Centre, just ten minutes' drive outside the city, and no one was surprised to see Anne Hebblethwaite take her son breakfast in bed every morning. Paul was clearly relieved to be back in the bosom of his family and was looking forward to going home to Yorkshire, meeting up with his mates in the pub, sleeping late and savouring his mother's shepherd's pie. However, this wasn't to be for long as he already had plans to go off sailing again. His big dream was to skipper an all-deaf crew round the world.

It had also been Liz Tring's dream to sail round the world again, though hers was a dream of a solo circumnavigation. Liz had turned out to be a sad casualty of the race. Shortly after leaving the boat at Sydney she'd suffered from a severe depression and was now living in a hostel in Edinburgh.

Although Stuart's experience of the race had also been mixed, he realized that he'd toughened up mentally and learnt not to dwell on things which previously would have preoccupied him for days. 'I've learnt how to approach a problem and see that there are different points of view and perspectives,' he said. 'You can't just blindly go on believing what you want to believe. The whole crew started out as a group of headstrong individuals who'd had a tough time in life because of struggling to overcome their disabilities, and because of that we didn't have the patience to understand other people's point of view. As the race has progressed, however, some of us have changed in that respect.' Like Nigel and Paul Hebblethwaite, Stuart had high hopes of continuing to work in the yachting world. Though he wasn't in any great hurry to get on a boat again, he hoped to play an administrative role in the next Global Challenge round-the-world yacht race.

Lesley, Carol and Carolyn cutting the cake at the homecoming party (© Ross Young Photographers)

For Paul Burns – one of the heroes of the race – the race had been a huge success but the end was also tinged with sadness. There was no doubt that his life would go forward from here on, but despite having the friendship of Brendan and Grahme and having grown close to both Carol and Lesley, he had been preoccupied with his marriage problems during the last two legs. It was his mother, rather than his wife, who spent time with him in Southampton, although on his return to Salisbury Sheila had arranged a welcome home celebration for him.

Initially it had seemed that the event would be ruined by the appearance in the *Sunday Times* on the morning of their arrival home of a second article which told of the Burns's marital problems in great detail. However, by the end of the day both Paul and Sheila recognized that perhaps the timing had been no bad thing, as it brought their marital situation out in the open, broke the ice and meant everyone steered clear of the subject. Also, as far as Paul was concerned, it had put a rubber stamp on the situation, even if the article had been biased in his favour. No marital breakup, he conceded, was ever that black and white.

For Paul returning home wouldn't mean adjusting to the old routine but finding a new one, and although he regretted that things would never be the same again, at the same time he was coming round to the opinion that perhaps Sheila had done him a favour: perhaps after all he needed to be independent and to live a life without restriction. As far as his health was concerned he had acquired the added injury of a chipped bone on his elbow, which caused him a great deal of discomfort. But one positive consequence of the race was that while in Salem he'd been fitted with a state-of-the-art artificial limb, which had a shock absorber built into the foot and therefore produced a flexibility he'd never known before. 'It was built for people to do crazy things with, like mountaineering, parachuting and running,' he said gleefully. This compensated for the fact that his foot was causing him increasing discomfort and pain, slowing him down and requiring a daily dose of painkillers. 'I'm just gritting my teeth and getting on with it,' he said. 'But at least I now know that when my foot has to come off this new technology will mean that I'll probably be more mobile than I am now and certainly in a lot less pain.'

While Paul was pleased to be back and was relieved the race was over, his crew mates had been with him solidly for the past ten months and he knew he'd find it hard to get the image of them out of his mind. Carol felt similarly caught up with the race, and in order to throw herself back into her old life she had decided to get an accountancy temping job immediately on her return to London, in order to start clearing her debts. Since her moments of melancholic reflection at the start of the last leg, she now felt a great deal more positive about life and was determined to use her experience on *Time & Tide* as something which would move her forward.

Lesley was returning to her work as a Macmillan nurse in a few weeks' time and although she was looking forward to going back to her house and garden she also knew she would miss everyone a lot – particularly Paul Burns and Carol, whom she had grown extremely fond of. For Lesley, as for Nigel, readjusting to normal life was going to be hard. Both of them lived alone and both had gained an inordinate amount from the race. While at times fear had paralysed her and her relationship with James hadn't always been smooth running, Lesley still felt that she'd come back a stronger and more confident person who from now on would be much more able to speak her mind.

Nigel, too, recognized that the race had given him a confidence and trenchancy that he'd never had before. 'If you can do this you can do anything,' he said proudly, certain that people would never view him in quite the same light again. As one commentator had noted at the race finish, 'Nigel started the race as a little pale chap, somewhat hesitant, and now here he is – this great strapping bronzed lad who's been working on the foredeck for the past ten months.' Although Nigel might find it harder to adjust to everyday life than most, he was certainly one of the success stories of the race and there was little doubt that he would use the experience to further himself and his career. In the eyes of James, Nigel had turned into 'a really beautiful person. He's quiet, with a droll sense of humour, still swears like a trooper but he's a very good guy,' he said proudly. Nigel had recently been told that he had won the first Douglas Bader Award of £5,000, for achieving great things as a leg amputee in the spirit of Douglas Bader, to be presented by Lady Bader.

Carolyn felt she had achieved an enormous amount, and because of that was not altogether sure how fulfilling she would find her job at BT when she returned to it. She wrote on the last page of her log:

> I am beginning to realize the enormity of what we and Time & Tide have achieved. I don't think we fully grasp the support that the people of the UK are giving us as we become ambassadors, if you like, for disabled people everywhere, trying to show that great things can be achieved by disabled people ... I know that this has been James's 'baby' for the past four years and you can't help admiring the fact that it has become a reality, when people did not think he would get the backing, never mind a boat! Without Susan much of this would have fallen apart as well, she has worked tirelessly and at her own expense for the Trust.

Out of everyone, James knew best what to expect from coming home. He'd completed many voyages before and knew he could adapt easily to the change of pace and lifestyle. For the past year there had been no let-up for him. Even during the stopovers he hadn't been able to relax. Like all the other skippers he'd had to act as an ambassador for The Challenge Business, regularly attending functions and always having to be on his best behaviour. Now, at long last, he was able to let his hair down and celebrate.

Most of all he was looking forward to going with Sarah to her home in north London, having a bath, cooking a good meal and enjoying a bottle of wine. As far as the *Time & Tide* crew were concerned, he would probably keep in contact with only very few, but he appreciated every one of them for the effort they'd made in helping make his dream a reality. He had been touched when arriving at Southampton by just how many relatives of the crew, even those who weren't his greatest supporters, had come up and thanked him for having brought their sons, daughters and husbands safely home. He had also been happily surprised when crew from the rest of the fleet had come up to shake his hand, congratulating him on having skippered the crew that no one wanted to take round the world. Some, in reference to the *Sunday Times* article, even told him, 'You're a saint compared to our skipper.'

On the Sunday after the race was over, as James was pushing a trolley round a supermarket in Enfield, chosing the ingredients for the dinner he was planning to cook for himself and Sarah that evening, an elderly woman who had spotted his white *Time & Tide* sweatshirt came up to him and asked him how he had been involved with the yacht. When he eventually admitted to having been the skipper, she was overcome with excitement, congratulating him on his incredible achievement. To James this said it all. If *Time & Tide* could reach the heart of an elderly lady in Enfield it had succeeded in touching lives all over the world. The fact that *Time & Tide* had come last no longer rankled. 'We've started something bigger than anyone could have imagined,' he said. 'We've touched lives all over the world. We raced the world to change attitudes and, judging from all the response we've had, I believe we've achieved our goal.'

Now that the voyage was over, the yacht home and the crew safe, the trustees of the *Time & Tide* Trust had to look to its future. *Time & Tide* had been an ambitious first project, yet its success had surpassed the Trust's wildest expectations. However, the Trust needed serious funding if it was to continue. The trustees hoped that the extraordinary amount of media coverage this story had generated would bring in further funding for other projects. James,

We did it! The Time & Tide crew raise a toast to their success (© Ross Young Photographers)

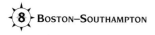

Susan and Guy were determined not to give up – they had come too far and made too many friends for that.

The *Time & Tide* homecoming party, arranged for the crew by Susan and Lucy in a marquee in the grounds of the New Place Management Centre, was a spectacular, rousing and highly emotional event. Many of those who attended claimed it was the best party they'd ever been to. Awards were given, speeches read and there wasn't a dry eye in the house. The fact that *Time & Tide* had crossed the finishing line and come home safely was all that mattered now. 'Just acheiving this had put the rest in second place,' Michael Nicholson had commented on *News at Ten* the day the crew came home.

All the sponsors were present at the homecoming party and Wendy May of Zurich Insurance uttered sentiments shared by all. 'You lived in our hearts for twelve months,' she said, 'and it was a great privilege to be part of it. For me life will never quite be the same again.' Presentations were made to each member of the crew (whether present or absent) as well as sponsors, workers and supporters, plus a few unsung heroes such as Maureen Ogg, who had tirelessly supported the project for the past two years, Eddie Edrich, who had taught the crew the basics of sailing when James was too busy, and even Michael Nicholson, whose news reports had helped bring the story to the nation. Following coverage of their arrival in Southampton there had been ninety phone calls from the world media asking for footage of *Time & Tide*.

Those who hadn't been able to make it were acknowledged and paid tribute to during the course of the day's proceedings. John Rich and Greg Hammond had sent good wishes from Australia, as had Liz Tring from Scotland. There were also a number of former leggers present – namely Mike Austin, John Spence, Steve Latter and John Anderson – all of them revelling in the memories and thoroughly enjoying the highly charged atmosphere of the party.

Mothers talked about 'the *Time & Tide* family' and telegrams were read out from the Prime Minister, Tony Blair, and Her Majesty The Queen. Then Sir Chay, who was present with his wife Lady Felicity, was presented with a woolly nightcap – intended to be a 'night hood' and meant to keep him going until Her Majesty presented him with his impending knighthood. In a short speech Sir Chay congratulated the crew for their fantastic achievement. 'I do believe you will have changed attitudes. Down in the grassroots people's hearts have been touched and it will have a huge effect.' He admitted to having initially been very 'iffy' about the whole project. He called them pioneers and said that although disabled people would probably do it again in the future, *Time & Tide* would always be first and no one could take that away from them.

When James stood up to give his speech the audience burst into spontaneous applause and even those who had at times been critical of his management style stood up to acknowledge their appreciation of his enormous achievement. He talked about his admiration for the crew and as usual his speech was not without humour. 'I know I was very tough on you,' he said; 'I know because I read it in the *Sunday Times*.' A little later a cake in the shape of the boat was presented to the crew. It showed James at the helm, in his usual dark glasses, and other crew members sitting along the rail, including one with a peg leg. The icing said, 'Well done, *Time & Tide*. Against all odds – you did it!'

Gary Champion and Lucy had brilliantly orchestrated a fantastic programme of entertainment in the evening, including Dolly James, a Tina Turner look-alike who sang all her hit songs and had the crew dancing on stage with her. In the midst of the euphoria any bad feeling that had existed on the boat simply faded away. Grahme, who had by now shaved off his long bushy beard and whose angular handsome face was unrecognizable to many, got the whole crew to sign his peg leg. By midnight everyone joined hands and sang 'Auld Lang Syne' before one final emotional blast of 'Simply the Best'.

Time & Tide gave Sir Chay a 'night hood' intended to keep him going until Her Majesty presented the real one (© Ross Young Photographers)

Leg 6 Final Results

	Team	Arrival time
1	Group 4	16/07/97 02:07
2	Toshiba Wave Warrior	16/07/97 03:40
3	Concert	16/07/97 05:08
4	Save the Children	16/07/97 15:32
5	Commercial Union	16/07/97 15:34
6	Nuclear Electric	16/07/97 19:11
7	Global Teamwork	16/07/97 19:29
8	Ocean Rover	16/07/97 19:54
9	Heath Insured II	16/07/97 20:06
10	3Com	16/07/97 20:10
11	Courtaulds Int.	16/07/97 20:10
12	Motorola	16/07/97 20:13
13	Pause to Remember	16/07/97 20:15
14	Time & Tide	17/07/97 09:35

All times BST (GMT +1hr).

Final Combined Times

	TEAM	TIME
1	Group 4	161d 05h 25m
2	Toshiba Wave Warrior	163d 11h 15m
3	Save the Children	165d 20h 51m
4	Motorola	165d 22h 41m
5	Commercial Union	167d 08h 02m
6	Global Teamwork	169d 20h 28m
7	Nuclear Electric	171d 01h 29m
8	Ocean Rover	171d 11h 47m
9	3Com	171d 11h 57m
10	Pause to Remember	172d 19h 13m
11	Courtaulds Int.	173d 19h 26m
12	Heath Insured II	174d 10h 04m
13	Concert	174d 21h 36m
14	Time & Tide	176d 18h 10m

All times rounded to the nearest minute.